my **revisi⊕n** notes

OCR A Level

PSYCHOLOGY

Sarah Byrne

HODDER
EDUCATION
AN HACHETTE UK COMPANY

The Publishers would like to thank the following for permission to reproduce copyright material.

Photo credits

p.40 © Spencer Platt/Getty Images; **p.51** © lithian – Fotolia; **p.65** © ALBERT BANDURA, STANFORD CENTER ON ADOLESCENCE, STANFORD UNIVERSITY; **p.66** © AVITA MEDICAL LTD; **p.94** Courtesy Autism Research Centre, Department of Psychiatry, University of Cambridge; **p.137** © kmwphotography – Fotolia; **p.142** © smart.art – Fotolia; **p.164** © Aliaksei Lasevich – Fotolia; **p.170** © nimon_t – Fotolia; **p.175** © Andrew Brown – Fotolia; **p.191** © Nina Ushakova – 123RF; **p.193** © P. G. Zimbardo Inc.; **p.208** © Retroman – Fotolia; **p.243** © gosphotodesign – Fotolia

Acknowledgements

p.178: Graph credited to R. Edward Geiselman; Ronald P. Fisher; David P. MacKinnon; Heidi L. Holland, taken from *The American Journal of Psychology*, Vol. 99, No. 3 (Autumn, 1986).

Although every effort has been made to ensure that website addresses are correct at time of going to press, Hodder Education cannot be held responsible for the content of any website mentioned in this book. It is sometimes possible to find a relocated web page by typing in the address of the home page for a website in the URL window of your browser.

Hachette UK's policy is to use papers that are natural, renewable and recyclable products and made from wood grown in well-managed forests and other controlled sources. The logging and manufacturing processes are expected to conform to the environmental regulations of the country of origin.

Orders: please contact Hachette UK Distribution, Hely Hutchinson Centre, Milton Road, Didcot, Oxfordshire, OX11 7HH. Telephone: +44 (0)1235 827827. Email education@hachette.co.uk Lines are open from 9 a.m. to 5 p.m., Monday to Friday.
You can also order through our website:
www.hoddereducation.com

ISBN: 978 1 4718 8268 5

© Sarah Byrne 2017

First published in 2017 by
Hodder Education,
An Hachette UK Company
Carmelite House
50 Victoria Embankment
London EC4Y 0DZ

www.hoddereducation.co.uk

Impression number   10 9 8 7 6 5 4 3

Year   2021

Cover photo © puckillustrations – Fotolia

Illustrations by Aptara Inc. and Barking Dog Art

Typeset in India by Aptara Inc.

Printed and bound by CPI Group (UK) Ltd, Croydon, CR0 4YY

A catalogue record for this title is available from the British Library.

Get the most from this book

Everyone has to decide his or her own revision strategy, but it is essential to review your work, learn it and test your understanding. These Revision Notes will help you to do that in a planned way, topic by topic. Use this book as the cornerstone of your revision and don't hesitate to write in it — personalise your notes and check your progress by ticking off each section as you revise.

Tick to track your progress

Use the revision planner on pages iv-vi to plan your revision, topic by topic. Tick each box when you have:

- revised and understood a topic
- tested yourself
- practised the exam questions and gone online to check your answers.

You can also keep track of your revision by ticking off each topic heading in the book. You may find it helpful to add your own notes as you work through each topic.

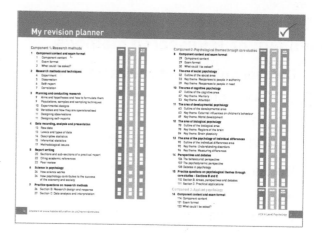

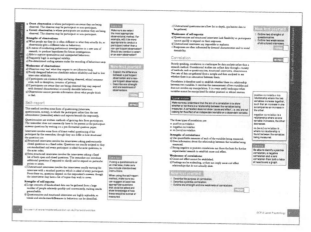

Features to help you succeed

Exam tips and summaries

Expert tips are given throughout the book to help you polish your exam technique in order to maximise your chances in the exam. The summaries provide a quick-check bullet list for each topic.

Typical mistakes

The author identifies the typical mistakes candidates make and explains how you can avoid them.

Now test yourself

These short, knowledge-based questions provide the first step in testing your learning. Answers can be found online.

Definitions and key words

Clear, concise definitions of essential key terms are provided where they first appear.

Exam practice

Practice exam questions are provided for each topic. Use them to consolidate your revision and practise your exam skills.

Online

Go online to check your answers to the Now test yourself, Check your understanding and Practice questions at **www.hoddereducation.co.uk/ myrevisionnotes**

My revision planner

REVISED TESTED EXAM READY

Component 2: Psychological themes through core studies

REVISED	TESTED	EXAM READY

Component 3: Applied psychology

REVISED	TESTED	EXAM READY

Now test yourself, Check your understanding and Practice answers at
www.hoddereducation.co.uk/myrevisionnotes

1 Component content and exam format

Component content

Research methods and techniques:
- Experiment
- Observation
- Self-report
- Correlation.

Planning and conducting research.

Data recording, analysis and presentation.

Report writing.

Science in psychology.

Exam format

Exam facts

H167 (AS level):
- This paper counts as 50 per cent of total AS level.
- It is a written paper of ONE AND A HALF hours.
- A total of 75 marks are available for this paper.

H567 (A level):
- This paper counts as 30 per cent of total A level.
- It is a written paper of TWO hours.
- A total of 90 marks are available for this paper.

Exam structure

The paper has THREE sections:
- Section A: Multiple choice
  - Candidates are required to answer ALL questions.
  - There will be questions from across the component content. Questions could also relate to the research methods used in the core studies.
- Section B: Research design and response
  - Candidates are required to answer ALL questions.
  - Assessment will focus on a novel source. The themes of the questions will be:
    a) the planning and design of research
    b) the evaluation of research
    c) improvements to research.
- Section C: Data analysis and interpretation
  - This section will require candidates to analyse and interpret novel data or a piece of hypothetical research using descriptive and/or inferential statistics.

What could I be asked?

The examination will require candidates to have knowledge and understanding of the following:

1.1 Research methods and techniques	Candidates should have knowledge and understanding of the following research methods and techniques and their associated strengths and weaknesses:
Experiment	● Laboratory experiment, field experiment, quasi experiment
Observation	● Structured and unstructured ● Naturalistic and controlled ● Participant and non-participant ● Overt and covert
Self-report	● Questionnaires and interviews (structured, semi-structured, unstructured)
Correlation	● Obtaining data for correlational analysis ● Positive correlation, negative correlation, no correlation
1.2 Planning and conducting research	Candidates should be familiar with the following features of planning and conducting research and their associated strengths and weaknesses:
Aims and hypotheses and how to formulate	● Research aim, research question ● Null hypotheses, alternative hypotheses, one-tailed (directional) hypotheses, two-tailed (non-directional) hypotheses
Populations, samples and sampling techniques	● Target population and sample ● Random sampling, snowball sampling, opportunity sampling, self-selected sampling
Experimental designs	● Repeated measures design, independent measures design, matched participants design
Variables and how they are operationalised	● Independent variable (IV), dependent variable (DV) ● Control of extraneous variables
Designing observations	● Behavioural categories, coding frames ● Time sampling and event sampling
Designing self-reports	● Open questions and closed questions ● Rating scales (Likert rating scale, semantic differential rating scale)
1.3 Data recording, analysis and presentation	Candidates should be able to demonstrate knowledge and understanding of the process and procedures involved in the collection, analysis and presentation of data. This will necessitate the ability to perform some calculations:
Raw data	● Design and use of raw data recording tables ● Standard and decimal form and significant figures ● Make estimations from data collected
Levels and types of data	● Nominal level data, ordinal level data, interval level data ● Quantitative data and qualitative data ● Primary data and secondary data
Descriptive statistics	● Measures of central tendency (mode, median, mean) ● Measures of dispersion (variance, range, standard deviation) ● Ratios, percentages, fractions ● Frequency tables (tally chart) ● Line graphs, pie charts, bar charts, histograms, scatter diagrams

Inferential statistics	<ul><li>Normal and skewed distribution curves</li><li>Probability and significance levels</li><li>Using statistical tables of critical values</li><li>Criteria for using a parametric test</li><li>Criteria for using a specific non-parametric inferential test (Mann-Whitney U test, Wilcoxon Signed-Rank test, Chi-square test, Binomial Sign test and Spearman's Rho)</li><li>Understand the use of specific non-parametric inferential tests (Mann-Whitney U test, Wilcoxon Signed-Rank test, Chi-square test, Binomial Sign test and Spearman's Rho)</li><li>Type 1 errors and Type 2 errors</li><li>Symbols: $=$, $<$, $\ll$, $\gg$, $>$, $\propto$, $\sim$</li></ul>
Methodological issues	<ul><li>Representativeness</li><li>Generalisability</li><li>Reliability (internal, external, inter-rater, test–retest, split-half)</li><li>Validity (internal, face, construct, concurrent, criterion, external, population, ecological)</li><li>Demand characteristics</li><li>Social desirability</li><li>Researcher/observer bias and research/observer effect(s)</li><li>Ethical considerations, including British Psychological Society's Code of Ethics and Conduct: respect (informed consent, right to withdraw, confidentiality), competence, responsibility (protection of participant, debrief), integrity (deception)</li></ul>
1.4 Report writing	Candidates should have knowledge of the conventions of reporting research in a practical report and demonstrate understanding of the role and purpose of each of the main sections and sub-sections:
Sections and sub-sections of a practical report	<ul><li>Abstract, introduction, method (design, sample, materials/apparatus, procedure), results, discussion, references, appendices</li></ul>
Citing academic references	<ul><li>Familiarity with citing academic research using the Harvard system of referencing</li></ul>
Peer review	<ul><li>Appreciate the role of the psychological community in validating new knowledge and ensuring integrity through the process of peer review</li></ul>
1.5 Practical activities	<ul><li>Candidates are expected to conduct and analyse their own small-scale research practicals, including appropriate risk assessment and management</li><li>Practicals should include: self-report, observation, experiment, correlation</li></ul>
1.6 How science works	<ul><li>Candidates should understand how society makes decisions about scientific issues and how psychology contributes to the success of the economy and society</li><li>Candidates should therefore have knowledge and understanding of the following concepts: the study of cause and effect, falsification, replicability, objectivity, induction, deduction, hypothesis testing, manipulation of variables, control and standardisation, quantifiable measurements</li></ul>

2 Research methods and techniques

This component introduces and develops knowledge and understanding of the process of planning, conducting, analysing and reporting psychological research across a range of experimental and non-experimental methodologies and techniques.

The four main techniques used for collecting and analysing data when conducting psychological research are experiment, observation, self-report and correlation.

Experiment

REVISED

Experiments involve the study of **cause and effect**, whereby one variable (the independent variable, IV) is altered or manipulated to see what effect it has on another variable (the dependent variable, DV). The dependent variable is the variable that is measured and the independent variable is the variable that is predicted to affect the dependent variable.

Other variables that could potentially influence the dependent variable, known as **extraneous variables**, should be eliminated or controlled whenever possible. Experiments are therefore frequently conducted in artificial environments so the researcher can control potential extraneous variables to prevent them becoming confounding variables (variables that actually affect the dependent variable strongly enough to influence the results).

> **cause and effect** refers to the belief that a cause can be established for every event. In an experiment, the independent variable is hypothesised as the cause and the resultant change in behaviour (the dependent variable) is the effect.
>
> **extraneous variables** are variables (which are not the independent variable) that could affect the dependent variables if not controlled, for example noise, temperature, age.

Laboratory experiments

Laboratory experiments are conducted in artificial environments, where the researcher manipulates the independent variable to measure its effect on a dependent variable while carefully controlling extraneous variables which could influence the results. By comparing two or more conditions, cause and effect can be tested.

> **Exam tip**
>
> Make sure you can state your independent and dependent variables.

Strengths:
a) Highly controlled so the effect of extraneous variables is minimised.
b) Easily replicable.
c) Can show cause and effect.

Weaknesses:
a) Low in **ecological validity**.
b) Often prone to **demand characteristics**.
c) Ethical concerns: deception is often used and stress may occur.

> **ecological validity** refers to the extent to which findings from one situation can be generalised to other situations, i.e. do the findings reflect real-life situations?
>
> **demand characteristics** are cues in the environment which give away the aim of the study. These can lead the participant to either behave in a way that will support the researcher or ensure the researcher does not get the anticipated results.

Field experiments

These are controlled experiments conducted in natural environments. In field experiments, the researcher has little control over extraneous variables but due to the manipulation of the independent variable, cause and effect can be inferred.

Answers at **www.hoddereducation.co.uk/myrevisionnotes**

Strengths:

a) High in ecological validity.

b) Demand characteristics can be minimised.

Weaknesses:

a) Low control over variables.

b) Difficult to replicate.

c) Difficult to record data.

d) Ethical concerns: lack of consent, deception, invasion of privacy, stress, no debriefing.

Quasi experiments

These make use of existing changes or differences in situations to create levels of an independent variable, i.e. the independent variable is naturally occurring and so cannot be manipulated by the researcher. Quasi experiments are usually conducted in a laboratory.

Strengths:

a) Naturally occurring independent variable.

b) Highly controlled so the effect of extraneous variables is minimised.

c) Can show cause and effect.

Weaknesses:

a) Low in ecological validity.

b) Not easy to replicate.

c) Often prone to demand characteristics.

d) Ethical concerns: deception is often used and stress may occur.

Exam tip

Make sure you know at least one strength and one weakness of each of the experimental methods.

Now test yourself

1 Describe one difference between a laboratory experiment and a field experiment.

2 Outline two weaknesses of a quasi experiment.

TESTED ☐

Observation

REVISED ☐

Observations involve the precise measurement of naturally occurring behaviour, the aim being to observe behaviour, record it, look for patterns in the observed behaviour and then make sense of it. In most cases observations are conducted in a natural, real-world environment where the people being monitored are unaware of the fact that their behaviour is being recorded. This is called naturalist observation.

- **Participant observation** involves the researcher becoming part of the group whose behaviour is being observed and monitored. This may be done either with (overt) or without (covert) the participants' knowledge.
- **Non-participant observation** involves the researcher recording participants' behaviour while not, themselves, being involved in the situation under observation. This may be overt or covert.
- **Structured (systematic) observation** involves the use of an explicitly designed coding framework/chart for recording behaviour. This may be participant or non-participant, overt or covert.
- **Unstructured observation** involves the observer recording a non-specified, wide range of behaviours including any that seem relevant to the study. This may be participant or non-participant, overt or covert.
- **Controlled observation** involves the recording of spontaneously occurring behaviour under conditions contrived by the researcher. Such observations can take place in either a laboratory or the participants' normal environment. This may be participant or non-participant, overt or covert.

- **Overt observation** is where participants are aware they are being observed. The observer may be participant or non-participant.
- **Covert observation** is where participants are unaware they are being observed. The observer may be participant or non-participant.

Strengths of observations:
a) What people say they do is often different to what they actually do, so observations give a different take on behaviour.
b) A means of conducting preliminary investigations in a new area of research, to produce hypotheses for future investigations.
c) Able to capture spontaneous and unexpected behaviour.
d) Frequently high in ecological validity.
e) Pre-determined coding systems make the recording of behaviours easy.

Weaknesses of observations:
a) Observers may 'see' what they expect to see (observer bias).
b) Poorly designed behaviour checklists reduce reliability and lead to low inter-rater reliability.
c) If participants are unaware they are being observed, ethical concerns arise, such as deception, invasion of privacy.
d) If participants are aware they are being observed they may respond with demand characteristics or socially desirable behaviour.
e) Observations cannot provide information about what people think or feel.

Self-report

REVISED

This method involves some form of questioning (interview, questionnaire, survey), in which the participant rather than the test administrator (researcher) selects and reports/records the response(s).

Questionnaires are written methods of gaining data from participants. The researcher does not necessarily have to be present as the participant answers questions by writing on a pre-formatted question paper.

Interviews involve some form of direct verbal questioning of the participant by the researcher, though they can differ in how structured the questions are:
a) Structured interviews involve the interviewer asking predominantly closed questions in a fixed order. Questions are usually scripted so they are standardised and every participant is asked the same questions, in the same order.
b) Semi-structured interviews involve the interviewer asking a fixed list of both open and closed questions. The researcher can introduce additional questions if required to clarify and/or expand on particular points or issues.
c) Unstructured interviews involve the interviewer usually starting the interview with a standard question which is asked of every participant. From there on, questions depend on the respondent's answers, though the interviewer may have a list of topics they wish to cover.

Strengths of self-reports:
a) Large amounts of standardised data can be gathered from a large number of people relatively quickly and conveniently, making results generalisable.
b) Questionnaires and structured interviews are highly replicable, so trends and similarities/differences in behaviour can be identified.

Exam tip

Make sure you select the most appropriate observational method. For example, will it be more appropriate to conduct a participant rather than a non-participant observation? Should you conduct a covert or an overt observation?

Now test yourself

3 Explain the difference between a participant observation and a non-participant observation.
4 Describe one strength and one weakness of observations.

TESTED

Exam tips

If using a questionnaire or an interview, make sure you include standardised instructions.

When using the self-report method, make sure you can suggest at least two appropriate questions that could be asked and show knowledge of how these would be scored or measured.

c) Unstructured questionnaires allow for in-depth, qualitative data to be gathered.

Weaknesses of self-reports:

a) Questionnaires and structured interviews lack flexibility so participants cannot qualify or expand on their responses.

b) Unstructured interviews are impossible to replicate.

c) Responses are often influenced by demand characteristics and/or social desirability.

Now test yourself

5 Outline two strengths of questionnaires.
6 Outline two weaknesses of structured interviews.

TESTED ☐

Correlation

REVISED ☐

Strictly speaking, correlation is a technique for data analysis rather than a research method. Correlational studies can collect data through a variety of methods, such as questionnaires, structured interviews, observations. Two sets of data are gathered from a sample and then analysed to see whether there is an association between them.

Correlation is therefore used to establish whether there is a relationship between two variables. It involves the measurement of two variables and does not involve any manipulation. It is a very useful technique when variables cannot be manipulated for either practical or ethical reasons.

> **Typical mistake**
>
> Make sure you understand that the aim of a correlation is to show whether or not there is a relationship between the variables being measured. A correlation does not show 'cause and effect', i.e. you are not looking for the effect of an independent variable on a dependent variable.

The three types of correlation are:
- **positive correlation**
- **negative correlation**
- **no (zero) correlation.**

Strengths of correlations:

a) Use quantifiable measures of each of the variables being measured.

b) Give information about the relationship between the variables being measured.

c) Strong negative or positive correlations can form the basis for further experimental research to establish cause and effect.

Weaknesses of correlations:

a) Cause and effect cannot be established.

b) Findings can be misleading, as they can imply cause and effect relationships that do not actually exist.

> **positive correlation** is a relationship where the two variables increase together, such that an increase in one accompanies an increase in the other.
>
> **negative correlation** is a relationship where as one variable increases, the other decreases.
>
> **no (zero) correlation** is where no relationship is found between the variables being measured.

> **Exam tip**
>
> Be able to identify a positive correlation, a negative correlation and a zero correlation from both a table of results and a graph.

Now test yourself

7 Describe the purpose of correlation.
8 Describe a positive correlation.
9 Outline one strength and one weakness of correlations.

TESTED ☐

Check your understanding

1 In an experiment, which of the following would be the dependent variable?
   A   A variable which might influence the findings
   B   The variable that is manipulated
   C   A naturally occurring variable
   D   The variable measured

2 Which of the following would be a covert, non-participant observation?
   A   An observation where the researcher records participants' behaviour while not being part of the investigation themselves
   B   An observation where the researcher is actually part of the group whose behaviour is being observed though the participants themselves are unaware they are being observed
   C   An observation where the participants know they are being observed though the researcher is removed from the situation and does not take part in the activity being observed
   D   An observation where the participants are unaware they are being observed and the researcher is removed from the situation and does not take part in the activity being observed

3 Which of these best describes a negative correlation?
   A   Where one variable increases, the other variable increases
   B   Where one variable decreases, the other variable does not change
   C   Where one variable decreases, the other variable decreases
   D   Where one variable decreases, the other variable increases

4 Which of the following studies was a field experiment?
   A   Baron-Cohen *et al.* (1997): Autism in adults
   B   Piliavin *et al.* (1969): Subway Samaritan
   C   Loftus and Palmer (1974): Eyewitness testimony
   D   Moray (1959): Auditory attention

5 What are demand characteristics?
   A   The tendency for participants to respond or behave in ways they think reflect what is acceptable in society rather than how they actually want to respond or behave
   B   The tendency for a researcher to act in ways that influence the results due to such things as their own beliefs, culture, gender
   C   Cues or features of an experiment or situation that indicate to participants the aim of the study and so influence their behaviour
   D   Influences researchers can have on a study by such things as their presence, beliefs, culture, gender

For practice questions relating to Sections B and C of the exam paper turn to Chapter 7.   ONLINE

Summary

By the end of this chapter you should:
● know and understand the four main techniques used for collecting and analysing data when conducting psychological research
● know and understand when each technique should be used
● know and understand at least one strength and one weakness of each technique.

3 Planning and conducting research

Students should be familiar with the following features of planning and conducting research and their associated strengths and weaknesses.

Aims and hypotheses and how to formulate them

Research aim: a statement that broadly points out what the research aims to accomplish and the desired outcomes of the research. It identifies the purpose of the investigation.

Research question: a question that asks about what a study intends to investigate.

Null hypothesis: predicts that there will be no difference or no relationship between the variables being studied and that any results are due to chance and are not significant in terms of supporting the idea being investigated.

Alternative hypothesis: predicts that there will be a difference or a relationship between the variables being studied and that the results are not due to chance but are significant in terms of supporting the idea being investigated.

One-tailed (directional) hypothesis: predicts the nature of the effect of the independent variable on the dependent variable (experiment) or the direction of the relationship (correlation).

Two-tailed (non-directional) hypothesis: predicts that the independent variable will have an effect on the dependent variable (experiment), or that there will be a relationship (correlation) but the direction of the effect is not specified.

> **Exam tips**
>
> Know the difference between a research aim and a hypothesis. Remember that a hypothesis is a prediction.
>
> Remember that a hypothesis for a correlation predicts that there will be a relationship/no relationship whereas for other research methods a hypothesis predicts a difference/no difference.

> **Typical mistakes**
>
> When writing hypotheses many students 'hedge their bets' and write, 'There will be a difference or a relationship between ... and ...', 'There will be no difference or relationship between ... and ...'. This will not score marks as there is no evidence of real understanding.
>
> Other mistakes include not clearly identifying the variables being measured when writing a hypothesis and not including how the variables will be operationalised when writing a hypothesis.

> **Now test yourself**
>
> 1 Describe the difference between a null hypothesis and an alternative hypothesis.
> 2 Describe the difference between a one-tailed hypothesis and a two-tailed hypothesis.
>
> TESTED

Populations, samples and sampling techniques

Target population and sample: the group of people the researcher is interested in and from which the sample is drawn.

Random sampling: the selecting of participants in a way that each member of the target population has an equal chance of being chosen. There is no bias in who is chosen so the sample is likely to be representative. There is, however, the chance of obtaining a freak sample as the researcher has no control over who will be selected.

Snowball sampling: relies on initial participants recruiting others to generate additional participants. The sample is unlikely to be representative, though it is an easy way of gathering a sample if specific sample features are required, for example gamblers, soccer players, health practitioners.

Opportunity sampling: produced by selecting people who are most easily available at the time of the study. The sample is unlikely to be representative, though again this is a quick and easy way of gathering a sample as the researcher just has to ask people who are around at the time of the investigation to be the participants.

Self-selected sampling: produced by asking people to volunteer to take part in a study. The study is unlikely to be representative, though participants who volunteer will usually be willing and co-operative so perform to the best of their ability.

Now test yourself

3 Describe the term 'random sampling'.
4 Describe why a self-selected sample is unlikely to be representative of the target population.

TESTED ☐

Experimental designs

Repeated measures design: each participant takes part in every condition under test. A strength of this experimental design is that fewer participants will be needed and individual differences will be controlled for as the same participants are used in all conditions. A weakness, however, is that participants may suffer from boredom, order effects and/or practice effects. Boredom and order effects tend to result in poorer performance in the second or subsequent conditions and practice effects often lead to improved performance in the second or subsequent conditions.

Independent measures design: different participants are used for each level of the independent variable. A strength of this experimental design is that there is no chance of boredom, order effects or practice influence performance in the second or subsequent conditions. A weakness of this design is that more participants will be needed and as different people will take part in each condition, individual differences may influence the results.

Exam tip

Know one strength and one weakness of each experimental design so that if an evaluation of the design is required, you can make both a supporting and a challenging comment.

Matched participants design: participants who are similar on key variables with one participant being placed in one experimental condition and the other in the other experimental condition. This design allows participants to be matched on features that are important to the study. For example, Bandura (1961) matched his participants on aggression levels, which was an important aspect of his study into the transmission of aggression. A disadvantage of this design is that it may be difficult to find an adequate number of participants who can be matched to the desired features.

Now test yourself

5 Describe the difference between a repeated measures design and an independent measures design.

TESTED ☐

Variables and how they are operationalised

Independent variable: the factor in an experiment that is manipulated, changed or compared by the researcher with the expectation that it will have an effect on the dependent variable. In a quasi experiment the IV is naturally occurring, it cannot be manipulated. For example, in Baron-Cohen's study (1997) he could not manipulate whether the participants were autistic, had Tourette syndrome or were 'normal'.

Dependent variable: the factor in an experiment that is measured by the researcher to assess the effects of the IV. The DV is therefore any observed changes in behaviour which result from the manipulation (or natural occurrence) of the IV.

Control of extraneous variables: the control of any factors other than the IV that might potentially affect the DV and so influence the findings. Environmental factors such as noise, temperature, time of day, etc., if not controlled, can influence findings. Likewise, individual factors such as gender, age, occupation, etc., if not controlled, can influence findings.

> **Typical mistake**
>
> Not making it clear to the examiner how the independent variable could be manipulated or how the dependent variable could be measured.

> **Exam tips**
>
> Understand that it is the independent variable that influences the dependent variable.
>
> Be able to suggest at least two controls that could be built into a research project to reduce the chances of the findings being caused by variables other than those being measured.

Designing observations

`REVISED`

Behavioural categories: objective methods used in an observation to break a continuous stream of activity into discrete recordable events. For example, if observing behaviour in a sixth form common room, behavioural categories could include talking/using a mobile phone/ working on a computer/reading/playing cards, etc.

Coding frames: lists of behavioural categories, each with a code. For example, behavioural categories for observing behaviour in a sixth form common room could be talking – to a friend/in a group, reading – a novel/an academic text/a magazine, playing cards – playing snap/ bridge/whist.

Time sampling: a data recording method that involves recording pre-determined behaviours at regular intervals, for example every five seconds, or taking a sample at different times of the day or month.

Event sampling: a data recording method that involves counting the number of behaviours in a specified time period, for example using a tally chart.

> **Exam tips**
>
> If conducting an observation, be able to suggest appropriate behavioural categories and coding frames.
>
> Know and understand the difference between time and event sampling. Bandura, in his study of aggression, used both time and event sampling.

> **Now test yourself**
>
> 6 Describe the difference between time sampling and event sampling.
>
> `TESTED`

Designing self-reports

`REVISED`

Open questions: allow participants to give full and detailed answers in their own words. They produce qualitative data, which is in depth and very detailed. However, because open questions usually give qualitative data, it is often difficult to identify trends and patterns or make comparisons between participants.

Closed questions: offer a small number of explicitly stated alternative responses from which the participant must choose. There is no opportunity to expand on answers and they produce quantitative data.

However, because closed questions usually collect quantitative data, which makes results easy to analyse, so trends and patterns can be identified and comparisons between individuals and/or groups can be made.

Rating scales: numerical scales on which participants indicate the strength of some measure. They produce quantitative data.

a) Likert rating scales: allow participants to indicate how much they agree or disagree by choosing an option.

b) Semantic differential rating scales: allow participants to choose between two extremes, rating their response towards an opposing pair of descriptive words. The participant chooses one of several numerical values.

A problem with the use of rating scales is that they are very subjective and therefore do not always give valid or useful findings. They do, however, produce quantitative data, which makes results easy to analyse.

Exam tip

Know a strength and a weakness of open and closed questions and rating scales.

Now test yourself

7 Describe one difference between open questions and closed questions.

TESTED ☐

Check your understanding

1 A researcher conducted an experiment to test the effect of time of day on reaction times. He tested one group of participants in the morning and a second group in the afternoon. Identify the research design used in the experiment.
   A   Repeated measures design
   B   Independent measures design
   C   Matched participants design
   D   Independent, matched participants design

2 Which of the following describes a random sample?
   A   Every third person on a list is selected
   B   The people most easily available at the time of the study
   C   Participants respond to an advertisement
   D   Every person in the target population had an equal chance of being selected

3 Which of the following refers to time sampling?
   A   A data recording method that involves counting the number of behaviours in a specified time period
   B   A data recording method where the researcher has a list of behavioural categories. A tick is inserted by a category every time the behaviour is observed
   C   A data recording method that involves the researcher timing how long a certain behaviour lasts
   D   A data recording method that involves recording pre-determined behaviours at regular intervals

For practice questions relating to Sections B and C of the exam paper turn to Chapter 7.   ONLINE ☐

Summary

By the end of this chapter you should:
● know how to formulate a hypothesis
● know and be able to evaluate the most common sampling techniques
● know and be able to evaluate the three experimental designs

● know how to design an observation so appropriate behaviours can be measured
● know and be able to evaluate how self-reports such as questionnaires and interviews can be designed.

4 Data recording, analysis and presentation

Candidates should be able to demonstrate knowledge and understanding of the processes and procedures involved in the collection, analysis and presentation of data. They will also need to be able to perform some calculations.

Raw data

Raw data recording tables include **tally charts/frequency tables**, summary tables, etc. They allow researchers to make a quick judgement in relation to the null or alternative hypothesis. To check knowledge and understanding of alternative and null hypotheses, refer to Chapter 3. Raw data is often gathered using tally charts/frequency tables. An example of a tally chart/frequency table is shown below.

Mobile phone usage by sixth formers in their common room			
	Texting	Speaking to someone else	Playing games	Using the internet
	✓✓✓✓✓✓	✓	✓✓✓	✓✓✓
Totals	6	1	3	3

> **raw data** (sometimes called source or primary data) is data that has not been processed for use.
>
> **tally chart/frequency table** is a grid used in an observation which shows the possible categories of results; a tick or tally is made each time the item is scored. These can be added together to give a total in each category.

Standard and decimal form

Standard form is a way of representing very small or very large numbers in a form in which they can be easily understood by showing how many 'times ten' the number is multiplied. For example, 3×10^4 means $3 \times 10 \times 10 \times 10 \times 10$ or 3 multiplied by 4 tens = 30,000.

Decimal form is a way of representing portions of numbers with values less than 1.

Significant figures

This is a way to simplify a long number. For example, 6640 to one significant figure becomes 7000 because the second figure is 5 or more. Meanwhile, 0.0536 to one significant figure becomes 0.05 because the next figure is less than 5. These numbers would become 6600 and 0.054 to two significant figures. The first digit is the most important as it shows the most about the ball-park amount. This makes it significant, but if the next figure is 5 or more, it is rounded up whereas if it is 4 or less it is not rounded up.

Make estimations from data collected

Making estimations means finding a value that is close enough to the right answer, usually with some thought or basic calculation involved.

Now test yourself

1 Sketch a tally chart to record behaviours displayed by passengers on a train.

Levels and types of data

Nominal level data: a level of measurement recording data in totals of named categories.

Ordinal level data: a level of measurement recording data as points along a scale where the gaps between the points are not necessarily equal.

Interval level data: a level of measurement recording data as points on a scale where the gaps between the points are equal.

Quantitative data: numerical data.

Qualitative data: descriptive data.

Primary data: data gathered first hand (directly) from the sample.

Secondary data: data gathered from research conducted by another researcher.

> **Exam tips**
>
> Know the difference between nominal, ordinal and interval level data.
>
> Know the difference between quantitative and qualitative data.

> **Typical mistake**
>
> Confusing quantitative with qualitative data – quantitative refers to the quantity, i.e. how much/how many; qualitative refers to the quality, i.e. descriptive information. This data cannot actually be measured, though rating scales are often used to make qualitative data measurable. For example, qualitative data in relation to mood states can be quantified using a rating scale.

> **Now test yourself**
>
> 2 Identify one core study that used secondary data.
>
> TESTED

Descriptive statistics

REVISED

Measures of central tendency: a mathematical way to describe a typical or average score from a data set.

a) Mode: the most frequent score(s) in a set of results.

b) Mean: the average score in a set of results, worked out by adding up all the scores and diving by the number of scores.

c) Median: the middle score in a data set when the data is in rank order.

Measures of dispersion: a mathematical way to describe the variance or spread of scores in a data set.

a) Variance: the average of the squared differences from the mean.

b) Range: the spread of scores within a data set, calculated by taking the smallest value from the largest value and adding 1 to the total.

c) Standard deviation: a measure of how spread out the scores are in a data set. It is the square root of the variance.

Ratio: a comparison between values within different categories.

Percentage: a fraction in which the common denominator is always 100. The resulting number is followed by the sign %.

Fraction: a representation of portions of a whole number calculated by dividing the number on the top by the number on the bottom.

Frequency table (tally chart): a grid showing the possible categories of results in which a tick or symbol is placed each time the behaviour is observed.

Line graph: a graph that uses points connected by lines to show how something changes in value.

Pie chart: a circular chart divided into sectors, with each sector showing the relative size of each value.

Bar chart: a graph which uses rectangular bars or columns to show how large each value is. Bars can be horizontal or vertical but should not touch each other.

Histogram: a graphical display where the data is grouped into ranges and then plotted in bars or columns. Because the data is related/continuous, bars/columns should touch each other.

Scatter diagram: a graph of plotted points to show the relationship between two sets of data.

> **Now test yourself**
>
> 3 Describe how you calculate the median in a set of numbers.
>
> 4 Identify the type of graph you would use when displaying data in a correlational analysis.
>
> TESTED

Inferential statistics

Normal distribution curve: a frequency distribution curve that rises gradually and symmetrically (in a bell shape) to a single maximum at the point of the mean, median and mode. A normal distribution curve should look like Figure 4.1.

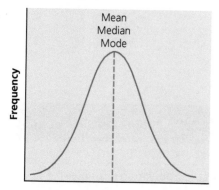

Figure 4.1 Normal distribution curve

Skewed distribution curve: a frequency distribution curve in which the measures of central tendency do not lie together in the middle, i.e. there is a greater spread of scores on one side. A skewed distribution curve could look like either of the ones shown here, depending on whether there is a negative (Figure 4.2) or a positive (Figure 4.3) skew.

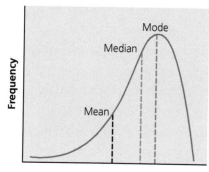

Figure 4.2 Negative skewed distribution curve

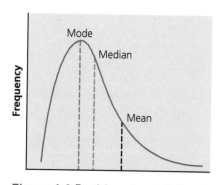

Figure 4.3 Positive skewed distribution curve

Probability: the chance that something will happen.

Significance level: the probability that a pattern in the results could have arisen by chance; the level at which psychologists reject the null hypothesis. This is usually at $p < 0.05$.

Tables of critical values: enable psychologists to compare the calculated/observed value of their data with critical values which mathematicians have identified to be the value at which data is significant.

4 Data recording, analysis and presentation

Criteria for using a parametric test:

a) The data has to be interval or ratio.

b) The data has to have a curve of normal distribution.

c) The variances should be similar.

Examples of parametric tests include t-tests and ANOVA tests. Detailed knowledge and understanding of these tests is not required for this specification. The only knowledge required is whether a parametric or a non-parametric test should be used. Generally, a non-parametric test is used when the gathered data does not show a normal distribution curve.

Criteria for using a specific non-parametric test are shown in the table.

Type of data	Experiment: independent design in test of difference	Experiment: repeated design in test of difference	Test for correlation
Nominal	Chi-square test	Binomial Sign test	X
Ordinal	Mann-Whitney U test	Wilcoxon Signed-Rank test	Spearman's Rho
Interval	X	X	Spearman's Rho

a) Mann-Whitney U test: a test of difference suitable for use with independent data. It can be used when at least an ordinal level of measurement has been achieved. It can therefore be used with data on an interval or ratio level of measurement which is converted to an ordinal level for the purpose of the test.

b) Wilcoxon Signed-Rank test: a test of difference that is suitable for use with related data. It can be used when at least an ordinal level of measurement has been achieved. It can therefore be used with data on an interval or ratio level of measurement which is converted to an ordinal level for the purpose of the test.

c) Chi-square test: a test of association for use with independent data which is measured at a nominal level (in the form of frequencies). It tests for differences by examining the association that exists between data categorised into rows and columns. It compares observed frequencies (those actually obtained) with expected frequencies (the average frequencies which would be observed if the null hypothesis were true).

d) Binomial Sign test: a test of difference suitable for use with related data which is measured at a nominal level of measurement. The test examines the direction of any difference between pairs of scores.

e) Spearman's Rho: a test of correlation suitable for use with pairs of scores. It can be used when at least an ordinal level of measurement has been achieved. It can therefore be used with data on an interval or ratio level of measurement which is converted to an ordinal level for the purpose of the test.

Type 1 errors: rejecting the null hypothesis when it is true, i.e. accepting the alternative hypothesis when it is not true.

Type 2 errors: accepting the null hypothesis when it is not true, i.e. rejecting the alternative hypothesis when it is true.

Symbols:

= equals

< smaller than

<< much smaller than

>> much greater than

Now test yourself

5 Describe a normal distribution curve.
6 Describe the difference between a type 1 and a type 2 error.

TESTED

> greater than

∝ proportional to

~ roughly equivalent to/approximately.

Methodological issues

Representativeness: the extent to which a sample is typical of the key features of the target population so is likely to produce findings that can be generalised.

Generalisability: the extent to which findings from one sample or situation can be applied to another sample or situation.

Reliability: the consistency of a measure.
a) **Internal:** the consistency of results of a test across items within the test.
b) **External:** the extent to which a test produces the same results in the same situation with the same people or the extent to which a test score varies from one time to another.
c) **Inter-rater:** the extent to which two researchers consistently rate, score or observe the same behaviour and the sets of ratings. If the two sets of ratings produce a positive correlation, inter-rater reliability has been established. Inter-rater reliability is frequently gained through a pre-test where the researcher has the opportunity to check that they are interpreting and recording behaviours in the same way.
d) **Test–retest:** a way to test reliability by using the same test twice. If the two sets of scores correlate well, the test has good reliability.
e) **Split-half:** a way to test internal reliability by comparing two halves of a test. If the scores on both halves of the test correlate well, the measure has good reliability.

> **Exam tips**
>
> Know the difference between internal and external reliability.
>
> Know what is meant by inter-rater reliability and how this can be achieved.

Validity: how accurate a piece of research or test is at measuring what it aims to measure.
a) **Internal:** the extent to which the procedures within a study achieve the intended manipulations and measures. High internal validity means researchers can be sure that changes in the dependent variable are caused by the independent variable.
b) **Face:** the extent to which a measure has 'face value' and appears to test what it claims to.
c) **Construct:** the extent to which the phenomenon being measured really exists.
d) **Concurrent:** the extent to which different measures of the same phenomenon produce similar results in the same circumstances, at the same time.
e) **Criterion:** the extent to which one measure of a phenomenon predicts the value of another measure of the same phenomenon.
f) **Population:** the extent to which the findings from one sample can be generalised to the whole of the target population.
g) **Ecological:** the extent to which findings from one situation generalise to other situations; the extent to which a piece of research is accurately measuring real life.

> **Typical mistake**
>
> Confusing the terms 'reliability' and 'validity' and/or using the terms interchangeably.

> **Exam tip**
>
> Know the difference between internal, face, construct and concurrent validity.

Demand characteristics: cues or features of an experiment or situation that indicate to participants the aim of the study and so influence their behaviour.

Social desirability: the tendency of participants to respond or behave in ways they think reflect what is acceptable in society rather than how they actually want to respond or behave.

> **Typical mistake**
>
> Confusing the terms 'demand characteristics' and 'social desirability' and/or using them interchangeably.

Researcher/observer bias:

- **Researcher bias:** the tendency for a researcher to act in ways that influence the results due to such things as their own beliefs, culture, gender.
- **Observer bias:** the tendency for an observer to 'see what they want to see' and so record behaviours they believe should or will occur rather than recording behaviours that actually occur.

Researcher/observer effects:

- **Researcher effects:** negative influences researchers can have on a study by such things as their presence, beliefs, culture, gender.
- **Observer effects:** influences that observers can have on a study by such things as their presence, beliefs, culture, gender, when the observer is overt or when their role becomes apparent to the participants.

Ethical considerations are based on the British Psychological Society's (BPS) Code of Ethics and Conduct. The area of RESPECT considers the following issues:

- **Informed consent:** participants should have sufficient knowledge about a study to decide whether or not they want to agree to take part.
- **Right to withdraw:** participants should be aware that they can remove themselves and their data from the study at any time.
- **Confidentiality:** participants' results and personal information should be kept safely and not released to anyone outside the study.

The area of COMPETENCE reflects the need for psychologists to work within their own capabilities, not giving advice to participants if not qualified to do so, and to check their research with peers. It clarifies the need for psychologists to monitor their own and others' competence in carrying out research appropriately.

The area of RESPONSIBILITY considers the following issues:

- **Protection of participant:** participants should not be put at any greater physical or psychological risk than they would expect in their everyday lives.
- **Debrief:** a full explanation of the aims and potential consequences of a study should be given to participants after they have taken part to ensure they leave in at least as positive a condition as they arrived.

The area of INTEGRITY considers the following issue:

- **Deception:** participants should not be deliberately misinformed about the aim or the procedure of the study.

> **Typical mistake**
>
> Confusing 'researcher' with 'observer' and/or using the terms interchangeably.

> **Exam tip**
>
> Be able to evaluate any given piece of research in relation to ethical considerations. Evaluations need not always be negative. Many pieces of research show at least some consideration has been given to ethics. For example, Milgram, after his study into destructive obedience (1863), debriefed his participants.

Now test yourself

7 Describe how you could ensure the findings from an observation had inter-rater reliability.

8 Describe how social desirability may influence the findings of a study.

9 Describe two ethical considerations a researcher must be aware of when conducting a covert observation and explain how they could be managed.

TESTED

Check your understanding

1 Which of the following is a type 1 error?
   A   Rejecting the null hypothesis when it is true
   B   Accepting the null hypothesis when it is not true
   C   Rejecting the alternative hypothesis when it is true
   D   Accepting the alternative hypothesis when it is true

2 What does the symbol p stand for?
   A   The possibility that the results are due to chance
   B   The probability that the results are significant
   C   The probability that the results are correct
   D   The probability of the results being due to chance

3 Which of the following statements describes the mean in a set of scores?
   A   The average score in a set of results, worked out by adding up all the scores and dividing by the number of scores
   B   The most frequent score(s) in a set of results
   C   The typical score from a data set
   D   The middle score in a data set when the data is in rank order

4 Which of the following statements describes how to calculate the range in a set of scores?
   A   Work out the average of the squared differences from the mean
   B   Work out the square root of the variance
   C   Take the smallest value from the largest value and add 1 to the total
   D   Take the smallest value from the largest value and subtract 1 from the total

5 49 participants are divided into two groups in a part-to-part ratio of 3:4. How many will be in each part?
   A   14:35
   B   21:28
   C   19:30
   D   23:26

6 A researcher investigated the relationship between students' ratings of enjoyment for homework and their performance in examinations. Identify the type of graph she would use to display her findings.
   A   Pie chart
   B   Scatter diagram
   C   Bar chart
   D   Line graph

7 A psychologist compared people who earned more than £40,000 per year with those who earned less than £20,000 per year by asking them how much control they felt they had over their futures. Which non-parametric inferential test should be used to analyse the data gathered?
   A   Wilcoxon Signed-Rank test
   B   Chi-square test
   C   Mann-Whitney U test
   D   Binomial Sign test

8 Which of the following is the usual level at which psychologists reject the null hypothesis?
   A $p < 0.05$
   B $p > 0.5$
   C $p < 0.005$
   D $p > 0.005$

9 Which ethical consideration does not come under the heading of 'Respect'?
   A   Competence
   B   Informed consent
   C   Right to withdraw
   D   Confidentiality

For practice questions relating to Sections B and C of the exam paper turn to Chapter 7.

ONLINE

Summary

By the end of this chapter you should:
● know how raw data can be presented
● understand about different levels and types of data
● know and understand the most common descriptive statistics used in psychological research
● understand inferential statistics and know which test to apply when analysing data
● have an understanding of the most common methodological issues that can be raised against psychological research.

5 Report writing

Psychologists use a conventional method when writing up their research. The sections and sub-sections of a psychological report generally follow the structure outlined below.

Sections and sub-sections of a practical report

Title

The title should be concise yet clear enough to give the reader an idea of the investigator's central concerns. Remember that your reader will initially see the title and nothing else, but wishes to know whether or not the report is relevant to his/her research interests. The title should be an accurate reflection of the content of the report and should not be more than 20 words, except under very unusual circumstances.

Abstract

The abstract is a self-contained and brief summary of the main points of the write-up. It enables an interested reader to quickly determine whether the content is likely to be of use to him/her. It should contain a brief statement of the topic being investigated, the design used, the participants investigated, the stimulus materials and apparatus involved, if appropriate, the principal results and their analysis, together with the main conclusions drawn.

> **Now test yourself**
>
> 1 Explain the purpose of an abstract.
>
> TESTED

Introduction

This should present the reasoning behind the particular topic being investigated. The introduction should provide the following information in the following order: (i) a review of the background material (existing findings and theories) relevant to the study, (ii) an outline of the precise topic being investigated and the way it is to be investigated, (iii) an outline of the aim and the hypothesis/hypotheses.

Method

The method describes in detail the operations performed by the researcher. The method should contain enough information for another researcher to be able to repeat the study.

a) **Design:** The research design (independent measures, repeated measures, etc.) if appropriate should be identified and justified. The independent variable(s) and how they were operationalised and the dependent variable and how it was measured should be described.

b) **Sample:** This should give information relating to the participants, i.e. the number, and other characteristics important for the topic under investigation and the conclusions you wish to draw, such as age, age range, sex ratio, educational level, occupation and how they were

> **Exam tips**
>
> Know that descriptions of the research design, sample, materials/apparatus and procedure should all be reported within the method section.
>
> Know that the procedure sub-section should contain adequate detail for another researcher to replicate the study.

selected. This information is very important as it may have implications for the generalisability of any findings.

c) **Materials/apparatus:** The apparatus and materials used should be described. If complex apparatus is used it should be described in sufficient detail to allow equivalent apparatus to be constructed. If special software is used, it should be named. Other materials, such as words, puzzles, questionnaires, etc., should be referred to and included in the appendices. The function of the equipment and the use to which it was put should also be described.

d) **Procedure:** This section should describe exactly what the researchers and the participants did. There should be enough information to enable another researcher to repeat the study. Such information as standardised instructions should be referred to, with the details included in the appendices.

Results

This section should provide a clear, concise summary of the data collected and the results of any statistical tests. A 'rule of thumb' guide for what should be included in this section is: (i) a summary table(s) of the results showing measures of central tendency and dispersion, (ii) if meaningful, visual diagrams, such as graphs of the findings, (iii) identification and justification of any statistical analysis conducted on the findings, (iv) if an inferential test has been used, the following information should be provided: the value of the test statistic, degrees of freedom (or number of participants), whether the test was one-tailed or two-tailed, and the observed p value. Reference should also be made to whether the null hypothesis was rejected and if a significant finding was observed, the direction of the effect. Large amounts of raw data and calculations should not be included in this section but rather in the appendices.

Typical mistakes

Putting far too much detail in the results section.

Not referencing in the main body of the text information that has been placed in the appendices.

Discussion

In this section the results can be interpreted and their meaning discussed. The discussion should relate to the issues raised in the introduction and provide more detail about these issues. The results may not have led to clear-cut answers to the questions initially raised, so the discussion may suggest further research which can be conducted in the future. Limitations of the study which have come to light should also be discussed, for example biases within the sample which may lead to findings having limited generalisability. This section should therefore be presented in three stages: (i) a short statement of results, (ii) an account and explanation of the findings, (iii) implications of the findings and limitations of the study. The final sentence or two should show how the study has benefited the research community and improved understanding of the issues and ideas raised in the introduction.

Now test yourself

2 In which section of a report should a description of the sample be placed?

TESTED ☐

Exam tips

Remember that any raw data and calculations should not be included in the results section but should appear in the appendices at the end of the report.

In this section refer to whether or not the null hypothesis was rejected and whether a significant finding was observed.

Now test yourself

3 Identify two things that should not be placed in the results section and state where they should be placed in the report.

TESTED ☐

Exam tips

Understand that the discussion section is not just an evaluation of the strengths and limitations of the study. There is also the opportunity in this section for the psychologist to make alternative suggestions relating to their findings and suggestions for further research. The psychologist may also consider implications for psychological theory and possible real-world applications.

Learn the Harvard referencing system as outlined on page 22.

Remember that each appendix should have a full title and be referenced somewhere in the main body of the report.

References

Use the Harvard referencing system.

Appendices

Any additional information such as raw data, statistical calculations, stimulus material, standardised instructions, copies of questionnaires, etc. should be placed here. Each appendix should have a full title and be referenced somewhere in the main body of the report.

Citing academic references

REVISED

Be familiar with citing academic research using the Harvard system of referencing. For example:

Loftus, E. F. and Palmer, J. C. (1974) Reconstruction of automobile destruction: An example of the interaction between language and memory. *Journal of Verbal Learning & Verbal Behaviour*, 13 (5), 585–589.

Milgram, S. (1963) Behavioural study of obedience. *Journal of Abnormal and Social Psychology*, 67 (4), 371–378.

Grant, H. M., Lane, C., Bredahl, J. C., Clay, J., Ferrie, J., Groves, J. E., McDorman, T. A. and Dark. V. J. (1988) Context-dependent memory for meaningful material: Information for students. *Applied Cognitive Psychology*, 12 (6), 617–623.

> **Exam tips**
>
> Look at how all the core studies have been referenced using the Harvard system. These can be found in the references section of any of the appropriate textbooks.
>
> Work with a friend. One person writes one of the references with either one or more aspect of the reference missing or incorrect, the other then completes or corrects the reference.

Peer review

REVISED

Appreciate the role of the psychological community in validating new knowledge and ensuring integrity through the process of peer review. Research papers, submitted for publication, are scrutinised by a panel of experts. This allows specialists to judge whether or not the article makes a significant contribution to the body of psychological knowledge or a particular area of psychology. Once published, an article is subject to further peer review through ongoing scrutiny by other researchers. This allows the original researcher and/or other researchers to comment on the work, follow it up and produce further research on the topic. However, as editors tend to prefer to publish positive results, as this will increase the standing of their journal, there can be a bias in publishing results that can lead to a misperception of the true facts.

> **Now test yourself**
>
> 4 Suggest one strength of peer reviews.
> 5 Suggest one weakness of peer reviews.
>
> TESTED

Check your understanding

1 Where, in a practical report, should tables of raw data be placed?
   A Method
   B Abstract
   C Appendices
   D Discussion
2 In the following academic reference, what is missing which should be included when using the Harvard referencing system?

Blakemore, C. and Cooper, G.F. Development of the brain depends on the visual environment. Nature, 228, 477–478.
   A The author's full name
   B The year of publication
   C The volume of the journal
   D The pages of the journal

For practice questions relating to Sections B and C of the exam paper turn to Chapter 7.

ONLINE

Summary

By the end of this chapter you should:
● have knowledge of the conventions of reporting research in a practical report
● understand the role and purpose of each of the main sections of a research report
● know and be able to apply the Harvard referencing system.

6 Science in psychology

How science works

REVISED

Students should understand the following scientific concepts:
- **The study of cause and effect:** experimental research aims to demonstrate a causal relationship by manipulating the independent variable so the effect on the dependent variable can be observed and measured.
- **Falsification:** the ability to demonstrate that a hypothesis is false.
- **Replicability:** the ability to repeat an original procedure in exactly the same way. If a finding from a study is valid, it should be possible to obtain the same finding if the study is repeated.
- **Objectivity:** the ability to take an unbiased external perspective by not being affected by an individual or personal viewpoint. If objectivity is achieved, different researchers will view things from the same perspective.
- **Induction:** a scientific method that uses observations to generate testable hypotheses, which are then developed into theories.
- **Deduction:** a scientific method that develops hypotheses from theories, then tests the hypotheses to see the extent to which they hold true.
- **Hypothesis testing:** a hypothesis is formulated once a theory has been identified or proposed. The hypothesis is then tested through empirical research – research that results in the collection, analysis and evaluation of data.
- **Manipulation of variables:** the manipulation of the independent variable to see the variation in results depending on whether it is or isn't present.
- **Control:** the extent to which any variable(s) is/are held constant or regulated by the researcher.
- **Standardisation:** ensuring that all procedures are the same for every participant so performances are comparable.
- **Quantifiable measurements:** recording behaviour in numbers for ease of analysis.

How psychology contributes to the success of the economy and society

REVISED

The following are examples of how psychological research has helped to improve the social and physical world:
- Improved understanding of the circumstances in which people will obey destructive orders.
- Improved understanding of how authorities can effectively question people who have been witnesses to important events such as accidents and crimes.
- Improved understanding of how observation can lead to the imitation of behaviours.
- Improved understanding of the localisation of brain functions.
- Improved understanding of the social interaction difficulties experienced by individuals on the autistic spectrum.
- Improved treatment of mental health issues.
- Improved understanding of child development, leading to better teaching and learning environments.

Exam tips

Make sure you can explain how the manipulation of an independent variable allows the researcher to infer cause and effect.

Understand how replicability can be enhanced through the use of controls.

Know that objectivity can be achieved through the use of quantifiable measurements.

Answers at **www.hoddereducation.co.uk/myrevisionnotes**

- Improved understanding of attachment, leading to family-friendly environments for hospitalised children.
- Improved understanding of how individuals can be encouraged to adopt positive attitudes to recycling.
- Increased understanding of how to reduce the chances of re-offending, saving the police, etc. time and money.
- Increased understanding about personal space and territory so working environments can be designed to maximise employee productivity and satisfaction.

Now test yourself

1 Give one example of how psychological research has helped to improve the social and physical world.
2 Identify one piece of psychological research that links to the example you have given.

TESTED

Check your understanding

1 Which of these is not a feature of scientific study?
  A   Case study method
  B   Studying cause and effect
  C   Having an independent variable
  D   Measuring a dependent variable
2 What is a definition of falsification?
  A   Demonstrating that data is flawed
  B   Demonstrating that a null hypothesis is false
  C   Demonstrating that a study lacks validity
  D   Demonstrating that a hypothesis is false
3 How can the objectivity be reduced in scientific research?
  A   Testing for inter observer reliability
  B   Using behavioural categories
  C   Allowing experimenter bias
  D   Collecting qualitative data
4 What is a definition of deduction?
  A   Developing a hypotheses from theories
  B   Using observations to generate testable hypotheses
  C   Testing hypotheses through empirical research
  D   Calculating a statistical significance
5 Which of these is a problem caused by lack of control?
  A   No hypothesis being formed
  B   Participants withdrawing
  C   Extraneous variables
  D   Qualitative data being collected
6 How might psychological research contribute to society?
  A   It provides universities with funds
  B   It can give an improved understanding of human behaviour
  C   It can form the basis of further research
  D   It can be carried out ethically

ONLINE

Summary

By the end of this chapter you should:
- know how science works within psychology
- know some ways in which psychology has contributed to the success of the economy and society.

7 Practice questions on research methods

Having reviewed the chapters in Component 1, you should be ready to attempt the following sample examination-style practice questions from Sections B and C.

Section B: Research design and response

1 A psychologist wanted to investigate the relationship between a person's level of happiness and their level of exposure to sunlight as some research suggests that people are happiest when the sun is shining. To do this, the psychologist gave a questionnaire to 15 employees at the G and H Superstore in Littlebridge, England as they reported for work at the beginning of the 18.00 to 24.00-hours shift.

   a) Describe the target population in this study. [2]

   b) The sampling technique used was opportunity sampling. Suggest one strength and one weakness of opportunity sampling as used in this study. [6]

   c) Write an alternative hypothesis for this study. [3]

   d) Describe an appropriate procedure the psychologist could have followed when conducting this study. [12]

In your answer you must refer to the following:
- How the two variables will be measured.
- How the questionnaire will be administered.
- At least two ethical considerations the psychologist would need to consider and how they could be managed.

   e) Explain why the data gathered in this study would be considered quantitative data. [2]

   f) Sketch an appropriate graph to present the data that might have been collected in this study. [4]

   g) State and justify which inferential (non-parametric) test the psychologist would have used to analyse the data gathered. [3]

2 A psychologist wants to investigate whether time of day has an effect on people's reading speed. To do this, she has decided to conduct an experiment using an independent measures design. She intends to gather a sample of 50 A level Psychology students from a local college in Cardiff, Wales – 25 of the students will be tested at 10 a.m. and the other 25 at 2 p.m.

   a) State a null hypothesis for this study. [2]

   b) Identify the independent and dependent variable in this study. [2]

   c) Outline one strength and one weakness of using an independent measures design in this study. [6]

   d) Describe how random sampling could be used to obtain participants for this study. [3]

   e) Describe how the dependent variable could be measured in this study. [4]

   f) Identify one extraneous variable that could affect the results of this study and suggest how it could be controlled. [3]

   g) Discuss ethical issues in relation to this study. [12]

Section C: Data analysis and interpretation

1 A psychologist conducted an observation to investigate what students did in lessons when not working on a task. He told a group of students that he was going to observe their behaviour. He then sat at the back of the classroom and observed them throughout a 40-minute geography lesson. The psychologist made a note each time he observed a behaviour listed on his tally chart. The results of the study are shown in the table below.

Chatting	Using mobile phone	Looking out of the window	Doodling	Drinking (water/soft drinks)	Eating/ chewing	Walking around/getting out of seat	Staring into space/ daydreaming
25	18	12	5	1	3	2	10

a) The tally chart contained eight behavioural categories. Describe one strength and one weakness of using behavioural categories in this observational study. [6]

b) This study gathered data through the event sampling method. Describe one strength and one weakness of event sampling. [4]

c) This was an overt observation.
   i) Explain what is meant by an overt observation. [2]
   ii) Describe one strength and one weakness of overt observations as used in this study. [6]

d) What is the mode for the type of behaviour observed during the 40-minute geography lesson? [1]

e) Sketch a bar chart to show the data recorded in this study. [4]

f) Outline two conclusions that can be drawn from the findings of this study. [6]

2 A researcher investigated the relationship between a person's levels of stress and their performance on a short-term memory test. The researcher placed a poster in a hospital canteen asking for nurses to volunteer to participate in the study. The first ten people to volunteer became the sample. Participants were first asked to rate themselves on a scale of 1 to 20 for how stressed they felt (with 20 being 'extremely stressed'). They were then asked to perform a short-term memory test which involved looking at 30 items displayed on a table in the centre of the room for one minute and then, once the items were covered, to write down as many as they could remember. The results of the investigation are shown in the table below.

Participant number	Self-rating of stress (1–20. 20 = extremely stressed)	Number of items recalled (/30)
1	2	28
2	12	18
3	11	21
4	15	30
5	4	26
6	8	23
7	5	24
8	20	10
9	14	17
10	10	22

a) Identify two findings from the table on page 27. [2]

b) What is the median for the self-rating of stress? Show your calculations. [2]

c) Describe one possible strength and one possible weakness of the volunteer sample used in this study. [6]

d) Sketch an appropriate graph to represent the results of this study. [4]

e) Draw two conclusions from the graph you have just sketched. [6]

f) Identify a suitable non-parametric inferential test that could be used to analyse the data and give one reason to justify your choice. [3]

8 Component content and exam format

Component content

Area	Key theme	Classic study	Contemporary study
Social	Responses to people in authority	Milgram (1963): Obedience	Bocchiaro et al. (2012): Disobedience and whistle-blowing
	Responses to people in need	Piliavin et al. (1969): Subway Samaritan	Levine et al. (2001): Cross-cultural altruism
Cognitive	Memory	Loftus and Palmer (1974): Eyewitness testimony	Grant et al. (1998): Context-dependent memory
	Attention	Moray (1959): Auditory attention	Simons and Chabris (1999): Visual inattention
Developmental	External influences on children's behaviour	Bandura et al. (1961): Transmission of aggression	Chaney et al. (2004): Funhaler study
	Moral development	Kohlberg (1968): Stages of moral development	Lee et al. (1997): Evaluations of lying and truth-telling
Biological	Regions of the brain	Sperry (1968): Split brain study	Casey et al. (2011): Neural correlates of delay of gratification
	Brain plasticity	Blakemore and Cooper (1970): Impact of early visual experience	Maguire et al. (2000): Taxi drivers
Individual differences	Understanding disorders	Freud (1909): Little Hans	Baron-Cohen et al. (1997): Autism in adults
	Measuring differences	Gould (1982): A nation of morons – bias in IQ testing	Hancock et al. (2011): Language of psychopaths

Exam format

Exam facts

H167 (AS level):
- This paper counts as 50 per cent of total AS level.
- It is a written paper of ONE AND HALF hours.
- A total of 75 marks are available for this paper.

H567 (A level):
- This paper counts as 35 per cent of total A level.
- It is a written paper of TWO hours.
- A total of 105 marks are available for this paper.

Exam structure

The paper has THREE sections:
- Section A: Core studies
  - Candidates are required to answer ALL questions.
  - Questions are based on the core studies individually, in their pairs or in terms of their key theme.

- Section B: Areas, perspectives and debates
  - ○ Candidates are required to answer ALL questions.
  - ○ Questions will focus on areas, perspectives and debates:
    - a) Areas: social, cognitive, developmental and biological psychology and the psychology of individual differences.
    - b) Perspectives: behaviourist and psychodynamic.
    - c) Debates: nature/nurture, freewill/determinism, reductionism/ holism, individual/situational explanations, usefulness of research, ethical considerations, conducting socially sensitive research and psychology as a science.
- Section C: Practical applications
  - ○ Candidates are required to answer ALL questions.
  - ○ Questions will require candidates to apply their knowledge and understanding of psychology to a novel source.

What could I be asked?

The examination will require candidates to be able to do the following:

Section A: Core studies	Content

Individual studies	'Tell the story' of each core study in terms of:
	● background
	● method
	  ○ design
	  ○ sample
	  ○ materials/apparatus
	  ○ procedure
	● results
	● conclusions

Core studies in their pairs	● How the two studies are similar ● How the two studies are different ● To what extent the contemporary study changes our understanding of the key theme ● To what extent the contemporary study changes our understanding of individual, social and cultural diversity
Methodological issues	● The strengths and weaknesses of the different research methods and techniques ● The strengths and weaknesses of different types of data ● Ethical considerations ● Validity ● Reliability ● Sampling bias ● Ethnocentrism
Key themes and areas of psychology	● How each core study relates to its key theme ● How each core study relates to the area of psychology it is placed within
Section B: Areas, perspectives and debates	
Areas ● Social ● Cognitive ● Developmental ● Biological ● Individual differences	● The defining principles and concepts of each area ● Research to illustrate each area ● Strengths and weaknesses of each area ● Applications of each area ● How each area is different from and similar to other areas

Perspectives • Behaviourist • Psychodynamic	• The defining principles and concepts of each perspective • Research to illustrate each perspective • Strengths and weaknesses of each perspective • Applications of each perspective • How each perspective is different from and similar to the other perspective
Debates • Nature/nurture • Freewill/determinism • Reductionism/holism • Individual/situational explanations • Usefulness of research • Ethical considerations • Conducting socially sensitive research • Psychology as a science	• The defining principles and concepts of each debate • Different positions within each debate • Research to illustrate different positions within each debate • Applications of different positions within each debate • How each debate is different from and similar to other debates
Section C: Practical applications	
The practical applications of psychology	• Recognise the psychological content in the source • Make evidence-based suggestions in relation to the source • Consider the strengths and weaknesses of the suggestion(s) they themselves are making

9 The area of social psychology

Outline of the social area

Social psychology can be defined as 'the scientific investigation of how the thoughts, feelings and behaviours of individuals are influenced by the actual, imagined or implied presence of others' (Allport, 1935). Social psychology is therefore about how people influence each other. People's behaviour is affected by the social situation they are in, so social psychologists are therefore particularly interested in the effects that environments (situations) have on people's behaviour.

Social psychology also considers how individuals think about other people. This is known as **social cognition** and it can involve such things as stereotyping, prejudice, helping behaviour and aggression.

The influence of others can cause individuals to change their behaviour. Social psychologists have conducted numerous studies of why people conform (change their behaviour to fit in with that of others) – for example, Asch, Zimbardo – and why they obey authority figures – for example, Milgram, Hofling.

An assumption of social psychology is that other people and the surrounding environment are major influences on an individual's behaviour, thought processes and emotions.

An implication of social psychology is that if we want an individual to behave in a certain way, we should ensure that person is placed in an environment where they can witness other people demonstrating the desired behaviour.

> **social cognition** is the process through which people store and apply information about other people and social situations.

Now test yourself

1 Briefly outline the social area of psychology.

TESTED

Key theme: Responses to people in authority

Classic study: Milgram (1963): Behavioural study of obedience

Relation to the social area

First, as Milgram himself suggested, the environment (Yale University) may have influenced participants as to the worthiness of the study and the competence of the experimenter, resulting in high levels of obedience which may not be found in a less prestigious setting. Second, the presence of what appeared to be a legitimate authority figure, dressed in a grey lab coat, carrying a clipboard, influenced the participants' behaviour as they believed him (through socialisation) to be a trustworthy and knowledgeable individual who should be obeyed.

Theory/theories on which the study is based

Obedience is the psychological mechanism that links individual action to political purpose. It is the dispositional feature that binds people to systems of authority. It is an active or deliberate form of social influence.

> **obedience** is a form of social influence that involves performing an action under the orders of an authority figure. It involves a person changing their behaviour because a figure of authority has told them to do so.

Obedience involves (a) being ordered or instructed to do something, (b) being influenced by an authority figure of superior status, (c) the maintenance of social power and status of the authority figure in a hierarchical situation. A person commanded by a legitimate authority usually obeys – it is a ubiquitous and indispensable feature of social life.

Background to the study

From 1933 to 1945, millions of innocent people were systematically slaughtered on command. Such inhumane actions may have originated in the mind of one person, but they could only have been carried out on such a massive scale because large numbers of people obeyed.

History and observation suggest that for many people obedience is such an ingrained behavioural tendency it will override training in ethics, empathy and moral values. This is because when given extreme commands by legitimate authority figures, subordinates adopt an **agentic state** where they become the instrument for carrying out another person's wishes.

The aim of this study was to investigate the process of obedience by testing how far an individual will go in obeying an authority figure, even when the command breaches the moral code that an individual should not hurt another person against their will.

Research method

This study is generally considered a controlled observation. Although Milgram refers to the study as an experiment and the study contains many experimental elements, there was in fact no independent variable. It has also been considered as a pre-test/pre-experiment.

The study took place in a laboratory at Yale University so conditions could be controlled, for example the design of the setting, who was teacher/learner, the learner's recorded and thus standardised responses, the experimenter's 'prods'.

Data was gathered through observations made by both the experimenter who was in the same room as the participant and others who observed the process through one-way mirrors. Most sessions were recorded on magnetic tape, occasional photographs were taken through the one-way mirrors and notes were made on unusual behaviours.

Prior to the study psychology students and professional colleagues estimated the percentage of participants who would administer the highest level of shock. Estimates ranged from 1–3 per cent (mean 1.2 per cent).

Outline of the procedure/study

Forty male participants aged between 20 and 50 years, from the New Haven area, were obtained by a newspaper advertisement and direct mail solicitation which asked for volunteers to participate in a study of memory and learning at Yale University. There was a wide range of occupations in the sample. Participants were paid $4.50 for simply presenting themselves at the laboratory.

Participants were always given the role of teacher (through a fixed lottery) and saw the learner (a confederate) strapped into a chair with (non-active) electrodes attached to his arms. Participants were given a trial shock of 45 volts to simulate genuineness.

agentic state is when individuals allow others to direct their actions and then pass the responsibility for the consequences to the person giving the orders.

Now test yourself

2 Briefly outline the event which was the stimulus for Milgram's study.

TESTED

Typical mistake

Stating that Milgram's study was a laboratory experiment.

Now test yourself

3 Suggest why this study is generally not considered an experiment.

TESTED

Exam tip

Know the procedure in relation to the teacher, learner and experimenter.

The 'teacher' then sat in front of an electric shock generator in an adjacent room. He had to conduct a paired word test on the learner and give him an electric shock of increasing intensity for every wrong answer. The machine had 30 switches ranging from 15 to 450 volts, in 15-volt increments. In reality no actual electrical shocks were administered to the 'learner'.

The 'learner' produced a set of predetermined responses, giving approximately three wrong answers to every correct one. At 300 volts he pounded on the wall and thereafter made no further replies.

If the 'teacher' turned to the experimenter for advice on whether to proceed, the experimenter responded with a series of four standardised prods, such as 'Please continue/Please go on'.

The study finished when the 'teacher' refused to continue (was disobedient) or reached 450 volts (was obedient). The participant was then fully debriefed and introduced to the 'learner' so he could see that no harm had been inflicted.

Typical mistake

Forgetting that Milgram debriefed his participants at the end of the study.

Now test yourself

4 Outline one way participants were deceived in this study.

TESTED

Key findings

All participants, $\frac{40}{40}$/100 per cent, continued to 300 volts.

$\frac{26}{40}$/65 per cent of participants continued to the full 450 volts.

Distribution of break-off points (/40 participants):

No. of participants	Voltage/shock level
26	450
1	375
1	360
1	345
2	330
4	315
5	300

Of the participants, 26 were obedient, 14 disobedient. Many showed signs of extreme stress while administering the shocks, for instance sweating, trembling, stuttering, laughing nervously. Three had full-blown, uncontrollable seizures.

On completion of the test many obedient participants heaved sighs of relief, mopped their brows or nervously fumbled for cigarettes. Some shook their head, apparently in regret; some remained calm throughout.

Milgram offered 13 possible explanations for the high levels of obedience shown by participants, such as the fact that the study was carried out at the prestigious University of Yale, which influenced participants as to the worthiness of the study and the competence of the researcher; the participants were told the shocks were not harmful; the situation was

Exam tips

Know at least three of Milgram's explanations for the results.

Know how this study is similar to the study by Bocchiaro et al. (2012).

Know why this study is different from the study by Bocchiaro et al. (2012).

Know how the study relates to the key theme 'Responses to people in authority'.

completely new for the participant so he had no experience to guide his behaviour.

Conclusions

People will obey others whom they consider legitimate authority figures even if what they are asked to do goes against their moral beliefs.

People obey because certain situational features lead them to suspend their sense of autonomy and become an agent of an authority figure.

Individual differences, such as personality, influence the extent to which people will be obedient.

Contemporary study: Bocchiaro *et al.* (2012): Disobedience and whistle-blowing

Relation to the social area

The study builds on Milgram's earlier study by focusing on **disobedience** and **whistle-blowing** as responses to people in authority who make immoral demands on their subordinates. Many of the participants who complied with the immoral request justified their behaviour by adopting an agentic state, allocating personal responsibility to external forces and saying such things as 'I co-operated because the experimenter asked me to', whereas participants who were defiant (disobedient) or who blew the whistle remained fully responsible for their actions by applying their internalised moral standards, which enabled them to resist the power of the situation.

Theory/theories on which the study is based

Independent behaviour/defiance involves the rejection of social influence/power to behave in accordance with one's internal attitudes, morals and beliefs.

Disobedience/defiance to unjust authority is a precondition for social progress.

In most situations, a lower level of whistle-blowing than disobedience would be anticipated because it involves a potential direct confrontation between the defiant person and the authority.

One might expect obedient individuals to be considerably different from defiants, the latter being, for example, more honest and pro-social. Therefore one might expect personality variables to influence an individual's decision to obey, disobey and openly defy an authority demanding them to act in unethical ways.

Background to the study

Although research has provided important information about the mechanisms of obedience, for example Milgram's study, there is still not a great deal of understanding about the nature of disobedience to unjust authority, with little being known about:

a) Who are the people who disobey or blow the whistle?

b) Why do they choose the challenging moral path?

c) Do they have personal characteristics that differentiate them from those who obey?

Now test yourself

5 Outline one key finding from this study.
6 Suggest one conclusion that can be drawn from the findings of this study.

TESTED

disobedience is when an individual refuses to comply with set rules or someone in authority.

whistle-blowing is when a person exposes any form of activity that is deemed illegal, unethical or not acceptable within either a private or a public organisation.

Now test yourself

7 Using your own words, define the terms 'disobedience' and 'whistle-blowing'.

TESTED

This study was one of the first to look at these topics. Participants were given the option to take personal action against an evil system (in this study an unethical experiment) by obeying, disobeying or blowing the whistle against authorities who encouraged immoral behaviours.

The study also aimed to replicate Milgram's findings by showing a wide gap between people's predictions of their own and others' degree of (dis)obedience and the actual behavioural outcomes.

Research method

Bocchiaro *et al.* consider this study to be a laboratory experiment. However, like Milgram, there was in fact no independent variable, so the study may be best viewed as a controlled laboratory study, or as Bocchiaro *et al.* say, a 'scenario study'.

The study took place in a laboratory at the VU University in Amsterdam, so conditions could be controlled – for example, the procedure was standardised so the experimenter–authority behaviour and cover story were consistent throughout the testing period, two specially prepared rooms were used, timings for when the researcher left the room were kept the same for all participants.

The sample consisted of 149 undergraduate students (96 women, 53 men, mean age = 20.8) who took part in the research in exchange for either €7 or course credit. They were recruited by flyers posted in the university cafeteria.

Data was gathered on the number of participants who obeyed by writing a statement in support of the sensory deprivation study, those who disobeyed by refusing to write the requested statement and those who became whistle-blowers by reporting the researcher's questionable conduct to the research committee. Data was also gathered through the scores on two personality inventories (the Dutch version of the 60-item HEXACO-PI-R), which measured the six major dimensions of personality, and a nine-item Decomposed Games measure, which measured Social Value Orientation (SVO).

In addition, 138 comparison students from the VU University were provided with a detailed description of the scenario setting and were then asked, 'What would you do?' and 'What would the average student at your university do?'

Outline of the procedure/study

Eight pilot tests were conducted to ensure the procedure was standardised, credible and morally acceptable.

In the actual study, participants were informed about their task, the potential benefits/risks of participation, and their right to withdraw at any time with no penalty. They were also assured of the confidentiality of the information collected and asked to complete a consent form.

Each participant was greeted in the laboratory by a male Dutch researcher who was formally dressed and had a stern demeanour. The researcher proceeded with a (seemingly unjustified) request for each participant to provide a few names of fellow students and then presented the cover story, the gist of which was:

> The researcher and an Italian colleague were investigating the effects of sensory deprivation on brain function. A recently conducted

Now test yourself

8 Outline how the sample was gathered and suggest one weakness of this approach.

TESTED

experiment on six participants in Rome who spent some time completely isolated, unable to see or hear anything, had disastrous effects – all panicked, their cognitive abilities were temporarily impaired, some experienced visual and auditory hallucinations, two participants asked to stop because of their strong symptoms but were not allowed to do so because invalid data may then have been collected. The majority said it had been a frightening experience.

The researcher wanted to replicate this study at the VU University using a sample of college students as there was currently no data on young people, but some scientists thought that their brains might be more sensitive to the negative effects of isolation.

Although it was difficult to predict what would happen, the researcher wanted to proceed with the experiment. A university research committee was evaluating whether to approve the study and was collecting feedback from students who knew its details to help them make their decision.

The researcher left the room for three minutes so the participants could reflect on the action-based decisions they were about to make.

Participants were then moved to a second room where there was a computer for them to use to write a statement to convince the students they had previously indicated to participate in the study. They were told to be enthusiastic when writing their statements and had to use two adjectives among 'exciting', 'incredible', 'great' and 'superb'. Negative effects of sensory deprivation were not to be mentioned. A mailbox and the research committee forms were also in this room. If a participant believed the proposed research on sensory deprivation violated ethical norms, they could anonymously challenge it by putting a form in the mailbox.

The researcher told participants to begin and left the room for seven minutes. The researcher then returned and asked the participant to follow him back to the first room where they completed two personality inventories, were probed for suspicion, fully debriefed and asked to sign a second consent form, this time fully informed.

The entire session lasted approximately 40 minutes.

Key findings

Of all the respondents in the comparison group:
- Only 3.6 per cent indicated that they would obey the researcher. Most believed they would be either disobedient (31.9 per cent) or whistle-blowers (64.5 per cent).
- When asked to predict the behaviour of other typical students at their university, only 18.8 per cent thought an average student at VU University would obey, while they believed most other students would either disobey (43.9 per cent) or whistle-blow (37.3 per cent).

Of the 149 participants in the actual laboratory situation:
- 76.5 per cent ($n = 114$) obeyed the experimenter, 14.1 per cent ($n = 21$) disobeyed and 9.4 per cent ($n = 14$) blew the whistle.
- Among whistle-blowers 6.0 per cent ($n = 9$) had written a message (anonymous whistle-blowers) and 3.4 per cent ($n = 5$) had refused to do so (open whistle-blowers).
- No significant differences were found in any of the groups in relation to gender, religious affiliation (Christian/Islamic) or religious involvement (defined in terms of church attendance). However, a significant difference was observed with regard to faith (defined as a confident belief in a transcendent reality).

Now test yourself

9 Outline the procedure followed in this study.
10 Describe why the researcher left the room for three minutes before participants were moved to the second room.

TESTED ☐

There were no significant differences in any of the six personality factors measured by the HEXACO-PI-R.

Results in terms of SVO showed that 'pro-social' and 'individualistic' participants were equally distributed among the three groups.

Exam tips

Know an outline of the cover story.

Know the procedure in relation to both the comparison group and the group tested in the laboratory.

Understand how this study is similar to the study by Milgram (1963).

Understand why this study is different from the study by Milgram (1963).

Know how the study relates to the key theme 'Responses to people in authority'.

Conclusions

Individuals tend to obey authority figures, even if the authority is unjust.

What individuals think/say they and others will do in a given situation often differs from what actually happens.

Individuals behave in completely different ways than expected when they find themselves in certain circumstances that are unfamiliar and somewhat extreme.

Behavioural acts of disobedience and whistle-blowing are psychologically, socially and economically demanding for people, notably whistle-blowers.

Whistle-blowers have more faith than either obedient or disobedient individuals.

Now test yourself

11 Outline the findings in relation to the comparison group.

12 Draw one conclusion from the findings of this study.

TESTED ☐

Section A practice questions

From Milgram's study of obedience:
1 Give one example of quantitative data and one example of qualitative data gathered in this study. [2]
2 Describe two reasons why participants found it difficult to withdraw from this study. [4]
3 Participants were observed to show a lot of tension
   a) Give one example of participants' behaviour that indicated extreme tension. [2]
   b) Milgram suggested that the tension was caused by the conflicts produced by the study. Outline this conflict. [2]

From Bocchiaro et al.'s study of disobedience and whistle-blowing:
4 Outline how two ethical guidelines were upheld in this study. [4]
5 Outline what this study tells us about disobedience. [4]
6 Describe two advantages of conducting this study in a laboratory. [4]
7 a) Identify the type of data gathered in this study. [1]
   b) Outline one finding from this study. [2]
8 This study used the self-report method to gather some of the data
   a) Describe one strength of the self-report method as used in this study. [2]
   b) Describe one weakness of the self-report method as used in this study. [2]
9 Explain why Milgram's study of obedience and Bocchiaro et al.'s study of disobedience and whistle-blowing can be related to the social area of psychology. [4]
10 Both Milgram, in his study of obedience, and Bocchiaro et al., in their study of disobedience and whistle-blowing used a comparison group. Outline the purpose of the comparison group in both of these studies. [4]

For practice questions linked to Sections B and C of the exam paper turn to Chapter 15. [4]

ONLINE ☐

Classic study: Piliavin *et al.* (1969): Subway Samaritan

Relation to the social area

The environment and situation are major influences on whether or not individuals will help another person. Piliavin *et al.*'s study showed that when in a closed area individuals tend not to diffuse responsibility by sharing it among those present; rather, they feel personally responsible and so offer help to a victim in need of assistance. Findings from the study showed that the more people there were present when the incident occurred, the more people went to help the victim. The researchers also found that the condition of a victim influences helping behaviour – if a victim is lame, people are more likely to help than if the victim is drunk. Also, if a victim is the same race as a potential helper, they are more likely to help them.

Theory/theories on which the study is based

Although pluralistic ignorance and/or genuine ambiguity make it less likely that an individual will define a situation as an emergency, in many situations the reason an individual may not help is because they diffuse responsibility.

Diffusion of responsibility is where the responsibility for the situation is spread (diffused) among the people present. This implies that the more people present, the more the bystander believes the responsibility is spread out so they feel less personal responsibility and are therefore less likely to help.

Another explanation for not helping a victim in need is that a bystander may believe that someone else will do what is necessary so there is no need for them to offer assistance. This is known as **bystander apathy**.

It is also suggested that individuals apply a cost–reward matrix when deciding whether or not to help an individual – they weigh up the costs of helping against the benefits and select the action that they feel is most likely to rid them of the unpleasant emotional state they find themselves in because of the situation.

Background to the study

Since the murder of Kitty Genovese in 1964 (a woman stabbed to death over a period of 30 minutes in front of 38 unresponsive witnesses), many social psychologists have studied the concept of good Samaritanism.

Research by Darley and Latané (1968) found that bystanders hearing an epileptic fit over earphones led to those who believed other witnesses to be present being less likely to help the victim than bystanders who believed they were alone.

Subsequent research by Latané and Rodin (1969) on the response to the victim of a fall confirmed this finding and suggested that assistance from bystanders was less likely if they were strangers than if they were acquaintances.

Field experiments conducted by Bryan and Test (1967) showed that individuals are more likely to be good Samaritans if they have just observed another individual performing a helpful act.

diffusion of responsibility is the tendency for multiple bystanders to be less likely to help in the event of an emergency than if they were there on their own. In such cases, the responsibility for action is shared (or diffused) among all the bystanders present. Because of the other people present, each individual feels less personal responsibility to help and is therefore less likely to do so.

bystander apathy is the tendency of people witnessing an emergency to ignore the problem.

Much of the work on victimisation has been conducted in laboratory settings, using non-visual emergency situations. This study was designed to investigate, under real-life conditions, the effect of several variables on helping behaviour.

Research method

The study was a field experiment. The field situation involved the A and D trains of the 8th Avenue New York subway (Figure 9.1) between 59th Street and 125th Street, a journey lasting about 7½ minutes.

The experiment had four independent variables:
1 Type of victim (drunk or carrying a cane).
2 Race of victim (black or white).
3 Effect of a model (after 70 or 150 seconds, from the critical or adjacent area), or no model at all.
4 Size of the witnessing group (a naturally occurring independent variable).

The dependent variables (recorded by two female observers seated in the adjacent area) were:
● frequency of help
● speed of help
● race of helper
● sex of helper
● movement out of critical area
● verbal comments by bystanders.

Outline of the procedure/study

Participants were about 4,500 men and women who used the subway on weekdays between 11 a.m. and 3 p.m. between 15 April and 26 June 1968. About 45 per cent were black, 55 per cent white.

There were four teams of four researchers: two female observers, two males – one acting as victim, one as the model.

The victims (three white, one black) were all male, General Studies students, aged 26 to 35 years and dressed alike. They either smelled of liquor and carried a liquor bottle wrapped tightly in a brown bag or appeared sober and carried a black cane. In all aspects they acted identically in both conditions.

The models (all white) were males aged 24 to 29 years. There were four model conditions:
1 Critical area – early (70 seconds after the victim collapsed).
2 Critical area – late (150 seconds after the victim collapsed).
3 Adjacent area – early (70 seconds after the victim collapsed).
4 Adjacent area – late (150 seconds after the victim collapsed).

The observers recorded the dependent variables.

The victim stood near a pole in the critical area. After about 70 seconds he staggered forward and collapsed. Until receiving help he remained supine on the floor, looking at the ceiling. If he received no help by the time the train stopped, the model helped him to his feet. At the stop the team disembarked and waited separately until other passengers had left the station. They then changed platforms to repeat the process in the opposite direction.

Between 6 and 8 trials were run on a given day, all using the same 'victim condition'.

Figure 9.1 The New York subway

Exam tip

Make sure you know the field situation.

Now test yourself

15 Explain why this study can be considered a field experiment.

TESTED

Typical mistake

Forgetting that the victim was dressed exactly the same in both the drunk and lame conditions.

Typical mistake

Confusing the victim and the model by calling the victim the model.

Exam tip

Know the procedure in relation to the victim, model and observers.

Now test yourself

16 Describe how the confederate played the role of the drunk victim.

TESTED

Key findings

The cane victim received spontaneous help 95 per cent of the time (62/65 trials) compared with the drunk victim 50 per cent of the time (19/38 trials).

Overall there was 100 per cent help for the cane victim compared with 81 per cent help for the drunk victim.

Help was offered more quickly to the cane victim (a median of five seconds compared with 109 seconds' delay for the drunk victim).

In 49/81 (60 per cent) trials, when help was given this was provided by two or more helpers.

90 per cent of the first helpers were males.

There was a slight tendency for same-race helping, especially in the drunk condition.

No diffusion of responsibility was found – in fact, response times were faster with larger groups than smaller ones.

More comments were made by passengers in the drunk than the cane condition and most comments were made when no help was given within the first 70 seconds.

> **Typical mistake**
>
> Not realising there was no inter-rater reliability as the observers collected data from different areas of the carriage.

> **Exam tips**
>
> Know the similarities and differences between this study and that of Levine *et al.* (2001).
>
> Know how the study relates to the key theme 'Responses to people in need'.

Conclusions

An individual who appears ill/lame is more likely to receive help than one who appears drunk.

With mixed groups of men and women, men are more likely than women to help a male victim.

With mixed-race groups, people are more likely to help those of the same race as themselves, particularly if they deem the victim's situation to be of his own making.

There is no strong relationship between number of bystanders and speed of helping when an incident is visible.

Individuals whom others consider not responsible for their situation are more likely to receive help than individuals whom others feel brought the situation upon themselves.

When escape is not possible and bystanders are face to face with a victim, help is likely to be forthcoming.

Bystanders conduct a cost–reward analysis before deciding whether or not to help a victim.

> **Now test yourself**
>
> 17 Describe one difference in helping behaviour towards the cane victim and the drunk victim.
>
> 18 Suggest why an individual who appears ill or lame is more likely to receive help than an individual who appears drunk.
>
> TESTED ☐

Contemporary study: Levine *et al.* (2001): Cross-cultural altruism

Relation to the social area

Helping behaviour refers to voluntary actions intended to help others and is a form of pro-social behaviour. This study found large cultural variations in the pro-social behaviour of helping, with countries such as Brazil, Mexico and Spain – countries with cultural values of being nice, friendly and having a concern for others, or **simpatia** – showing higher rates of helping behaviours than cities such as New York or Kuala Lumpur, Malaysia. The study also found that overall levels of helping across cultures were inversely related to a country's economic productivity, suggesting that individuals in poorer countries are more prepared to offer help than those in countries with greater purchasing power.

All of the variables against which levels of helping behaviour were correlated in this study were social variables, i.e. how many people lived in each city, how well off the people were in each city, how individualistic/collectivist the people in each city were and how quickly the people moved around each city centre.

Theory/theories on which the study is based

Theories about helping behaviour include:
- Kin selection theory: this refers to the tendency to perform behaviours that may favour the chance of survival of people with a similar genetic base (for example, Hoffman, 1981).
- Reciprocal altruism: this suggests that an individual's helping behaviour is based on the expectation that other people will perform altruistic (helping) acts in return.
- Responsibility–pro-social value orientation: this holds that a strong influence on helping behaviour is a feeling of and belief in one's responsibility to help, especially when combined with the belief that one is able to help the other person (Staub, 2003).
- Social exchange theory: people help because they want to gain goods from the one being helped. They calculate rewards and costs of helping others, aiming to maximise the rewards and minimise the costs (Foa and Foa, 1975).

Milgram (1970) proposed that people in urban areas are less helpful than those in rural areas because they cope with stimulus overload differently: urban dwellers restrict their attention mainly to personally relevant events. Strangers, and their situations of need, may therefore go unnoticed.

Background to the study

Studies conducted in several countries (including the USA, Saudi Arabia and Sudan) have found that people living in urban areas tend to be less helpful than those in rural settings (Hedge and Yousif, 1992; Yousif and Korte, 1995).

Virtually all of the studies of community differences in helping have focused on the single variable of population size, most often testing the hypothesis that the tendency to help strangers declines as the size of the city increases – see Steblay (1987).

Triandis (1991) found a major cultural difference in helping behaviour to be the difference between **collectivism** and **individualism**. Collectivists attend more to the needs and goals of the group they belong to, while individualists focus on themselves. Therefore, collectivists would be more likely to help in-group members but less likely than individuals to help strangers.

Although many studies have demonstrated that helping rates differ between communities in a single country, almost no systematic cross-cultural research of helping behaviour had been conducted prior to this

simpatia has no English translation, but it is generally understood to refer to a feeling of community, work ethic and compassion shown particularly in Spanish and Portuguese communities, which place great value on being nice, friendly and sympathetic towards others.

Now test yourself

19 Outline one theory of helping behaviour.

TESTED

collectivism is a type of social arrangement or culture where the good of the group is considered more important than the good of the individual. The social outlook emphasises the significance of groups.

individualism refers to any culture where the main type of social arrangement is the nuclear family (parent(s) and children). Here the social outlook emphasises significance of the individual.

study. The aim of this study was therefore to look at helping behaviour, in a wide range of cultures, in large cities around the world in relation to the four specific community variables of population size, economic well-being, cultural values (individualism–collectivism, simpatia) and walking speed (pace of life).

This study had three main goals:

1 To determine whether a city's tendency to offer non-emergency help to strangers is a cross-culturally stable characteristic of a place.
2 To obtain a descriptive body of data on helping behaviour across cultures using identical procedures.
3 To identify country-level variables that might relate to differences in helping.

In addition to population size, three overlapping cultural variables were assessed for community-level differences in helping behaviour, none of which had been previously considered in cross-cultural research. These were economic prosperity, cultural values and pace of life.

Research method

This can be considered a quasi experiment conducted in a natural environment which used an independent measures design. Correlational analysis was used to analyse the data.

The field situation was 23 large cities around the world, including Rio de Janeiro (Brazil), Calcutta (India), Madrid (Spain), Shanghai (China), Budapest (Hungary), Rome (Italy), New York (USA) and Kuala Lumpur (Malaysia).

> **Exam tip**
>
> Make sure you name the field situation.

The experiment had three measures of helping behaviour (Figure 9.2):

1 Whether the victim dropped a pen.
2 Whether the victim had a hurt/injured leg.
3 Whether the victim was blind and trying to cross the street.

Each of the three helping measures and the walking speed measure were administered in two or more locations, in main downtown areas, during main business hours, on clear days, during the summer months of one or more years between 1992 and 1997.

Figure 9.2 The three helping measures

For the dropped pen and hurt leg situations, only individuals walking alone were selected. Children (younger than 17 years old) and people who were physically disabled, very old, carrying packages, etc. (i.e. those who might not be fully capable or expected to help) were excluded.

Participants were drawn from large cities in the 23 countries. Participants were the second person who crossed a predetermined line at the site of the investigation. The helping rate of the 23 individual cities was calculated to give each city an Overall Helping Index. The three measures of helping were correlated with statistics reflecting population size, economic well-being, cultural values (individualism–collectivism, simpatia) and the pace of life for each of the 23 locations.

Outline of the procedure/study

All experimenters were college age and dressed neatly and casually. To control for experimenter gender effects and to avoid potential problems in some cities, all experimenters were men.

To ensure standardisation in scoring and to minimise experimenter effects:

- all experimenters received both a detailed instruction sheet and on-site field training for acting their roles, learning the procedure for participant selection and scoring of participants
- the experimenters practised together
- no verbal communication was required of the experimenter.

The three helping measures were:

1 Dropped pen: walking at a carefully practised, moderate pace (15 paces/ 10 seconds), experimenters walked towards a solitary pedestrian passing in the opposite direction. When 10 to 15 feet from the participant, the experimenter reached into his pocket and accidentally, without appearing to notice, dropped his pen behind him, in full view of the participant, and continued walking past the participant. A total of 214 men and 210 women were approached. Participants were scored as having helped if they called back to the experimenter that he had dropped the pen and/or picked up the pen and brought it to the experimenter.

2 Hurt leg: walking with a heavy limp and wearing a large and clearly visible leg brace, experimenters accidentally dropped and unsuccessfully struggled to reach down for a pile of magazines as they came within 20 feet of a passing pedestrian. A total of 253 men and 240 women were approached. Helping was defined as offering to help and/or beginning to help without offering.

3 Helping a blind person across the street: experimenters, dressed in dark glasses and carrying a white cane, acted the role of a blind person needing help getting across the street. Experimenters attempted to locate downtown corners with crosswalks, traffic signals and moderate, steady pedestrian flow. They stepped up to the corner just before the light turned green, held out their cane and waited until someone offered help. A trial was terminated after 60 seconds or when the light turned red, whichever occurred first, after which the experimenter walked away from the corner. A total of 281 trials were conducted. Helping was scored if participants, at a minimum, informed the experimenter that the light was green.

Key findings

NB: For purposes of analyses, each of the 23 cities/countries was treated as a single participant.

Now test yourself

20 Outline two aims of this study.

21 Identify two helping behaviours measured in this study.

TESTED

Typical mistake

Forgetting that, to control for gender effects, all the experimenters were men.

Exam tip

Know the procedure in relation to the participants, the experimenters and the three measures of helping.

Now test yourself

22 Describe the 'hurt leg' condition.

TESTED

Inter-correlations of helping measures are shown in the table below.

Helping measure			
	Blind person	**Dropped pen**	**Hurt leg**
Dropped pen	28**		
Hurt leg	.21	.36***	
Blind + Pen + Leg	.67****	.77****	.73****

**p < .10. ***p < .05. ****p < .01 using 1-tailed significance test. n = 23 in all cases.

The table shows that two of the three correlations were significant. All three inter-correlations were in the positive direction.

No significant gender differences in helping behaviour were found in the two conditions in which relatively equal numbers of male and female participants were targeted by the experimenter (dropped pen, hurt leg).

An overall helping index was calculated, combining results for the three helping measures. Results showed that the most helpful cities/countries were (1) Rio de Janeiro (Brazil), 93 per cent, (2) San Jose (Costa Rica), 91 per cent, (3) Lilongwe (Malawi), 86 per cent. The least helpful cities/countries were (23) Kuala Lumpur (Malaysia), 40 per cent, (22) New York (USA), 45 per cent, (21) Singapore (Singapore), 48 per cent.

Correlations between helping measures and other community characteristics showed that on average there were low correlations between the community variables and helping measures. The only statistically reliable relationship was between the economic productivity measure and overall helping: cities that were more helpful tended to have lower PPP (purchasing power parity).

Although statistically insignificant, there was a small relationship between walking speed and overall helping, with participants in faster cities somewhat less likely to help.

More individualistic countries showed somewhat less overall helping and less helping in the hurt leg situation than collectivist countries, but none of the correlations reached significance. There was no relationship between population size and helping behaviour.

Simpatia countries (Brazil, Costa Rica, El Salvador, Mexico and Spain) were, on average, more helpful than non-simpatia countries.

Overall, a city's helping rate was relatively stable across all three measures.

Conclusions

Helping strangers is a cross-culturally meaningful characteristic of a place. There are large cross-cultural variations in helping rates. Helping across cultures is inversely related to a country's economic productivity. Countries with the cultural tradition of simpatia are, on average, more helpful than countries with no such tradition.

Although faster cities tend to be less helpful than slower cities, the link between economic health and helping is not a by-product of a fast pace of life in affluent societies.

The value of collectivism–individualism is unrelated to helping behaviours.

Typical mistake

Forgetting how helping behaviour was scored in each of the three situations.

Now test yourself

23 Outline one finding in relation to the helping behaviours shown in simpatia countries.

24 Suggest one conclusion that can be drawn from the findings of this study in relation to helping behaviours.

TESTED

Exam tips

Know how this study is similar to and different from the study by Piliavin et al. (1969).

Know how the study relates to the key theme 'Responses to people in need'.

Section A practice questions

From Piliavin *et al.*'s subway Samaritan study:

1 (a) Describe the sampling method used in this study.   [2]
   (b) Suggest one weakness of using this sampling method for this study.   [2]
2 Outline two practical difficulties the researchers may have encountered whilst conducting
   this study.   [4]
3 Suggest how the participants who did not help the victim might have applied the
   cost-reward matrix.   [4]
4 (a) Explain what is meant by 'diffusion of responsibility'.   [2]
   (b) Suggest one reason why diffusion of responsibility did not occur in this study.   [2]
5 Describe two controls used in the study by Levine at al. on cross-cultural altruism.   [4]

From Levine *et al.*'s study on cross-cultural altruism:

6 (a) Outline how the experimenters were prepared for this study.   [2]
   (b) Suggest one advantage of preparing the experimenters in this study.   [2]
7 Outline two of the three ways helping behaviour was tested.   [4]
8 (a) Define the term 'simpatia'.   [2]
   (b) Outline the difference in relation to helping behaviour found in simpatia countries compared
       to non-simpatia countries.   [2]
9 Describe how the studies by Piliavin *et al.* and Levine *et al.* relate to the key theme
   'Responses to people in need'.   [4]
10 Explain why both Piliavin *et al.*'s subway Samaritan study and Levine *et al.*'s study into
   cross-cultural altruism are considered field studies.   [4]

For practice questions linked to Sections B and C of the exam paper turn to Chapter 15.

ONLINE ☐

Summary

By the end of this chapter for the two AS-level studies and/or the four A-level studies you should:

- know the research method and sample
- know the key findings
- be able to suggest at least one way in which each study could be improved and possible implications of the suggestion(s) for methodology, ethics, reliability, validity, usefulness, practicality, etc.
- know how each study relates to the area of social psychology
- know strengths/weaknesses of conducting research under controlled conditions, snapshot studies, observation and self-reports (including rating scales) as ways to gather data, quantitative and qualitative data, the sample
- be able to consider the issues of reliability, validity and ecological validity, ethnocentrism
- understand how each study links to the psychological debates of nature/nurture, freewill/determinism, reductionism/holism, individual/situational explanations, usefulness of research, ethical considerations, conducting socially sensitive research, psychology as a science.

Answers at **www.hoddereducation.co.uk/myrevisionnotes**

10 The area of cognitive psychology

Outline of the cognitive area

Cognitive psychology is based on an analogy between the mind and the digital computer. Individuals receive information through their senses (sight, hearing, taste, touch, smell) and cognitive psychology focuses on how a person makes sense of this information. So, like a computer, individuals receive, process and respond to received information, the response being the behaviour the individual displays.

Cognitive psychology therefore involves the study of all mental processes such as memory, perception, thinking, attention, reasoning, problem solving and language. It is impossible to see thinking or memory; one can see only the end result of these cognitive processes as they are displayed in behaviour. The cognitive area sees psychologists trying to explain behaviour through the effects of mental processes.

An assumption of cognitive psychology is that humans, like computers, are information processors. The brain receives, interprets and responds to information in a similar way to a computer, with the response being displayed through an individual's behaviour.

An implication of cognitive psychology is that if individuals receive, process and respond to information in different ways, then their behaviour will be different.

> **Now test yourself**
>
> 1 Describe one assumption of the cognitive area of psychology.
>
> TESTED

Key theme: Memory

Classic study: Loftus and Palmer (1974): Eyewitness testimony

Relation to the cognitive area

Cognitive processes include how we attain, retain and regain information through the processes of perception, attention, memory, problem solving, decision-making, language and thought. This study is concerned with eyewitness testimony (EWT) and shows that memory is reconstructive. Bartlett's (1932) theory of reconstructive memory proposes that individuals reconstruct the past by fitting new information into their existing understanding of the world – **a schema**.

Loftus and Palmer showed that EWT is influenced by people's tendency to reconstruct their memories of events to fit their schemas.

Theory/theories on which the study is based

Schema theory proposes that memory is influenced by what an individual already knows and that their use of past experience to deal with a new experience is a fundamental feature of the way the human mind works.

Knowledge is stored in memory as a set of schemas – simplified, generalised mental representations of everything an individual understands by a given type of object or event based on their past experiences.

> **Now test yourself**
>
> 2 Outline Bartlett's theory of reconstructive memory.
>
> TESTED

> **a schema** in psychology is a cognitive framework or concept that helps an individual organise and interpret information. A schema informs a person about what to expect from a variety of experiences and situations. Schemas are developed based on information provided by life experiences which are then stored in memory.

Background to the study

Memory involves interpreting what is seen or heard, recording bits of it and then reconstructing these bits into memories when required. This infers recall can be distorted or biased by certain features of the situation.

Loftus and Palmer conducted a good number of studies investigating ways in which memory can be distorted, many of which show that EWT is highly unreliable because it can be influenced by such things as subtle differences in the wording of questions.

This study focuses on the effects of 'leading questions' on an individual's ability to accurately remember events. The expectation was that any information subtly introduced after the event through leading questions – questions phrased in a way suggesting the expected answer – would distort the original memory.

Research method

Experiment 1

This was a laboratory experiment using an independent measures design.

The independent variable (IV) was the wording of a critical question hidden in a questionnaire. This question asked: 'About how fast were the cars going when they hit/smashed/collided/contacted/bumped each other?'

The dependent variable (DV) was the estimated speed given by the participant.

Experiment 2

This was also a laboratory experiment using an independent measures design. The IV was the wording on a question in a questionnaire:
- One group was asked: 'About how fast were the cars going when they smashed into each other?'
- A second group was asked: 'About how fast were the cars going when they hit each other?'
- A third group was not asked about speed.

One week later, all participants were asked to complete another questionnaire which contained the critical question: 'Did you see any broken glass?' The DV was whether the answer to this question was Yes or No.

Outline of the procedure/study

Experiment 1

Forty-five students were divided into five groups, with nine participants in each group. All participants were shown the same seven film clips of different traffic accidents which were originally made as part of a driver safety film.

After each clip participants were given a questionnaire which asked them first to describe the accident and then answer a series of questions about the accident.

There was one critical question in the questionnaire: 'About how fast were the cars going when they hit each other?'

One group was given this question while the other four groups were given the verbs 'smashed', 'collided', 'contacted' or 'bumped' instead of 'hit'.

Experiment 2

One hundred and fifty students were divided into three equal groups. All participants were shown a one-minute film which contained a four-second multiple car crash. They were then given a questionnaire which asked them to describe the accident and answer a set of questions about the incident.

There was a critical question about speed:

- One group was asked: 'About how fast were the cars going when they smashed into each other?'
- Another group was asked: 'About how fast were the cars going when they hit each other?'
- The third group did not have a question about vehicular speed.

One week later, all participants, without seeing the film again, completed another questionnaire about the accident which contained the further critical question: 'Did you see any broken glass – Yes/No?' There had been no broken glass in the original film.

Key findings

Experiment 1

a) The table shows speed estimates for the verbs used in the critical question.

Verb	Mean speed estimate (mph)
Smashed	40.5
Collided	39.3
Bumped	38.1
Hit	34.0
Contacted	31.8

'Smashed' produced the fastest speed estimates and 'contacted' the slowest.

b) For the four-staged films where speeds were measured accurately:
- the film of a crash at 20 mph was estimated to be 37.7 mph
- the film of a crash at 30 mph was estimated to be 36.2 mph
- the films of crashes at 40 mph were estimated to be 39.7 mph and 36.1 mph.

Experiment 2

a) The table shows speed estimates for the verbs used in the question about speed.

Verb	Mean speed estimate (mph)
Smashed	10.46
Hit	8.00

'Smashed' produced the highest speed estimates.

b) Responses to the question 'Did you see any broken glass?' are shown in the table.

Response	Smashed	Hit	Control
Yes	16	7	6
No	34	43	44

Now test yourself

5 Outline the procedure followed in Experiment 2.

TESTED

Typical mistakes

Forgetting that in Experiment 1 participants watched seven short clips of car crashes and were asked to complete a questionnaire after watching each film but that in Experiment 2 participants watched only one short clip which involved multiple cars crashing.

Forgetting that, in Experiment 2, participants were asked the question about speed immediately after watching the film of the multiple car crash but that the question relating to seeing broken glass was not asked until a week later.

Exam tip

Know the key findings for each experiment and be able to draw conclusions from them.

Now test yourself

6 Outline one key finding from Experiment 1.
7 Outline one key finding from Experiment 2.

TESTED

More participants in the 'smashed' condition than either the 'hit' or control groups reported seeing broken glass. The majority of participants in each group correctly recalled that they had not seen any broken glass.

Conclusions

The verb used in a question influences a participant's response, i.e. the way a question is phrased influences the answer given.

People are not very good at judging vehicular speed.

Contemporary study: Grant *et al.* (1998): Context-dependent memory

Relation to the cognitive area

This study is concerned with memory, a cognitive process. An individual's ability to remember information can be enhanced if the environment in which they are asked to recall the information is the same as the one in which the information was originally received or learned. When information is memorised, cues from the environment are subtly encoded and, when the information is recalled, the same environmental cues can enhance the memory. There is therefore a context-dependent aspect to the cognitive process of remembering.

Theory/theories on which the study is based

Context-dependent memory refers to improved recall of specific episodes or information when the context present at encoding and retrieval are the same.

A number of factors are thought to affect how contextual information interacts with memory recall. An analysis of the literature on environmental context-dependency memory by Smith and Vela (2001) suggests that in cases where contextual information is not particularly salient, context-dependent effects on memory are reduced.

Context effects differ when it comes to what sort of task is being performed. Research by Godden and Baddeley (1975, 1980) showed the effects of context change on memory retrieval are much greater in recall tests than in recognition tests, suggesting there are differences in the retrieval process involved in the two types of tests.

Background to the study

Grant *et al.* were interested in studying whether environmental context-dependency effects are found with the type of material and the type of tests typically encountered in school.

Observations had shown that many students study material in environments very different from those in which they are tested – study environments often include background noise from either family, friends or television, while test environments are frequently silent.

Grant *et al.* therefore aimed to show that environmental context can have a more positive effect on performance in a meaningful memory test when the test takes place in the same environment in which the to-be-remembered material was originally studied (the matching condition) than when the test occurs in a different environment (mismatching condition).

Now test yourself

8 Draw one conclusion from the findings of this study.

TESTED

Exam tips

Know how this study is similar to and different from the study by Grant *et al.* (1998).

Know how the study relates to the key theme 'Memory'.

context-dependent memory is a state-dependent form of memory that makes things easier to recall if a person is in the same place during both memory encoding (or storage) and recall.

Now test yourself

9 Outline the aim of this study.

TESTED

Research method

This was a laboratory experiment using an independent measures design. The IVs were:

- whether the participant read the two-page article under silent or noisy conditions
- whether the participant was tested under matching or mismatching conditions.

The first IV – study context (silent versus noisy) – and the second IV – test context (silent versus noisy) – were manipulated in a between-subjects factorial design, producing four conditions.

The DV was the participant's performance on (a) a short-answer recall test and (b) a multiple-choice recall test.

Outline of the procedure/study

Eight members of a psychology laboratory class served as experimenters. Each experimenter recruited five acquaintances to serve as participants. There were 39 participants, ranging in age from 17 to 56 years (17 female, 23 male – 1 participant's results were omitted from the analyses).

Each experimenter worked with one participant for each of the four conditions and an additional participant for one of the conditions was assigned by the instructor. Experimenters randomly assigned their participants to their five conditions.

Stimuli

a) Each experimenter provided their own cassette player and headphones. The eight cassettes were exact copies made from a master tape of background noise recorded during lunchtime in a university cafeteria. The background noise consisted of occasional distinct words/phrases embedded within a general conversational hum that was intermixed with the sounds produced by movement of chairs and dishes. The tape was played at a moderately loud level.

b) A two-page, three-column article on psychoimmunology (Hales, 1984) was selected as the to-be-studied material.

c) Sixteen multiple-choice questions, each consisting of a stem and four alternatives, were generated, all of which tested memory for points stated in the text. Ten short-answer questions were derived from those multiple-choice stems that could easily be restated to produce a question that could be answered unambiguously by a single word or phrase. The order of the questions on each test followed the order in which the tested points were made in the text. The short-answer test was always administered first to ensure that recall of information from the article was being tested and not recall of information from the multiple-choice test.

Procedure

Instructions, describing the experiment as a class project and stating that participation was voluntary, were read aloud. Participants were asked to read the given article once, as if they were reading it for a class assignment. They were allowed to highlight and underline as they read. Participants were informed that their comprehension would be tested with both a short-answer test and a multiple-choice test.

All participants wore headphones while they read (Figure 10.1). Those in the silent condition were told they would not hear anything over

Exam tip

Make sure you know the research design used in this study.

Now test yourself

10 Identify the dependent variable in this study.

TESTED

Typical mistake

Forgetting that although the experimenters were all psychology students, the participants weren't – they were merely acquaintances of the experimenters.

Typical mistake

Forgetting that the short-answer test was given, followed by the multiple-choice test, not vice versa.

Figure 10.1 Participants were all asked to wear headphones throughout the experiment

Exam tip

Know the procedure followed and at least two controls used in this study.

the headphones while those in the noisy condition were told they would hear moderately loud background noise but that they should ignore it.

Reading times were recorded by the experimenters.

A break of approximately two minutes between the end of the study phase and the beginning of the test phase was incorporated to minimise recall from short-term memory. The short-answer test was given, followed by the multiple-choice test.

Participants were tested in either silent or noisy conditions and were informed of the condition before testing. Regardless of testing condition, all participants wore headphones. At the end of the testing phase participants were debriefed concerning the purpose of the experiment.

The entire procedure lasted about 30 minutes.

Key findings

Mean reading time (in minutes) and mean number of correct answers on the two tests are shown in the table.

| Test condition | Study condition | | | |
| | Silent | | Noisy | |
	Mean	Standard deviation	Mean	Standard deviation
Reading time (mins)				
Silent	15.0	7.08	13.8	6.78
Noisy	11.8	3.07	14.0	8.24
Short-answer test (out of 10)				
Silent	6.7	1.22	5.4	1.9
Noisy	4.6	1.17	6.2	2.2
Multiple-choice test (out of 16)				
Silent	14.3	1.58	12.7	1.64
Noisy	12.7	1.64	14.3	1.77

Results suggest participants in all groups spent roughly equal amounts of time studying the material. Therefore reading time was used as a co-variable in the analysis of test performance.

There was a reliable Study Condition × Test Condition interaction for both the short-answer test and the multiple-choice test, showing that studying and testing in the same environment produced better results.

There was no overall effect of noise on performance.

Conclusions

There are context-dependency effects for newly learned meaningful material regardless of whether a short-answer test or a multiple-choice test is used to assess learning.

Studying and testing in the same environment leads to enhanced performance.

Exam tips

Know how this study is similar to and different from the study by Loftus and Palmer (1974).

Know how the study relates to the key theme 'Memory'.

Now test yourself

11 Outline the sample used in this study.
12 Describe how the sample was gathered.
13 Suggest why all participants wore headphones.

TESTED

Now test yourself

From the table:
14 Identify one finding in relation to the short-answer test completed by participants in the silent study/silent test condition.
15 Identify one finding in relation to the multiple-choice test completed by participants in the silent study/noisy test condition.
16 Suggest why students are likely to perform better in exams if they study for them in a quiet environment.

TESTED

Section A practice questions

From the study by Loftus and Palmer on eyewitness testimony:
1 a) Identify the independent variable (IV) and the dependent variable (DV) in the first experiment. [2]
  b) Outline how the independent variable (IV) was manipulated in the first experiment. [2]
2 Outline two ways the procedure was standardised. [4]
3 Describe one strength and one weakness of the experimental method as used in this study. [4]
4 Loftus and Palmer proposed that 'two kinds of information go into one's memory for some complex occurrence'. Describe these two kinds of memory in relation to this study. [4]

From Grant *et al.*'s study on context-dependent memory:
5 Explain what is to be understood by the term 'context-dependent memory'. [4]
6 Identify the four testing conditions. [4]
7 Outline two key findings from this study. [4]
8 Suggest two conclusions that can be drawn from this study. [4]
9 Describe how the study by Loftus and Palmer on eyewitness testimony and the study by Grant *et al.* on context-dependent memory relate to the key theme of 'Memory'. [4]
10 Explain why the study by Loftus and Palmer on eyewitness testimony and the study by Grant *et al.* on context-dependent memory can both be considered experiments. [4]

For practice questions linked to Sections B and C of the exam paper turn to Chapter 15.

ONLINE

Key theme: Attention

REVISED

Classic study: Moray (1959): Auditory attention

Relation to the cognitive area

An individual's brain receives an incredible amount of information from the surrounding environment via their senses. **Attention** is the cognitive process that enables individuals to select certain information while rejecting other information. Attention allows an individual to focus on one thing while blocking out or ignoring other things. This cognitive process is known as either **selective attention** or **focused attention**. Although the brain seems to have the ability to selectively block unwanted information, some information seems able to break through this attentional barrier. This study aimed to investigate factors that would enable information that was not being focused on to break through the **cognitive attentional barrier** so they become noticed.

Theory/theories on which the study is based

Broadbent (1958) argued that as the world is composed of many more sensations than can be handled by the perceptual and cognitive capabilities of the human observer, to cope with the flood of available information humans must selectively attend to only some information and somehow 'tune out' the rest. Attention, therefore, is the result of a limited-capacity information-processing system.

There are two main methods of studying attention:
a) Selective attention: here people are presented with two or more simultaneous 'messages' and are instructed to process and respond to only one of them.

Now test yourself

17 What is attention?

TESTED

attention is the act of careful observing or listening.

selective/focused attention is simply the act of focusing on a particular object for a period of time while simultaneously ignoring irrelevant information that is also occurring. The two terms are synonymous.

cognitive attentional barrier refers to the sensory filter mechanism that, early in the processing of information, selects only one channel of incoming sensory information and blocks off all the others, allowing attention to be focused.

b) Divided attention: this is a dual-task technique in which people are asked to attend and respond to both (or all) the messages. Whereas **shadowing** focuses attention on a particular message, the dual-task method deliberately divides people's attention.

Background to the study

Cherry's (1953) method of 'shadowing' one of two dichotic messages for his study of attention in listening found participants who shadowed a message presented to one ear were ignorant of the content of a message simultaneously presented to the other ear.

The first experiment in this study aimed to test Cherry's findings more rigorously while the second and third experiments aimed to investigate other factors that can affect attention in **dichotic listening** (Figure 10.2).

Research method

All tasks were laboratory based and highly controlled. They were therefore all laboratory experiments.

In all tasks the apparatus used was a Brenell Mark IV stereophonic tape recorder modified with two amplifiers to give two independent outputs through attenuators, one output going to each of the earpieces of a pair of headphones. Matching for loudness was approximate, by asking participants to say when two messages that seemed equally loud to the experimenter were subjectively equal to them.

Experiment 1

This used a repeated measures design. The IVs were:
a) the dichotic listening test in which the participant was asked to recall all they could from the unattended message
b) the recognition test, which consisted of 21 words. Seven of these were from the shadowed passage, seven were from the list of words in the unattended message and seven were similar words but not present in either passage.

The DV was the number of words recognised correctly in the rejected message.

Experiment 2

This also used a repeated measures design. The IV was whether or not instructions were prefixed by the participant's name.

The DV was the number of affective instructions (instructions preceded by the participant's name).

Experiment 3

This used an independent measures design. The IVs were:
a) whether digits were inserted in both messages or only one
b) whether participants had to answer questions about the shadowed message at the end of each passage or whether participants had to merely remember all the numbers they could.

The DV was the number of digits correctly reported.

Now test yourself

18 Describe the term 'divided attention'.

TESTED ☐

---

shadowing refers to the process of repeating out loud words as they are being heard.

dichotic listening is an experimental technique in which different messages are transmitted into each ear of a subject to test 'selective attention' or the ability to concentrate on one message to the exclusion of the other.

Figure 10.2 A dichotic listening task

Exam tips

Know that Experiments 1 and 2 used a repeated measures design while Experiment 3 used an independent measures design.

Know the independent variables and dependent variables for each experiment.

Outline of the procedure/study

Participants were undergraduates and research workers of both sexes. Participant numbers are not given for Experiment 1 but 12 participants took part in the experimental conditions in Experiment 2 and two groups of 14 participants were used in Experiment 3.

Experiment 1

A short list of simple words was repeated in the unattended ear while the words shadowed a prose message in the attended ear. The word list was faded in after shadowing had begun and was equal in intensity to the shadowed message. At the end of the prose passage it was faded out so as to become inaudible as the prose finished.

The word list was repeated 35 times. The participant was then asked to report all they could of the content of the unattended message. About 30 seconds later the participant was then given the recognition test.

The gap between the end of shadowing and the beginning of the recognition test was about 30 seconds.

Experiment 2

This experiment was conducted to find out the limits of the efficiency of the attentional block.

Participants shadowed ten short passages of light fiction. They were told that their responses would be recorded and that the object of the experiment was for them to try to score as few mistakes as possible.

In some of the passages instructions were **interpolated**, but with the exception of two instances, the participants were not warned of these. In half of the cases with instructions these were prefixed by the participant's name.

The order of presentation is shown in the table.

interpolated means to insert material into a text.

Passage	Instructions at start of passage	Instructions within passage
1	Listen to your right ear.	All right, you may stop now.
2	....	No instructions.
3	....	John Smith, you may stop now.
4	....	No instructions.
5	....	Change to your other ear.
6	....	No instruction.
7	....	John Smith, change to your other ear.
8	Listen to your right ear: you will receive instructions to change ears.	Change to your other ear.
9		No instructions.
10	Listen to your right ear.	John Smith, change to your other ear.
	Listen to your right ear: you will receive instructions to change ears.	

The 'no instructions' passages were interpolated in the table at random. The passages were read in a steady monotone at about 130 words per minute. Participants' responses were tape-recorded and later analysed.

Experiment 3

Experiment 2 indicated that when participants were given a warning at the start of a passage to expect instructions to change ears there was a slight increase in the mean frequency with which they heard instructions in the unattended message. Experiment 3 tested this point further.

Two groups of 14 participants shadowed one of two simultaneous dichotic messages. In some of the messages digits were interpolated towards the end of the message. These were sometimes present in both messages, sometimes only in one. The position of the numbers in the message and relative to each other in the two messages was varied and controls with no numbers were also used, randomly inserted.

One group of participants were told they would be asked questions about the content of the shadowed message at the end of each message, the other group were specifically instructed to remember all the numbers that they could.

Typical mistake

Confusing the three experiments – make sure you know the specific procedure for each.

Exam tip

Know how at least two controls were implemented in the study.

Now test yourself

21 Outline the purpose of Experiment 2.

TESTED

Key findings

Experiment 1

The table shows recognition scores for words from shadowed and rejected messages.

	Mean number of words recognised
Words presented in shadowed message	4.9 out of 7
Words presented in rejected message	1.9 out of 7
Words presented for the first time in recognition test	2.6 out of 7

There was no trace of material from the rejected message being recognised. The difference between the new material and that from the shadowed message was significant at the 1 per cent level. The 30-second delay was unlikely to have caused the rejected material to be lost because words from early in the shadowed message were recognised.

These findings support those found by Cherry (1953).

Experiment 2

Most participants ignored the instructions that were presented in the passages they were shadowing and said they thought this was merely an attempt to distract them. Relative frequencies of hearing affective and non-affective instructions when presented in the rejected message (pooled for 12 participants) are shown in the table.

	Affective (instructions preceded by name)	**Non-affective (instructions not preceded by name)**
Number of times presented	39	36
Number of times heard	20	4

There should have been 36 sets of instructions preceded by the participant's name presented in the rejected message. However, the discrepancy is due to three participants who heard the instructions and actually changed over, so that the second set of instructions which would normally have been heard as part of the shadowed message was now heard as part of the rejected message. These all occurred in passage 10.

The mean number of instructions heard when presented in the rejected message was calculated and the difference between the 'names' and 'no names' was found to be significant at 1 per cent.

On only four out of the 20 occasions in which the 'names' instructions were heard did the participants actually make a change to the other message.

Experiment 3

Results showed no significant difference, even at 5 per cent, in the mean scores of digits recalled correctly between the condition in which participants had been told they would be asked about the content and the condition in which participants were told specifically to listen for digits.

Conclusions

In a situation where a participant directs his attention to the reception of a message from one ear and rejects a message from the other ear, almost none of the verbal content of the rejected message is able to penetrate the block set up.

A short list of simple words presented as the rejected message shows no trace of being remembered, even when presented many times.

Subjectively 'important' messages, such as a person's own name, can penetrate the block – thus a person will hear instructions if they are presented with their name as part of the rejected message.

While perhaps not impossible, it is very difficult to make 'neutral' material important enough to break through the block set up in dichotic shadowing.

Contemporary study: Simons and Chabris (1999): Visual inattention

Relation to the cognitive area

Visual perception is another cognitive process in which an individual interprets, organises and elaborates on information that enters the brain via the eyes. The brain has to perceive or interpret the visual information it receives via the optic nerve. But visual perception, like auditory perception, is selective and limited physiologically and cognitively. Not 'everything' collected in the image can be seen. There is too much information to process, so the brain filters out what is relevant and essential, while omitting what is not. As a result, what an individual sees is highly influenced by their brain and depends on what they decide to focus on. What is not seen is the result of **inattentional blindness**. This study shows that if an individual is focused on a particular task involving visual perception, other events, even unusual or unexpected events, go unnoticed due to inattentional blindness.

Theory/theories on which the study is based

Focused visual attention: the cluttered scenes of everyday life present more objects than an individual can respond to simultaneously, and

---

Now test yourself

22 Outline one finding from Experiment 2.

TESTED

Exam tips

Know how this study is similar to and different from the study by Simons and Chabris (1999).

Know how the study relates to the key theme 'Attention'.

Now test yourself

23 Draw one conclusion from the findings of this study.

TESTED

---

inattentional blindness refers to not noticing something because attention is focused on something else.

Now test yourself

24 Describe the term 'visual perception'.

TESTED

---

often more than can be fully perceived at any one time. Accordingly, mechanisms of attention are required to select objects of interest for further processing. In the case of vision, one such mechanism is provided by eye movements (Driver, 1996). Attention is necessary for change detection.

Change blindness: individuals often do not detect large changes to objects and scenes from one view to the next, particularly if those objects are not the centre of interest in the scene (Rensink *et al.*, 1997). Individuals perceive and remember only those objects and details that receive focused attention.

Inattentional blindness: when attention is diverted to another object or task. Observers often fail to perceive an unexpected object, even if it appears at fixation (for example, Mack and Rock, 1998).

Background to the study

Previous studies had investigated the precision of visual representations. In those studies observers had to engage in a continuous task that required them to focus on one aspect of a dynamic visual scene while ignoring others. At some point during the task an unexpected event occurred. Results showed that the majority of observers did not report seeing the unexpected event even though it was clearly visible to others not engaged in the concurrent task (consider Becklen and Cervone, 1983; Stoffregen and Becklen, 1989).

Although those previous studies have had profound implications for the understanding of perception with and without attention (for example, change blindness, inattentional blindness), the empirical approach has recently fallen into disuse. One goal of this study was therefore to revive the empirical approach used in the earlier studies.

This study therefore builds on classic studies of divided visual attention to examine inattentional blindness for complex objects and events in dynamic scenes.

To overcome the fact that previous research did not systematically consider the role of task difficulty in detection, and no direct comparisons were made between performance with a superimposed version of the display and a live version, for this study several video segments with the same set of actions, in the same location, on the same day, were filmed. A large number of naive observers were asked to watch the video recordings and later answer questions about the unexpected events.

Research method

This is primarily a laboratory experiment that used an independent measures design, though an additional task was completed at the end which was a controlled observation.

The IVs were whether the participant took part in:
a) the Transparent/Umbrella woman condition
b) the Transparent/Gorilla condition
c) the Opaque/Umbrella woman condition
d) the Opaque/Gorilla condition

For each of the four displays there were four task conditions:
a) White/Easy.
b) White/Hard.
c) Black/Easy.
d) Black/Hard.

Overall there were therefore 16 individual conditions.

The DV was the number of participants in each of the 16 conditions who noticed the unexpected event (Umbrella woman or Gorilla).

A controlled observation was subsequently conducted in which participants watched a different video and had to attend to the White team and engage in the Easy monitoring task.

Materials

Four video tapes, each 75 seconds in duration, were created showing two teams of three players, one team wearing white shirts, the other black shirts. Players moved around in a relatively random fashion in an open area in front of a bank of three elevator doors.

The members of each team passed a standard orange basketball to each other in a standardised order. Passes were either bounce or aerial. Players would also dribble the ball, wave their arms and make other movements consistent with their overall pattern of action.

After 44 to 48 seconds of action, either of two unexpected events occurred: in the Umbrella woman condition, a tall woman holding an open umbrella walked from off camera on one side of the action to the other, left to right. In the Gorilla condition, a shorter woman wearing a gorilla costume that fully covered her body walked through the action in the same way. In either case, the unexpected event lasted five seconds and the players continued their actions during and after the event.

There were two styles of video: in the Transparent condition, the white team, black team and unexpected event were all filmed separately and the three video streams were rendered partially transparent and then superimposed by using digital video-editing software. In the Opaque condition, all seven actors were filmed simultaneously and could thus occlude one another and the basketballs. (This required some rehearsal before filming to eliminate collisions and other accidents and to achieve natural-looking patterns of movement.)

In a separate Opaque-style video recording, the gorilla walked from right to left into the live basketball-passing event, stopped in the middle of the players as the action continued all around it, turned to face the camera, thumped its chest and then resumed walking across the screen.

Outline of the procedure/study

For the experiment

There were 228 participants (referred to as 'observers' throughout the original study), almost all undergraduate students. Each participant volunteered to participate without compensation, received a large candy bar for participating, or was paid a single fee for participating in a larger testing session including another, unrelated experiment.

NB: data from 36 participants was discarded so results were used from 192 participants. These were equally distributed across the 16 conditions.

For the controlled observation

Twelve different participants watched the video in which the gorilla thumped its chest. Twenty-one experimenters tested the participants. To ensure standardisation of procedures, a written protocol was devised and reviewed with the experimenters before data collection was begun. All participants were tested individually and gave informed consent in advance.

> **Typical mistake**
>
> Forgetting the controlled observation part of the study.

> **Typical mistake**
>
> Remembering all the conditions, i.e. the Transparent/Gorilla/Hard task, Transparent/Gorilla/Easy task, Transparent/Umbrella woman/Hard task, Transparent/Umbrella woman/Easy task, Opaque/Gorilla/Hard task, Opaque/Gorilla/Easy task, Opaque/Umbrella woman/Hard task, Opaque/Umbrella woman/Easy task.

Now test yourself

27 Identify the four independent variables.
28 Describe the transparent style of video.

TESTED

Before viewing the video tape, participants were told they would be watching two teams of three players passing basketballs and that they should pay attention to either the team in white (the White condition) or the team in black (the Black condition). They were told to keep either a silent mental count of the total number of passes made by the attended team (Easy condition) or separate silent mental counts of the number of bounce passes and aerial passes made by the attended team (Hard condition).

After viewing the video tape and performing the monitoring task, participants were immediately asked to write down their count(s) on paper. They were then asked the following additional questions:

a) While you were doing the counting, did you notice anything unusual in the video?
b) Did you notice anything other than the six players?
c) Did you see a gorilla/woman carrying an umbrella walk across the screen?

After any 'yes' responses, participants were asked to provide details of what they noticed. If at any point a participant mentioned the unexpected event, the remaining questions were skipped.

After questioning, participants were asked whether they had previously participated in a similar experiment, heard of such an experiment or heard of the general phenomenon. If they said 'yes', they were replaced and their data was discarded.

Participants were debriefed; this included replaying the video tape on request.

Each testing session lasted 5 to 10 minutes.

Key findings

From the experiment

NB: data from 36 participants was discarded for the following reasons:
a) They already knew about the phenomenon and/or experimental paradigm ($n = 14$).
b) They reported losing count of the passes ($n = 9$).
c) Passes were incompletely or inaccurately recorded ($n = 7$).
d) Answers could not be clearly interpreted ($n = 5$).
e) The participant's total pass count was more than three standard deviations away from the mean of the other participants in the condition ($n = 1$).

The remaining 192 participants were distributed equally across the 16 conditions of the $2 \times 2 \times 2 \times 2$ design (12 per condition).

The table shows the percentage of participants noticing the unexpected event in each condition.

	Easy task		Hard task	
	White team	**Black team**	**White team**	**Black team**
Transparent				
Umbrella woman	58	92	33	42
Gorilla	8	67	8	25
Opaque				
Umbrella woman	100	58	83	58
Gorilla	42	83	50	58

Exam tips

Know the procedure followed in both the experimental and controlled observation parts of the study.

Know at least two controls used in this study.

Now test yourself

29 Describe what participants were told before they viewed the video tape.
30 Describe what participants were asked to do as they watched the video.

TESTED ☐

Out of all 192 participants across all conditions, 54 per cent noticed the unexpected event and 46 per cent failed to notice the unexpected event, revealing a substantial level of sustained inattentional blindness for a dynamic event.

The umbrella woman was noticed more often than the gorilla overall (65 per cent versus 44 per cent). This relation held regardless of the video type, monitoring task or attended team. The gorilla was noticed by more participants who attended to the actions of the black team than those who watched the white team (Black 58 per cent, White 27 per cent per condition). However, there was little difference between those attending to the black team and those attending to the white team in noticing the umbrella woman (Black 62 per cent, White 66 per cent per condition).

From the controlled observation

Only 50 per cent noticed the event (roughly the same as the percentage that noticed the normal Opaque/Gorilla walking event (42 per cent) under the same task conditions).

> **Exam tip**
>
> Know the key findings in relation to both the experiment and the controlled observation.

Conclusions

Individuals have a sustained inattentional blindness for dynamic events. Individuals fail to notice an ongoing and highly salient but unexpected event if they are engaged in a primary monitoring task. The level of inattentional blindness depends on the difficulty of the primary task.

Individuals are more likely to notice unexpected events if those events are visually similar to the events they are paying attention to.

> **Exam tips**
>
> Know how this study is similar to and different from the study by Moray (1959).
>
> Know how the study relates to the key theme 'Attention'.

> **Now test yourself**
>
> Using the table:
> 31 Identify one finding in relation to the Transparent/Gorilla/Hard task.
> 32 Identify one finding in relation to the Opaque/Umbrella woman/Easy task.
>
> TESTED ☐

> **Now test yourself**
>
> 33 Outline how the findings from this study show that 'individuals have a substantial level of sustained inattentional blindness for dynamic events'.
>
> TESTED ☐

Section A practice questions

From Moray's study into auditory attention:
1 (a) Describe the sample used. [2]
  (b) Describe one weakness of the sample used in this study. [2]
2 Outline two findings from Experiment 1. [4]
3 Describe the procedure followed in Experiment 3. [4]
4 Outline two things Moray's study tells us about auditory attention. [4]

From the study by Simons and Chabris on visual inattention:
5 Identify the four task conditions used in this study. [4]
6 (a) Describe the 'umbrella-woman' condition. [2]
  (b) Describe the 'gorilla' condition. [2]
7 (a) Identify the technique used to gather the sample. [1]
  (b) Describe one strength of the way the sample was gathered in this study. [2]
8 Outline how two ethical issues were upheld in this study. [4]
9 Outline one similarity between the samples used in Moray's study into auditory attention and the study of visual inattention by Simon and Chabris and suggest a weakness of these samples. [4]

10 Describe how the study by Moray into auditory attention and the study by Simons and Chabris on visual inattention differ in relation to the key theme of 'Attention'.   [4]

For practice questions linked to Sections B and C of the exam paper turn to Chapter 15.

ONLINE ☐

Summary

By the end of this chapter for the two AS-level studies and/or the four A-level studies you should:
- know the research method and sample key findings
- be able to suggest at least one way in which each study could be improved and possible implications of the suggestion(s) for methodology, ethics, reliability, validity, usefulness, practicality, etc.
- know how each study relates to the area of cognitive psychology
- know strengths/weaknesses of conducting research under controlled conditions, independent versus repeated measures designs, snapshot studies, observation and self-reports (including rating scales) as ways to gather data, quantitative and qualitative data, the sample
- be able to consider the issues of reliability, validity and ecological validity, ethnocentrism
- understand how each study links to the psychological debates of: nature/nurture, freewill/determinism, reductionism/holism, individual/situational explanations, usefulness of research, ethical considerations, conducting socially sensitive research, psychology as a science.

11 The area of developmental psychology

Outline of the developmental area

REVISED

This is the branch of psychology that is concerned with change and development in experience and behaviour over an individual's lifespan.

Developmental psychologists aim to discover, describe and explain how development occurs, from its earliest origins into adulthood and old age.

Intellectual development is concerned with the origins and acquisition of thought and language, whereas social development is concerned with the integration of the individual into the social world and how the social world interacts with the individual as they grow and mature.

An assumption of developmental psychology is that there are clearly identifiable, systematic changes that occur in an individual's behaviour from conception to death.

An implication of developmental psychology is that if there are clearly identifiable stages of development that individuals go through as they grow and mature, learning and experiences within any of the stages of development can have a significant positive or negative effect on subsequent behaviour.

Key theme: External influences on children's behaviour

REVISED

Classic study: Bandura *et al.* (1961): Transmission of aggression

Relation to the developmental area

This area is concerned with the study of psychological changes that occur throughout a person's lifespan. There are many changes which interest psychologists, for example cognitive processes such as thinking and problem-solving, social processes such as developing relationships, and the acquisition of moral understanding. Bandura *et al.*'s study focuses on the social process of how children learn about behaving aggressively. The study therefore links with the development of moral understanding and behaviour. The researchers argue that children develop views of the world through a process known as social learning so, as children grow, through these processes they learn to be aggressive.

Theory/theories on which the study is based

Social learning theory (SLT) explains human behaviour in terms of a continuous interaction between cognitive, behavioural and environmental influences.

According to SLT, aggressive behaviours are learned through reinforcement and the imitation of aggressive 'models' (Bandura, 1965, 1973, 1974). Imitation is the reproduction of learning through observation (observational learning) and involves observing other people who serve as models for behaviour.

Bandura *et al.* (1961, 1963) showed how a child's aggressive tendencies can be strengthened through vicarious reinforcement (seeing others being rewarded for behaving aggressively, i.e. not being punished).

Background to the study

Previous research has shown that children will readily imitate behaviour demonstrated by an adult model if the model remains present (Bandura and Hudson, 1961). However, although such research has provided convincing evidence for the influence and control exerted by role models on the behaviour of others, until this study little was known about how the behaviour displayed by a model might affect an individual in novel settings when the model is absent.

This study therefore first exposed children to aggressive and non-aggressive adult models and then tested the amount of imitative learning demonstrated by the children in a new situation in the absence of the model.

The aim was to demonstrate that learning can occur through mere observation of a model and that imitation of learned behaviour can occur in the absence of that model. There were four hypotheses:
1 Children shown aggressive models will show significantly more imitative aggressive acts resembling those of their models than those shown non-aggressive or no models.
2 Children shown non-aggressive, subdued models will show significantly less aggressive behaviour than those shown aggressive or no models.
3 Boys will show significantly more imitative aggression than girls.
4 Children will imitate same-sex model behaviour to a greater degree than opposite-sex behaviour.

Research method

This was a laboratory experiment which used an independent measures, matched participants design. The independent variables were:
a) whether the child witnessed an aggressive or a non-aggressive adult model in the first phase of the experiment (a control group was not exposed to an adult model)
b) the sex of the model (male or female)
c) the sex of the child (boy or girl).

The dependent variable was the amount of imitative behaviour and aggression shown by the child in Phase 3, measured by the male model and at times a second researcher observing each child through a one-way mirror and noting down at five-second intervals: displays of imitative physical aggression, imitative verbal aggression, imitative non-aggressive physical and verbal acts, and partially imitative physical and verbal acts.

The 72 children (36 boys, 36 girls), aged 37 to 69 months (mean 52 months), from Stanford University Nursery School, were matched through a procedure which pre-rated them for aggressiveness. Each child participated in only one of the experimental conditions.

> **Now test yourself**
>
> 1 Outline the social learning theory.
> 2 Describe the aim of Bandura *et al.*'s study.
>
> TESTED ☐

> **Exam tip**
>
> Know the experimental and control conditions.

> **Now test yourself**
>
> 3 Describe how the dependent variable was measured in this study.
>
> TESTED ☐

> **Typical mistake**
>
> Not being able to accurately describe how the participants were matched for aggressiveness.

Outline of the procedure/study

Phase 1

Children in the experimental conditions were individually taken into a room and sat at a table to play with potato prints and picture stickers for ten minutes while:

- the aggressive model began by assembling a tinker toy set but after about a minute turned to a Bobo doll (Figure 11.1) and spent the remainder of the period physically and verbally aggressing it using a standardised procedure
- the non-aggressive model assembled the tinker toys in a quiet, subdued manner, totally ignoring the Bobo doll.

The control group did not participate in Phase 1.

Figure 11.1 A Bobo doll

Phase 2

All the children were then taken individually to an anteroom and subjected to mild aggression arousal. Initially they were allowed to play with some very attractive toys but after about two minutes the experimenter took the toys away, saying they were reserved for other children. However, they could play with any of the toys in the next room.

Phase 3

Children were then taken individually into a third room which contained both aggressive and non-aggressive toys, for example a 3ft high Bobo doll, a mallet, dart guns, and non-aggressive toys, such as a tea set, cars, dolls. They were observed through a one-way mirror for 20 minutes while observers recorded behaviour (with inter-scorer reliabilities of 0.90 product-moment coefficients) in the following categories:

a) Imitative aggression (physical, verbal and non-aggressive speech).
b) Partially imitative aggression.
c) Non-imitative physical and verbal aggression.
d) Non-aggressive behaviour.

Exam tip

Make sure you know the procedure – in all three phases.

Now test yourself

4 Describe the aggression arousal phase.

TESTED

Key findings

Children in the aggressive condition showed significantly more imitation of physical and verbal aggressive behaviour than children in the non-aggressive or control conditions.

Children in the aggressive condition showed more partial imitation and non-imitative physical and verbal aggression than those in the non-aggressive or control conditions. However, results here were not always significant.

Children in the non-aggressive condition showed very little aggression, although results were not always significantly less than the control group.

Children who saw the same-sex model imitated the model's behaviour significantly more in the following categories:

a) Boys imitated male models more than girls for physical and verbal aggression, non-imitative aggression and gun play.
b) Girls imitated female models more than boys for verbal imitative aggression and non-imitative aggression. However, results were not significant.

The behaviour of the male model exerted greater influence than the female model. Overall boys produced more imitative physical aggression than girls.

> **Typical mistake**
>
> Not showing knowledge of the fact that the aggressive and non-aggressive models, regardless of sex, followed a standardised procedure.

Conclusions

Children will imitate aggressive/non-aggressive behaviours displayed by adult models, even if the model is not present.

Children can learn behaviour though observation and imitation.

Behaviour modelled by male adults has a greater influence on children's behaviour than behaviour modelled by a female adult.

Both boys and girls are more likely to learn highly masculine-typed behaviour such as physical aggression from a male adult rather than from a female.

Boys and girls are likely to learn verbal aggression from a same-sex adult.

Contemporary study: Chaney *et al.* (2004): Funhaler study

Relation to the developmental area

Good and bad behaviours can develop over an individual's lifespan. Many of these behaviours develop as a result of external influences on the individual. If an external influence such as a child's role model, such as a parent, teacher or sports star, is seen to encourage or reward a child's behaviour in any way, or if the child's behaviour results in pleasant and satisfying consequences, the child is likely to continue displaying that behaviour. This study shows that health-enhancing behaviours can be developed in children through positive reinforcement – they are able to breathe more easily as a consequence of using a Funhaler (Figure 11.2) so are encouraged to use the inhaler as prescribed, which will improve their overall health status.

Theory/theories on which the study is based

Operant conditioning is a form of associative learning, whereby associations and connections are formed between stimuli and responses that did not exist before learning occurs.

Operant conditioning involves learning through the consequences of behavioural responses. The principles of operant conditioning were first investigated by Thorndike, who found that any response that led to desirable consequences was more likely to be repeated, whereas any response that led to undesirable consequences was less likely to be repeated – a principle which became known as the Law of Effect.

The principles of operant conditioning were further developed by Skinner, who applied them to explain how many aspects of human behaviour develop.

Background to the study

Behaviour therapy and behaviour modification (based on classical and operant conditioning) have been major approaches used by both clinical

> **Exam tip**
>
> Be able to describe at least three findings accurately.

> **Now test yourself**
>
> 5 Outline one finding in relation to the imitation of verbal aggression when the model was female.
> 6 Outline one finding in relation to the male aggressive model.
> 7 Draw one conclusion from the findings of this study.
>
> TESTED ☐

> **Exam tips**
>
> Know how this study is similar to and different from the study by Chaney *et al.* (2004).
>
> Know how the study relates to the key theme 'External influences on children's behaviour'.

Figure 11.2 **A Funhaler**

> **operant conditioning** refers to learning by consequences. If consequences of an action are rewarding, they are likely to be repeated whereas if consequences are negative, there is a strong tendency not to repeat the action.

> **Now test yourself**
>
> 8 Outline 'operant conditioning'.
>
> TESTED ☐

psychologists and health practitioners to improve adherence to prescribed medical regimes.

Poor adherence to prescribed frequency and technique remains a major problem for paediatric asthmatics on inhaled medication (Watt *et al.*, 2003). Reasons for poor adherence are varied, so Chaney *et al.* decided to find out whether rewards could be used to increase health behaviours in young asthmatics.

The aim of this study was therefore to show that the use of a novel asthma spacer device, known as the Funhaler, which incorporates incentive toys isolated from the main inspiratory circuit by a valve while not compromising drug delivery, can provide positive reinforcement which leads to improved adherence in young asthmatics.

Research method

This was a field experiment, conducted in the participants' home settings in Australia, which used a repeated measures design.

> **Typical mistake**
>
> Forgetting about how the study used the repeated measures design.

The IVs were:
a) whether the child used a standard/small volume spacer device – the Breath-a-Tech (Scott-Dibben, Australia)
b) whether the child used a Funhaler (InfMed Ltd, Australia).

The DV was the amount of adherence to the prescribed medical regime.

Outline of the procedure/study

The sample consisted of 32 children who were a mix of boys and girls (age range 1.5 to 6 years, mean age 3.2 years; average duration of asthma 2.2 years), prescribed drugs delivered by pMDI (pressurised metered dose inhaler) and spacer. The children's parents were contacted by phone and visited in their homes. They gave informed consent and completed a questionnaire about their child's use of their current inhaler – this gave baseline measurements in relation to adherence against which Funhaler usage and effects could be compared. Throughout the study parents helped (where necessary) in the use of the inhalers.

Participants were asked to use a Funhaler for two weeks instead of their normal pMDI and spacer inhaler to administer their medication. The Funhaler incorporates a number of features to distract the child's attention from the drug delivery event itself and to provide a means of self-reinforcement through the effective use of the technique.

The Funhaler makes spacers appealing to children in the following ways:
a) It isolates incentive toys (e.g. spinner and whistle) in a separate branch to the standard inhalation circuit, placing them outside the expiratory valve of the spacer to avoid problems of contamination and interference of drug delivery.
b) The design attempts to link the optimal function of the toys to a deep breathing pattern conducive to effective medication.
c) The design anticipates the potential for boredom of children with particular incentive toys in its modular arrangement, which would allow the replacement of the incentive toy module with a range of different toys.

> **Now test yourself**
>
> 9 Outline the aim of this study.
> 10 Explain why this was a repeated measures design.
>
> TESTED ☐

> **Typical mistake**
>
> Forgetting the role played by the children's parents.

Matched questionnaires were completed (by parents) after sequential use of the normal inhaler and the Funhaler.

Exam tips

Know that adherence in relation to the use of inhaler devices was measured both before and after the experiment. The first questionnaire measured the first independent variable and the second questionnaire measured the second independent variable.

Know how the study was conducted.

Key findings

- The use of the Funhaler was associated with improved parental and child compliance.
- When surveyed at random, 81% (22/27) of children using the Funhaler were found to have been medicated the previous day compared to 59% of children (16/27) using the existing small volume spacer device.
- 30% more children took the recommended four or more cycles per aerosol delivery (24/30 – 80% versus 15/30 – 50%; p = 0.02) when using the Funhaler compared with the standard/small volume spacer.
- When using the standard/small volume spacer only 3/30 parents reported being always successful in medicating their children compared to 22/30 when using the Funhaler (p ≤ 0.001).
- Of the parents who were unsuccessful with the conventional spacer, 17 became successful with time and practice in medicating their children, leaving 11 who never succeeded. When these 11 were changed to the Funhaler, 7 were immediately successful, 1 became successful with time and only 3 continued to have problems.
- Use of the Funhaler was associated with fewer problems than when using the existing device.

Conclusions

Improved adherence, combined with satisfactory delivery characteristics, suggests that the Funhaler may be useful for management of young asthmatics.

The use of the Funhaler could possibly be translated to improved measures of clinical outcome.

Now test yourself

11 Outline the sample used in this study.
12 Describe one finding from this study.

TESTED

Exam tips

Know how this study is similar to and different from the study by Bandura *et al.* (1961).

Know how the study relates to the key theme 'External influences on children's behaviour'.

Section A practice questions

From Bandura et al.'s study of aggression:
1 (a) How were the children matched in this study? [2]
  (b) Outline why the children were matched in this study. [2]
2 Describe two ways in which this study can be considered low in ecological validity. [4]
3 One of the independent variables (IVs) in this study was the behaviour of the model (aggressive or non-aggressive). Identify the other two independent variables (IVs). [2]
4 Describe how the children's behaviour was measured in Phase 3. [4]

From Chaney et al.'s Funhaler sudy:
5 Explain why this study is generally considered a field experiment. [4]
6 Describe the role of the children's parents in this study [2]
7 Describe two ways in which the Funhaler was thought to be appealing to children. [4]
8 Draw one conclusion from the findings of this study. [2]
9 Both Bandura et al. and Chaney et al. used children as participants. Outline two ethical issues which can arise when using children in psychological research. [4]
10 Describe what Bandura et al.'s and Chaney et al.'s studies tell us about the key theme 'External influences on children's behaviour. [4]

For practice questions linked to Sections B and C of the exam paper turn to Chapter 15.

ONLINE

Key theme: Moral development

Classic study: Kohlberg (1968): Stages of moral development

Relation to the developmental area

Everyone is born amoral, i.e. lacking a system of personal values and judgements about right and wrong. **Morals** develop and change over time as children interact with their environment and learn what is and what is not acceptable in the society or societies within which they interact. This study links to the developmental area of psychology as it shows how moral thinking develops through prescribed, identifiable stages which are invariant. Each stage has to be passed through and the skills acquired used to move on to the next stage.

morals are beliefs about what is right and wrong.

Now test yourself

13 Outline how this study relates to the developmental area.

TESTED

Theory/theories on which the study is based

Freud's psychoanalytic theory (circa 1930)

Freud proposed the existence of a tension between the needs of society and the individual. According to Freud, moral development proceeds when the individual's selfish desires are repressed and replaced by the values of important socialising agents in one's life, such as parents.

Piaget's cognitive theory (1965)

To understand adult morality, Piaget believed that it was necessary to study both how morality manifests in the child's world and the factors that contribute to the emergence of central moral concepts such as welfare, justice and rights.

Figure 11.3 Moral development: weighing up self versus humanity

Background to the study

Kohlberg was inspired by Piaget's pioneering effort to apply a structural approach to moral development, so he expanded on Piagetian notions of moral development. Kohlberg saw moral development as a more gradual process than Piaget. He provided a systematic three-level, six-stage sequence of development which reflected changes in moral judgement throughout the lifespan. Specifically, Kohlberg argued that development proceeds from a selfish desire to avoid punishment (personal), to a concern for group functioning (societal), to a concern for the consistent application of universal ethical principles.

Over the years Kohlberg gradually elaborated a typological scheme which described general structures and forms of moral thought. The typology contains three distinct levels of moral thinking and within each of these levels distinguishes two related stages, shown in the table. Everyone progresses through the levels and stages in order.

Stage	Moral reasoning	What is the value of human life
Preconventional		
Stage 1: Orientation towards obedience to avoid punishment and belief in right of authority	Obey rules to avoid punishment.	The value of a human life is based on the status or physical attributes of the person.
Stage 2: Orientation to behaviour that satisfies one's own needs and occasionally the needs of others.	Conform to obtain rewards, have favours returned, and so on.	The value of a human life is seen in how much it satisfies a person's needs.

Stage	Moral reasoning	What is the value of human life
Conventional level		
Stage 3: Orientation to behaviour that pleases others and is approved by them.	Conform to avoid disapproval, dislike by others.	The value of a human life is based on how much others value the person.
Stage 4: Orientation toward authority, rules and social order.	Conform to avoid the displeasure of authority figures.	The value of human life depends on its place in society.
Postconventional level		
Stage 5: Orientation to behaviour that is agreed upon by the whole society and meets it's standards	Conform to maintain the respect of the others in society.	The value of human life depends on its contribution to community welfare and is a universal human right.
Stage 6: Orientation toward behaviour that meets one's own ethical principles	Conform to avoid self-condemnation.	The value of human life is due to a universal respect for each individual.

> **Exam tip**
>
> Know and understand the main features of Kohlberg's theory of moral development.

In this study Kohlberg aimed to find evidence to support his theory of moral development.

Research method

This was a longitudinal study which followed the development of the same group of boys for 12 years by presenting them with hypothetical moral dilemmas. The aim was to show how, as young adolescents develop into young manhood, they move through the distinct levels and stages of moral development proposed by Kohlberg in his theory.

Kohlberg also studied moral development in other cultures using hypothetical moral dilemmas. This study therefore has a cross-cultural element.

Outline of the procedure/study

Seventy-five American boys aged 10 to 16 at the start of the study were followed at three-year intervals through to ages 22 to 28. Participants were presented with hypothetical moral dilemmas in the form of short stories to solve. The stories were to determine each participant's stage of moral reasoning for each of 25 moral concepts/aspects. Aspects assessed included:

- motive given for rule obedience or moral action
- the value of human life: tested by asking the participant:
  - Aged 10: 'Is it better to save the life of one important person or a lot of unimportant people?'
  - Aged 13, 16, 20 and 24: 'Should the doctor "mercy kill" a fatally ill woman requesting death because of her pain?'

Boys of other cultures were also used. Taiwanese boys, aged 10 to 13, were asked about a story involving theft of food: 'A man's wife is starving to death but the store owner won't give the man any food unless he can pay, which he can't. Should he break in and steal some food? Why?'

Young boys in Great Britain, Canada, Mexico and Turkey were tested in a similar way.

> **Now test yourself**
>
> 14 Identify Kohlberg's three levels of moral development.
> 15 Identify the two stages Kohlberg included in his conventional level of moral development.
> 16 Identify what Kohlberg used to study moral development.
>
> TESTED

> **Exam tip**
>
> Know the research method and sample in relation to both the American and the cross-cultural aspects of the study.

> **Exam tip**
>
> Know how the study was conducted.

Key findings

In relation to 'motive given for rule obedience or moral action'

Each of Kohlberg's six stages were shown as follows:
1 Obey rules to avoid punishment.
2 Conform to obtain rewards, have favours returned, etc.
3 Conform to avoid disapproval, dislike by others.
4 Conform to avoid censure by legitimate authorities and resultant guilt.
5 Conform to maintain the respect of the impartial spectator judging in terms of community welfare.
6 Conform to avoid self-condemnation.

In relation to the value of human life

The six stages were shown as follows:
1 The value of a human life is confused with the value of physical objects and is based on the social status or physical attributes of its possessor.
2 The value of human life is seen as instrumental to the satisfaction of the needs of its possessor or of other people.
3 The value of human life is based on the empathy and affection of family members and others towards its possessor.
4 Life is conceived as sacred in terms of its place in a categorical moral or religious order of rights and duties.
5 Life is valued both in terms of its relation to community welfare and in terms of life being a universal human right.
6 Belief in the sacredness of human life as representing a universal human value of respect for the individual.

Results showed that in about 50 per cent of each of the six stages a participant's thinking was at a single stage, regardless of the moral dilemma involved, and participants showed progress through the stages with increased age.

Not all participants over the period of the study progressed through all the stages and reached Stage 6. Participants progressed through the stages one at a time and always in the same order. Once a participant had reached a particular stage, they either stopped or continued to move upwards. No adults in Stage 4 had been through Stage 6, but all Stage 6 adults had gone through at least Stage 4.

A child at an earlier stage of development tends to move forward when confronted with the views of a child one stage further along and they seem to prefer this next stage.

Cross-cultural findings

- Taiwanese boys aged 10 to 13 tended to give 'classic' Stage 2 responses.
- Middle-class urban boys aged 10 in the USA, Taiwan and Mexico showed the order of use of each stage to be the same as the order of its difficulty or maturity.
- In the USA, by age 16, Stage 6 was little used. At age 13, the good-boy, middle stage (Stage 3) was not used.
- Mexico and Taiwan showed the same results in that development followed the same stages but the development through the stages was a little slower.
- At the age of 16, Stage 5 thinking was much more salient in the USA than in either Mexico or Taiwan.
- Results for two isolated villages, one in Yucatán, one in Turkey, also showed that moral thought increased steadily from ages 10 to 16

though it had not achieved a clear ascendency over pre-conventional thought.

- Trends for lower-class urban groups were intermediate in the rate of development between those for middle-class and for village boys. In these three divergent cultures therefore, middle-class children were found to be more advanced in moral judgement than matched lower-class children.
- No important differences were found in the development of moral thinking among Catholics, Protestants, Jews, Buddhists, Muslims or atheists.

Typical mistake

Forgetting that the study included cross-cultural findings in relation to moral development as well as findings in relation to American boys.

Conclusions

There is an invariant developmental sequence in an individual's moral development.

Each stage of moral development comes one at a time and always in the same order. An individual may stop at any given stage and at any age.

This six-stage theory of moral development is not significantly affected by widely ranging social, cultural or religious conditions. The only thing that is affected is the rate at which individuals progress through the sequence.

Contemporary study: Lee *et al.* (1997): Evaluations of lying and truth-telling

Relation to the developmental area

As shown in the study by Kohlberg, morals develop and change over time as children interact with their environment and learn what is and what is not acceptable in the society or societies within which they interact. One aspect of moral thinking is honesty and Kohlberg saw this as a universal component of morality. However, it appears that in some situations honesty can conflict with other moral values and this may be different in different cultures, for example Eastern and Western cultures. This study links to the developmental area of psychology as it shows how moral thinking develops differently in different cultures, something Kohlberg suggested did not happen.

Theory/theories on which the study is based

Children's moral judgements about lying and truth-telling rely primarily on the extent to which a verbal statement differs from factuality and whether or not the lie is punished (Piaget, 1932/1965).

There is now a general consensus that preschool children and young school-aged children are distinctly capable of distinguishing lying from behavioural misdeeds and can make consistent and accurate moral judgements in a similar way to that of older children and adults when both the falsity of a statement and the speaker's intention to deceive are highlighted, for example Wimmer *et al.*, 1984.

Background to the study

Since the early 1980s, developmental psychologists have showed renewed interest in children's understanding and moral judgements of lying and truth-telling, for example Wimmer, Gruber and Perner, 1984, and Peterson, 1995.

Now test yourself

17 Outline one finding in relation to 'value of human life'.
18 Outline one cross-cultural finding.

TESTED

Exam tips

Know how this study is similar to and different from the study by Lee *et al.* (1997).

Know how the study relates to the key theme 'Moral development'.

Despite the advances of research in recent years, understanding of the development of children's moral development of lying is still somewhat restricted. One of the limitations is that nearly all previous research was conducted with children in Western countries. These children were raised in industrialised environments that emphasise individualism, self-assertion/promotion and competition. It was therefore unclear whether the findings with these children could be generalised to children of other socio-cultural backgrounds.

This study was conducted to bridge the gap between this literature by directly testing the posited effect of culture on children's moral evaluations of lying and truth-telling.

This study compares the moral judgements of Canadian children and Chinese children from the People's Republic of China (PRC) in situations in which pro- and antisocial actions were denied or acknowledged.

Research method

This was a laboratory experiment which used an independent measures design to investigate cross-cultural differences in children's understanding and moral valuations of lying.

The IVs were:
a) whether the participant was Chinese or Canadian (a naturally occurring IV)
b) the age of the participant – 7, 9 or 11 years (a naturally occurring IV)
c) whether the participant heard the social story or the physical story
d) whether the participant heard (pro-social) stories involving a child who intentionally carried out a good deed (a deed valued by adults in both countries) or (antisocial) stories involving a child who intentionally carried out a bad deed (a deed viewed negatively in both cultures).

There were therefore four conditions: Pro-social behaviour/Truth-telling stories, Pro-social behaviour/Lie-telling stories, Antisocial behaviour/Truth-telling stories, Antisocial behaviour/Lie-telling stories.

The DVs were:
a) the rating given to the story character's deed (ranging between very, very good and very, very naughty)
b) the rating given to what the character said (verbal statement) (ranging between very, very good and very, very naughty).

The fact that participants were read four scenarios (two pro-social and two antisocial) and asked to apply the same rating scale to both the character's deed and its response in each story means the study had elements of a repeated measures design within it.

Outline of the procedure/study

The sample

- 120 Chinese children: 40 7 year olds (M age = 7.5 years, 20 male, 20 female), 40 9 year olds (M age = 9.4 years, 20 male, 20 female) and 40 11 year olds (M age = 11.3 years, 20 male, 20 female). They were recruited from elementary schools in Hangzhou, Zhejiang Province, a medium-sized city (provincial capital) in the PRC.
- 108 Canadian children: 36 7 year olds (M age = 7.4 years, 20 male, 16 female), 40 9 year olds (M = 9.6 years, 24 male, 16 female) and 32 11 year olds (M age = 11.5 years, 14 male, 18 female). They were recruited from elementary schools in Fredericton, New Brunswick.

Now test yourself
19 Outline the purpose of this study.
TESTED

Now test yourself
20 Identify two of the independent variables manipulated in this study.
TESTED

Like Hangzhou, Fredericton is a provincial capital but its population is considerably smaller than that of Hangzhou.

- Although the socio-economic status of the Chinese children was not known (no such categorisation exists in the PRC), most Canadian children were from middle-class families.

Exam tip

Know the research method and sample in relation to both the Chinese and the Canadian participants.

The procedure

Half of the Chinese children participated in the social story condition and the other half were placed in the physical story condition. The children were randomly assigned to each condition.

From the Canadian sample: 19 7 year olds, 20 9 year olds and 17 11 year olds were randomly assigned to the social story condition and the other children were assigned to the physical story condition.

Participants were read four scenarios accompanied by illustrations, two pro-social, two antisocial. All eight stories can be found in the appendix of the original article; however, the Pro-social behaviour/Lie-telling story went as follows:

Here is Alex. Alex's class had to stay inside at recess time because of bad weather, so Alex decided to tidy up the classroom for his teacher.

(Question 1: Is what Alex did good or naughty?)

So Alex cleaned the classroom, and when the teacher returned after recess, she said to her students, 'Oh, I see that someone has cleaned the classroom for me.' The teacher then asked Alex, 'Do you know who cleaned the classroom?' Alex said to his teacher, 'I did not do it.'

(Question 2: Is what Alex did good or naughty?)

Typical mistake

Forgetting that there were four scenarios accompanied by illustrations, two pro-social, two antisocial – making eight stories in all.

Each participant was tested individually.

Participants were first instructed about the meaning of the words and the symbols for rating the deeds and verbal statements on a seven-point rating chart. These were: very, very good (3 red stars), very good (2 red stars), good (1 red star), neither good nor naughty (blue circle), naughty (1 black cross), very naughty (2 black crosses), very, very naughty (3 black crosses).

Participants were then read either the four social or the four physical stories. The story's 'deed' section was read first and then the participants would indicate their rating verbally, non-verbally or both on the rating chart.

They were then read the second section of the story and would then indicate, in the same way, their rating for the character's verbal statement.

The meaning of each symbol was repeated every time a question was asked. The words 'good' and 'naughty' in the two questions were altered within subjects.

To control for **order effects**, for each condition two orders of the four stories were first determined using a randomisation table. About half of the participants in each condition were read the stories in one predetermined order and the other half were read them in the other order.

Participants were then involved in post-experimental discussions.

Now test yourself

21 Describe how the possibility of 'order effects' was controlled for in this study.

TESTED ☐

order effects refer to how the positioning of questions or tasks influences the outcome.

Key findings

NB: Participants' ratings were converted according to the following scale: very, very good = 3, very good = 2, good =1, neither good nor naughty = 0, naughty = −1, very naughty = −2, very, very naughty = −3.

Exam tip

Know how the study was conducted.

Preliminary analyses of the effects of order and gender showed no significant differences so the data for these two dimensions were combined for subsequent analyses.

Pro-social behaviour/Truth-telling situations

A 2 (culture: Canadian and Chinese) × 2 (condition: physical and social stories) × 3 (age: 7, 9, 11 years) analysis of covariance with the ratings of deeds as covariates was conducted on participants' ratings of truth-telling. This indicated that children of both cultures rated the pro-social behaviours similarly. The age and culture main effects were significant, with Canadian children at each age giving similar ratings to truth-telling whereas Chinese children's ratings became less positive as age increased.

Pro-social behaviour/Lie-telling situations

A 2 × 2 × 3 analysis of covariance with the ratings of deeds as covariates was conducted on participants' ratings of lie-telling. This indicated that children from the two cultures rated the pro-social behaviours differently both in different age groups and in the two conditions. However, only the interaction between age and culture was found to be significant.

Overall, Canadian children rated lie-telling in this situation negatively, but as age increased their ratings became somewhat less negative. Overall, Chinese children's ratings of lie-telling in this situation changed from negative to positive as age increased.

Antisocial behaviour/Truth-telling situations

A 2 × 2 × 3 analysis of covariance with the ratings of deeds as covariates was conducted on participants' ratings of truth-telling. This indicated that children from both cultures rated the antisocial behaviours similarly, both rating truth-telling in this situation very positively.

Antisocial behaviour/Lie-telling situations

A 2 × 2 × 3 analysis of covariance with the ratings of deeds as covariates was conducted on participants' ratings of lie-telling. This indicated that children of both cultures rated the antisocial behaviours differently in different age groups in the two conditions.

Both Chinese and Canadian children rated lie-telling negatively in this condition. Overall, negative ratings increased with age, irrespective of culture.

Chinese 7 year olds rated lie-telling less negatively than older children in the physical story condition, whereas Canadian 7 year olds rated lie-telling less negatively than older children in the social story condition.

Conclusions

Specific social and cultural norms have an impact on children developing moral judgements, which in turn are modified by age and experience in a particular culture.

The emphasis on self-effacement and modesty in Chinese culture increasingly exerts its impact on Chinese children's moral judgements.

Moral development is a highly contextualised process and is affected by the culture and/or social environment in which individuals are socialised.

Typical mistake

Not knowing how the deeds and verbal statements were rated.

Now test yourself

22 Outline one of the findings from the Antisocial behaviour/Truth-telling situation.

TESTED

Exam tips

Know how this study is similar to and different from the study by Kohlberg (1968)

Know how the study relates to the key theme 'Moral development'.

Section A practice questions

From Kohlberg's study of moral development:
1 Outline the first level (Pre-conventional) of Kohlberg's theory of moral development. [4]
2 Outline the aim of this study. [2]
3 a) Explain why this can be considered a longitudinal study. [2]
  b) Suggest one strength of this study being longitudinal. [2]
4 Suggest why this study can be said to support the 'nature' side of the nature/nurture debate. [2]

From Lee et al.'s study on lying and truth-telling:
5 Identify two of the independent variables manipulated in this study. [2]
6 a) Outline what a 'pro-social' story involved. [2]
  b) Outline what an antisocial story involved. [2]
7 a) Identify how the children were allocated to the social story and the physical story conditions. [1]
  b) Suggest one strength of the way the children were allocated to the social story and the physical story conditions. [2]
8 a) Outline one finding in relation to the Pro-social Behaviour/Truth-Telling situation. [2]
  b) Outline one finding in relation to the Antisocial Behaviour/Lie-Telling situation. [2]
9 Outline how Lee et al.'s study builds on Kolberg's study and changes our understanding of moral development. [4]
10 Outline why both Kohlberg's study and Lee et al.'s study can be placed in the developmental area of psychology. [4]

For practice questions linked to Sections B and C of the exam paper turn to Chapter 15.

ONLINE

Summary

By the end of this chapter for the two AS-level studies and/or the four A-level studies you should:
- know the research method and sample
- know the key findings
- be able to suggest at least one way in which each study could be improved and possible implications of the suggstion(s) for methodology, ethics, reliability, validity, usefulness, practicality, etc.
- know how each study relates to the area of developmental psychology
- know strengths/weaknesses of conducting research under controlled conditions, snapshot versus longitudinal studies, observation and self-reports (including rating scales) as ways to gather data, quantitative and qualitative data, the sample, cross-cultural research
- be able to consider the issues of reliability, validity and ecological validity, ethnocentrism
- understand how each study links to the psychological debates of nature/nurture, freewill/determinism, reductionism/holism, individual/situational explanations, usefulness of research, ethical considerations, conducting socially sensitive research, psychology as a science.

12 The area of biological psychology

Outline of the biological area

REVISED

The biological approach explains behaviour in terms of biological or genetic factors and explores human behaviour and experience by looking at people as if they are biological machines. This idea has some value because it is clear that our biology affects our behaviour and experience. It has also been observed for a long time that damage to the brain and nervous system can have a significant effect on behaviour and experience.

The action of chemicals and the structure of the nervous system are therefore the two main themes of biological psychology. However, the question that arises is, how much does our biology affect us and what other factors intervene to affect the response?

An assumption of biological psychology is that all that is psychological is first biological – that since the mind appears to reside in the brain, all thoughts, feelings and behaviours ultimately have a biological cause.

An implication of biological psychology is that behavioural problems can be treated by drugs. Another implication of the biological area is that because it requires specialist equipment, trained operators are needed.

> **Now test yourself**
>
> 1 Outline one implication of the biological area.
>
> TESTED

Key theme: Regions of the brain

REVISED

Classic study: Sperry (1968): Split-brain study

Relation to the biological area

The physiological approach could explain the difficulties experienced by individuals with a 'split brain' because their brains work differently to those of 'normal' people. As a result of having their corpus callosum severed, the two hemispheres of the brain work independently and unlike a 'normal' brain do not transfer information from one side to another. This inability to transfer information means split-brain patients cannot do certain things a 'normal' person can. This was demonstrated in Sperry's study, which showed, for example, that if an object was presented to the left visual field which was registered by the right hemisphere of split-brain patients, they were unable to name what they had seen. A 'normal' person would have no difficulty naming the object. This is because the language centre of the brain is in the left hemisphere and in split-brain patients, information presented to the right hemisphere cannot be transferred to the left for identification through language.

> **Now test yourself**
>
> 2 Outline how Sperry's study related to the biological area of psychology.
>
> TESTED

Theory/theories on which the study is based

Although the right and left hemispheres are in many ways mirror images of each other, there are distinct areas dealing with speech production and comprehension (Broca's area and Wernicke's area, respectively) showing their functional localisation. Functional **lateralisation** also exists because Broca's and Wernicke's areas are found only in the left hemisphere.

The primary motor cortex is situated in the frontal lobe and areas in the right hemisphere receive information from and are concerned with the activities of the left side of the body and vice versa.

Sperry believes that studies involving split-brain patients reveal the 'true' nature of the two hemispheres because a **commissurotomy**, which deconnects (disconnects) the two hemispheres, means they can only work independently.

Background to the study

Research by Sperry on both humans and monkeys which had undergone surgical section of the corpus callosum suggested the behavioural effects of this surgery may be less severe than other forms of cerebral surgery such as frontal lobotomy. Research by Akelaitis (1944) also showed no important behavioural effects of surgical section of the corpus callosum in humans, provided other brain damage was excluded.

More recent research by Sperry *et al.* using appropriate tests has actually shown a large number of behavioural effects that correlate directly with the loss of the neocortical commissures in man as well as animals.

Sperry therefore set out in this study, using split-brain patients, to show that each hemisphere:
● possesses an independent stream of conscious awareness
● has its own separate chain of memories that is inaccessible to the other.

Research method

This is usually considered a quasi/natural experiment because the independent variable – having a split brain or not – was not directly manipulated by the researchers. Participants with split brains had already undergone hemisphere deconnection to reduce severe epilepsy. No actual control group was necessary for comparison in the study because the functions and abilities of the visual fields and hemispheres in non–split-brain individuals were already known.

The dependent variable was the participant's ability to perform a variety of visual and tactile tests.

It has been argued, however, that because such extensive tests were carried out on a very small sample (11 split-brain patients in total), this study can be considered a collection of case studies. Qualitative data was gathered through the self-reports of the participants as they responded to the various stimuli/tasks.

Outline of the procedure/study
Presenting visual information

The participant, with one eye covered, centred his gaze on a fixed point in the centre of an upright translucent screen. Visual stimuli on 35 millimetre transparencies were arranged in a standard projector and were then back-projected at one tenth of a second or less – too fast for eye movements to get the information into the wrong visual field. Everything projected to the left of the central meridian of the screen is passed via the left visual field (LVF) to the right hemisphere and vice versa (regardless of which eye is used).

lateralisation of brain function refers to how some neural functions or cognitive processes tend to be more dominant in one hemisphere than the other.

a **commissurotomy** is when the corpus callosum connecting the two hemispheres of the brain is severed to some degree. If this is a complete severance it is commonly called a split-brain operation.

Exam tip

Know how both visual and tactile tests were conducted.

Typical mistake

Referring to the right/left eye instead of the right/left visual field.

Presenting tactile information

Below the translucent screen there was a gap so that participants could reach objects but not see their hands. Objects were then placed in either the participant's right/left hand or both hands. Information about objects placed in the left hand is processed by the right hemisphere and vice versa.

Participants undertook a variety of both visual and tactile tests, details of which can be found in the original study. The apparatus used is called a tachistoscope.

Key findings

Visual tests

Information shown and responded to in one visual field could be recognised again only if shown to the same visual field.

Information presented to the RVF (LH system of a typical right-handed patient) could be described in speech and writing (with the right hand). If the same information was presented to the LVF (RH), the participant insisted that he either did not see anything or that there was only a flash of light on the left side, i.e. the information could not be described in speech or writing. However, the participant could point with his left hand (RH) to a matching picture/object presented among a collection of pictures/objects.

If different figures were presented simultaneously to different visual fields, for instance a $ sign to the LVF and ? to the RVF, the participant could draw the $ sign with his left hand but reported that he had seen a ?.

Tactile tests

Objects placed in the right hand (LH) could be described in speech or writing (with the right hand). If the same objects were placed in the left hand (RH) participants could only make wild guesses and often seemed unaware they were holding anything.

Objects felt by one hand were only recognised again by the same hand, for example objects first sensed by the right hand could not be retrieved by the left. When two objects were placed simultaneously in each hand and then hidden in a pile of objects, both hands selected their own object and ignored the other hand's object.

Conclusions

People with split brains have two separate visual inner worlds, each with its own train of visual images.

Split-brain patients have a lack of cross-integration where a second hemisphere does not know what the first hemisphere has been doing.

They seem to have two independent streams of consciousness, each with its own memories, perceptions and impulses, i.e. two minds in one body.

Contemporary study: Casey *et al.* (2011): Neural correlates of delay of gratification

Relation to the biological area

Biological and genetic factors are known to influence the way individuals behave. This study links with the biological area because it investigates

Now test yourself

3 Describe how visual information was presented to a participant's right hemisphere.

TESTED

Typical mistake

Confusing the tactile tests in which no visual material was presented to either visual field with the visual tests in which material was presented to either or both visual fields.

Now test yourself

4 Describe how a participant responded when information was presented to the right visual field.
5 Describe how a participant responded when an object was placed in their right hand.
6 Draw one conclusion from the findings of this study.

TESTED

Exam tip

Know: RVF → LH → Right hand

LVF → RH → Left hand

Exam tip

Know the key findings for both visual fields in relation to both tactile and visual tests.

how specific areas of the brain, i.e. Metcalfe and Mischel's 'hot' and 'cool' processing systems, found respectively in the ventral striatum and inferior frontal gyrus, seem to impact on a person's ability to resist the temptation of rewarding stimuli, thus delaying gratification.

Theory/theories on which the study is based

The ability to resist temptation in favour of long-term goals is an essential component of individual, societal and economical success. Alluring situations can diminish control. What serves as an alluring situation that requires a capacity to control impulses changes as a function of age.

Delay of gratification depends importantly on cognitive control. Individuals use different cognitive strategies to delay gratification and there appear to be naturally existing differences in the spontaneous use of these strategies.

Correlation has shown a relationship between an avoidance of risky behaviour and greater excitation in the right inferior frontal gyrus. It has also been found that functionally, the ventral striatum facilitates and balances motivation with both higher-level and lower-level functions, such as inhibiting one's behaviour in a complex social interaction. This region has been found to be the region in the basal ganglia neural circuit most closely associated with reward.

Brain imaging has shown that a region of the prefrontal cortex, the inferior frontal gyrus, is critically involved in resolving interference among competing actions (for example, to go or not to go), i.e. cognitive control during delay of rewards, whereas limbic or emotional brain regions, including the ventral striatum, have been shown to be associated with more immediate choices and rewards.

Background to the study

Previous research (Eigsti, 2006) showed performance on a delay-of-gratification task in childhood predicted the efficiency with which the same individuals performed a cognitive control task (go/no go task) as adolescents and young adults. The findings suggested that performance in preschool delay of gratification may predict the capacity, in adulthood, to control thoughts and actions, as reflected in performance on cognitive control tasks.

The aim of this study was to build on previous research to assess whether delay of gratification in childhood predicts impulse control abilities and sensitivity to alluring or social cues (happy faces) at the behavioural and neural level when participants were in their forties, i.e. adults.

The alluring qualities of targets in an impulse control task were manipulated to examine behavioural and neural correlates of delay of gratification using **functional magnetic resonance imaging** (fMRI).

Research method

This can be considered a quasi/natural experiment.

The IV – whether the participant was a high delayer or a low delayer – was naturally occurring and so could not be manipulated or controlled by the researchers.

The DV was the performance on the impulse control task (in terms of reaction times and accuracy) in Experiment 1 and the performance on

Exam tip

Although you will not be required to have detailed knowledge of the brain for the exam, you should be aware of the specific brain areas mentioned here and their functions in order to understand Casey et al.'s study.

Figure 12.2 The marshmallow test studies a child's self-control

Now test yourself

7 Outline one piece of research that this study builds on.

TESTED

functional magnetic resonance imaging is a neuroimaging procedure using MRI technology that measures brain activity by detecting changes associated with blood flow.

the impulse control task (in terms of reaction times and accuracy) and imaging results using fMRI in Experiment 2.

The fact that some participants completed self-control scales when in their twenties and thirties, and that those participating in Experiment 1 did both the 'hot' and 'cool' go/no go tasks, means the study had, in parts, a repeated measures design.

This was a longitudinal study which followed some of the original participants from the age of four years until they were in their forties.

Outline of the procedure/study

During the late 1960s and early 1970s 562 four-year-old pupils from Stanford University's Bing Nursery School completed a delay-of-gratification task. Of these, 155 completed self-control scales when in their twenties (1993) and then 135 when in their thirties (2003).

117 of the 135 individuals who were above average or below average in their original delay-of-gratification performance as well as in the self-report measures of self-control were contacted in relation to participating in this study. 59 (23 males, 36 females) agreed to participate in this longitudinal behavioural study (Experiment 1). Participants were classified as low or high delayers from the results of (a) their delay-of-gratification performance and (b) the self-control measures. In Experiment 1 there were 32 high delayers (12 male, 20 female) and 27 low delayers (11 male, 16 female).

Of the 59 who participated in Experiment 1, 27 (13 males, 14 females) agreed to be part of a functional neuroimaging study (Experiment 2). In Experiment 2 there were 15 high delayers (5 male, 10 female) and 11 low delayers (7 male, 4 female).

NB: One 41-year-old man was excluded from all analyses because of poor performance, so results for Experiment 2 were based on the performance of 26 participants.

Experiment 1: Behavioural correlates of delay of gratification 40 years on

This tested whether individuals who were less able to delay gratification as children and young adults (low delayers) would, as adults in their forties, show less impulse control in suppression of a response to 'hot' relative to 'cool' cues.

The 59 participants, already classified as high or low delayers, consented to take part in a behavioural version of a 'hot' and 'cool' impulse control task. Participants completed two versions of the go/no go task. The 'cool' version of the task consisted of male and female stimuli, which were presented, one sex as a 'go' (i.e. target) stimulus to which participants were instructed to press a button, and the other sex as a 'no go' (i.e. non-target) stimulus to which participants were instructed to withhold a button press. Before the onset of each run, a screen appeared indicating which stimulus category served as the target.

Participants were instructed to respond as quickly and accurately as possible. Each face appeared for 500 ms, followed by a 1s inter-stimulus interval. A total of 160 trials were presented per run in pseudo-randomised order (120 go, 40 no go). The task was therefore a 2 (trial type: go, no go) × 2 (stimulus sex: male, female) factorial design.

Now test yourself

8 Describe why this study can be considered a quasi/natural experiment.

TESTED

Exam tip

Know the procedure followed in both Experiment 1 and Experiment 2.

Accuracy and response latency data (reaction times) were acquired in four runs representing each combination of stimulus sex (male, female) and trial type (go, no go). The 'hot' version of the go/no go task was identical to the 'cool' version except happy faces were used in the 'hot' version and neutral or fearful faces were used in the 'cool' version.

The tasks were presented using programmed laptop computers sent to participants' homes.

Experiment 2: Neural correlates of delayed gratification 40 years on

fMRI was used to examine neural correlates of delay of gratification. It was anticipated that low delayers would show diminished activity in the right prefrontal cortex and amplified activity in the ventral striatum compared with high delayers.

Twenty-seven participants from Experiment 1 agreed (consented) to complete the imaging study. Participants completed a 'hot' version of the go/no go task similar to that used in Experiment 1. Differences were in timing, number of trials and apparatus.

Each face stimulus was presented for 500 ms, followed by a jittered inter-trial interval ranging from 2 to 14.5 s in duration (mean 5.2 s). A total of 48 trials were presented per run in pseudo-randomised order (35 go, 13 no go). In total, imaging data was acquired for 26 no go trials and 70 go trials for each expression.

The task was viewable with a rear projection screen and a NeuroScreen five-button response pad recorded button responses and reaction times.

One participant was excluded for excessively poor behavioural performance on the fMRI version of the task, leaving 26 participants for group analysis.

Key findings

Experiment 1

Reaction times (outside the scanner)
● There were no effects of delay group on reaction time measures to correct 'go' trials.

Accuracy (outside the scanner)
● Both low and high delayers performed with a high level of accuracy for correctly responding to 'go' trials during both the 'cool' (99.8 per cent correct) and 'hot' tasks (99.5 per cent correct).
● Accuracy for 'no go' trials was more variable, with low delayers committing more false alarms than high delayers.
● Low and high delayers performed comparably on the 'cool' task but the low delayers trended towards performing more poorly on the 'hot' task than the high delayers; only the low delay group showed a significant decrement in performance for the 'hot' trials relative to the 'cool' trials.
● Overall, therefore, the go/no go task produced differences between the delay groups only in the presence of emotional 'hot' cues, i.e. individuals who, as a group, had more difficulty in delaying gratification at four years of age showed more difficulty as adults in suppressing responses to happy faces.

Experiment 2

Reaction times (inside the scanner)
● The two delay groups did not differ significantly in reaction times in correct 'go' trials.

Now test yourself

9 Explain how the tasks were presented in this study.

TESTED

Typical mistakes

Forgetting that the sample size decreased as the study progressed.

Confusing the purpose of the two experiments – Experiment 1 was to study behavioural correlates, Experiment 2 was to study neural correlates.

Now test yourself

10 Outline one finding from Experiment 1.

TESTED

Accuracy (inside the scanner)

- Overall, accuracy rates for the 'hot' go/no go task were uniformly high for 'go' trials (mean 98.2 per cent correct hits), with more variable performance than 'no go' trials (12.4 per cent false alarm rate).
- Differences between the two delay groups in 'no go' accuracy were consistent with the observed differences in the 'hot' task performance in Experiment 1, with low delayers committing more false alarms than high delayers.

Imaging results

The 'no go' vs. 'go' trials identified candidate regions of the brain differentially engaged as a function of cognitive control tasks. The right inferior frontal gyrus was involved in accurately withholding a response.

Compared with high delayers, low delayers had diminished recruitment (lower activity) of the inferior frontal gyrus for correct 'no go' relative to 'go' trials.

The ventral striatum demonstrated significant difference in recruitment between high and low delayers. This reward-related region of the brain showed a three-way interaction of group × trial × emotion, with elevated activity to happy 'no go' trials for low delayers relative to high delayers.

These results showed that the prefrontal cortex differentiated between 'no go' and 'go' trials to a greater extent in high delayers, while the ventral striatum showed exaggerated recruitment in low delayers.

Conclusions

Sensitivity to environmental hot cues plays a significant role in an individual's ability to suppress actions toward alluring cues.

Resistance to temptation as measured originally by a delay-of-gratification task is a relatively stable individual difference that predicts reliable biases in frontostriatal circuitries that integrate motivational and control processes.

The capacity to resist temptation varies by context – the more tempting the choice for the individual, the more predictive are the individual differences in people's ability to regulate their behaviour.

Behavioural correlates of delay ability are a function not only of cognitive control but also of the compelling nature of the stimuli that must be suppressed.

Individuals who at the age of four years have difficulty delaying gratification and who continue to show reduced self-control abilities have more difficulty as adults in suppressing responses to positive social cues than those who do not.

> **Exam tip**
>
> Know at least two results from each experiment.

> **Now test yourself**
>
> 11 Outline one finding from Experiment 2.
>
> TESTED ☐

> **Exam tips**
>
> Know how the study by Sperry (1968) is similar to and different from the study by Casey *et al.* (2011).
>
> Know how these studies relate to the key theme 'Regions of the brain'.

Section A practice questions

From Sperry's split brain study:
1 a) Give one reason why the participants had previously undergone an operation to disconnect the two hemispheres of the brain. [2]
   b) Outline one problem with generalising from the sample used in this study. [2]
2 a) Outline how information was presented to a participant's left visual field (LVF). [2]
   b) Explain why participants were unable to identify in words information presented to their left visual field. [2]
3 Describe two findings from the tactile tests used in this study. [4]

4 a) Explain why a participant was able to point with his right hand to pictures flashed to his right visual field (RVF). [2]
   b) Describe how a participant responded when two images were flashed simultaneously, one to his right visual field (RVF) and one to his left visual field (LVF). [2]

From Casey et al.'s study on delayed gratification:
5 a) Identify the independent variable (IV) in both Experiment 1 and Experiment 2. [2]
   b) Identify the dependent variables (DVs) in both Experiment 1 and Experiment 2. [2]
6 Outline the main difference between the 'hot' and 'cool' versions of the go/nogo task in Experiment 1. [2]
7 a) Explain why this is generally considered a longitudinal study. [2]
   b) Suggest one weakness of longitudinal studies in relation to this study. [2]
8 Describe two findings from Casey et al/'s study on delayed gratification. [4]
9 Explain why both Sperry's split brain and Casey et al.'s delayed gratification studies are useful when trying to understand human behaviour. [4]
10 Suggest how the study by Casey et al. into delayed gratification builds on the split brain study of Sperry. [4]

For practice questions linked to Sections B and C of the exam paper turn to Chapter 15.

ONLINE ☐

Key theme: Brain plasticity

REVISED ☐

Classic study: Blakemore and Cooper (1970): Impact of early visual experience

Relation to the biological area

Biological workings of the brain influence the behaviour of both human beings and animals. This study shows that, in the visual cortex of the brain, orientation-specific cells can change the kind of stimulus they respond to depending on an animal's, in this case a cat's, early visual environment. The study shows the plasticity of a kitten's brain as neurones originally conditioned to respond to either horizontal or vertical orientation can switch to responding to the opposite orientation when required.

Theory/theories on which the study is based

Research has shown that the physical structure of the brains of humans and cats is very similar: both have cerebral cortices with similar lobes, both are gyrencephalic, i.e. they have a surface folding, both have grey and white matter.

Kittens' brains have a neuroplasticity: control of visual stimuli correlated with changes in RNA structures. Cats possess visual-recognition memory and have flexibility of cerebral encoding from visual information, adaptability corresponding to changing environmental stimuli (Grouse et al., 1979; Okujava et al., 2005, Okujava et al., 2009).

In a normal cat, neurones of the visual cortex are selective for the orientation of lines and edges in the visual field, and the preferred orientations of different cells are distributed throughout the visual field (Hubel and Wiesel, 1962).

Now test yourself

12 Outline one similarity between the physical structure of the brains of humans and cats.

TESTED ☐

Background to the study

Hirsch and Spinelli (1970) reported that early visual experience can change neural organisation in kittens. They reared kittens with one eye viewing vertical stripes, the other horizontal, and found that out of 21 neurones with elongated receptive fields, all were monocularly driven, and in all but one case the orientation of the receptive field closely matched the pattern experienced by that eye.

Blakemore and Cooper therefore began a related project, though their approach is slightly different to that of Hirsch and Spinelli in that they allowed kittens normal binocular vision in an environment consisting entirely of horizontal or vertical stripes.

The aim of this study was therefore to investigate the development of the primary visual cortex (in cats) and to find out whether some of its properties, such as orientation selectivity, are innate (as suggested by Hubel and Wiesel) or learned.

Research method

This was a laboratory experiment which used an independent measures design.

The IV was whether the kittens were reared in a horizontal or a vertical environment (Figure 12.3).

The DV was their visuomotor behaviour once they were placed in an illuminated environment, i.e. whether the horizontally raised kittens could detect vertically aligned objects and/or whether the vertically raised kittens could detect horizontally aligned objects.

Outline of the procedure/study

Kittens (studied from birth until this report was compiled) were randomly allocated to one of the two conditions. Two of the kittens (one reared in a horizontal and one in a vertical environment) were used to study neurophysical effects.

The kittens were housed from birth in a completely dark room. From the age of two weeks they were put into a special apparatus for an average of about five hours per day. The kitten stood on a clear glass platform inside a tall cylinder, the entire inner surface of which was covered with high-contrast black-and-white stripes, either vertical or horizontal. There were no corners to its environment, no edges to its floor, and the upper and lower limits to its world of stripes were a long way away. It could not even see its body as it wore a wide black collar that restricted its visual field to a width of about 130 degrees. (The kittens did not seem upset by the monotony of their surroundings and sat for long periods inspecting the walls of the tube.)

This routine was stopped when the kittens were five months old. They were then taken for several hours each week from their dark cage to a small, well-lit room, furnished with tables and chairs. Their visual reactions were observed and recorded/noted.

At 7.5 months, two of the kittens (one reared in the horizontal and one reared in the vertical environment) were anaesthetised so that their neurophysiology could be examined.

Key findings

Regardless of whether the kittens had been exposed to vertical or horizontal stripes, they were initially extremely visually impaired:

● Their **pupillary reflexes** were normal but they showed no visual placing when brought up to a table top and no startle response when an object was thrust towards them.

Figure 12.3 Some kittens were exposed to an entirely vertical environment

Now test yourself

13 Describe how the independent measures experimental design was used in this study.

    TESTED ☐

Typical mistake

Confusing 'vertical' with 'horizontal'.

Exam tips

Know the procedure followed in the study.

Know how data was gathered – through observation and neurophysiological examination.

Now test yourself

14 Outline what happened to two of the kittens when they were 7.5 months old.

    TESTED ☐

pupillary reflex refers to the ability of the eye's pupils to respond to light intensity.

- They guided themselves mainly by touch.
- They were frightened when they reached the edge of the surface they were standing on.
- They showed 'behavioural blindness' in that the kittens raised in the horizontal environment could not detect vertically aligned objects and vice versa.
- Only the eyes of the kitten brought up in vertical stripes followed a rod held vertically and only the eyes of the kitten reared in horizontal stripes followed the rod if it was held horizontally, i.e. both kittens remained blind to contours perpendicular to the stripes they had lived with.

The kittens quickly recovered from many of the deficiencies and within a total of about ten hours of normal vision they showed startle responses and visual placing and would jump with ease from a chair to the floor. However, some of their defects were permanent:
- They always followed moving objects with clumsy, jerky head movements.
- They often tried to touch things moving on the other side of the room, well beyond their reach.

The neurophysiological examination showed:
- no evidence of severe **astigmatism**, which might have explained the behavioural responses
- horizontal plane recognition cells did not 'fire off' in the kitten from the vertical environment and vertical plane cells did not 'fire off' in the kitten from the horizontal environment so there was distinct orientation selectivity, showing the kittens suffered from 'physical blindness'
- about 75 per cent of cells in both cats were clearly binocular and in almost every way the responses were like that of a normal kitten
- the distributions of preferred orientation were totally abnormal, however in the horizontally raised kitten there were no neurones in the vertical orientation and in the vertically raised kitten there were no neurones in the horizontal orientation.

astigmatism is a visual defect which results in distorted images, as light rays are prevented from meeting at a common focus.

Now test yourself

15 Outline one finding from the neurophysiological examination.

TESTED ☐

Conclusions

Visual experiences in the early life of kittens can modify their brains and have profound perceptual consequences.

A kitten's visual cortex may adjust itself during maturation to the nature of its visual experience.

A kitten's nervous system adapts to match the probability of occurrence of features of its visual input.

Brain development is determined by the functional demands made upon it rather than pre-programmed genetic factors.

Exam tips

Know how this study is similar to and different from the study by Maguire *et al.* (2000).

Know how the study relates to the key theme 'Brain plasticity'.

Contemporary study: Maguire *et al.* (2000): Taxi drivers

Relation to the biological area

The biological area explains behaviour through an understanding of biological and neurological processes. The biological workings of the body and brain therefore determine how an individual behaves. Maguire *et al.* hypothesised that experiences can cause changes in the brain and discovered that people who use navigational skills constantly in their work show differences in the part of the brain (the **hippocampus**, Figure 12.4)

the **hippocampus** is a small, curved formation in the brain that plays an important role in the limbic system. The hippocampus is involved in the formation of new memories and is also associated with learning and emotions.

that deals with these skills compared with those who don't – London taxi drivers, for example, have a significantly greater posterior hippocampal volume than non-taxi drivers.

Because the brain is lateralised and symmetrical, there are actually two hippocampi. They are located just above each ear and about an inch and a half inside the head.

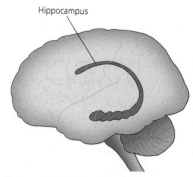

Hippocampus

Figure 12.4 The hippocampus

Theory/theories on which the study is based

The hippocampus plays an important role in the laying down of new memories. It is found inside each hemisphere of the brain and is thought to be significant in facilitating spatial memory and navigation.

Recent research has indicated that lesions to the hippocampus affect an individual's ability to remember the location of different places and things.

Background to the study

Research has shown increased hippocampal volume relative to brain and body size in small mammals and birds which show behaviour requiring spatial memory, such as food storing.

In some species, hippocampal volumes enlarge specifically during seasons when spatial ability is greatest. However, past research has not shown:
● whether differences in brain structure are susceptible to plastic change in response to environmental stimulation
● the precise role of the hippocampus in humans
● whether the human brain responds to experiences requiring spatial memory in the same way as smaller mammals and birds.

Maguire *et al.* therefore aimed to show that the hippocampus in the human brain is the structure associated with spatial memory and navigation. Her sample of London taxi drivers was ideal because they have to acquire extensive spatial and navigational information (pass 'The Knowledge') on the city of London to gain their taxi driving licence. Her use of a group of taxi drivers with a wide range of navigational experience allowed her to examine the direct effect of spatial experience on brain structure.

Research method

This was a quasi/natural experiment because the IV – whether the participant was a London taxi driver or a person who did not drive taxis – was naturally varying and so could not be manipulated or controlled by the researchers. The DV was the volume of the hippocampi, including their anterior, body and posterior regions, measured by analysing MRI scans of participants' brain using the two techniques of **VBM** and **pixel counting**.

The study used an independent measures, matched participants design.

Outline of the procedure/study

The experimental group of 16 taxi drivers were all healthy, right-handed, male London taxi drivers, mean age 44 years (range 32 to 62 years), mean time as a licensed London taxi driver (passed 'The Knowledge') 14.3 years (range 1.5 to 42 years).

The control group who did not drive taxis (50 for the VBM analysis, 16 for the pixel counting) were matched for health, handedness, sex, mean age and age range.

> **Now test yourself**
>
> 16 Outline one important role of the hippocampus.
> 17 Suggest why taxi drivers made an excellent sample for this study.
>
> TESTED

> **voxel-based morphometry (VBM)** is a technique which enables the brain to be examined in an objective and unbiased way. VBM identifies differences in the density of grey matter in different parts of the brain.
>
> **pixel counting** (in this situation) is a technique where the pixels (a pixel is a single point on a graphic image) are counted from images produced by MRI scans.

> **Now test yourself**
>
> 18 Outline why this study is generally considered a quasi/natural experiment.
>
> TESTED

> **Exam tip**
>
> Know the procedure followed.

The scans of the control group were selected from the structural MRI scan database at the same unit where the taxi drivers were scanned. The MRI scans of all participants were analysed using:

- VBM, which is an automatic procedure that 'normalises' the scans to a template to eliminate overall brain size as a variable and then identifies differences in grey matter density in different regions of the brain. The brains of the 16 taxi drivers were compared with those of 50 non-taxi drivers to see whether there were any differences in structure
- pixel counting to compare the volume of anterior, body and posterior cross-sections of the taxi drivers' hippocampi with those of a previously age, gender and handedness-matched sample of 16 controls taken from the 50 used in the VBM analysis. The images were analysed by one person experienced in the technique and blind to whether the scan was of a taxi driver or a control and the VBM findings. This procedure allowed the total hippocampal volume to be calculated.

Key findings

VBM analysis showed no significant differences between the brains of the two groups except:

- taxi drivers had significantly increased grey matter volume in the right and left posterior hippocampi compared with controls
- in the controls there was a relatively greater grey matter volume in the anterior hippocampi compared with taxi drivers.

Pixel counting showed that although there was no significant difference in overall volume of the hippocampi between the two groups:

- taxi drivers had a significantly greater posterior hippocampal volume than controls
- controls had a significantly greater anterior right hippocampal volume than the taxi drivers and a significantly greater hippocampal body volume on the right than the left.

Regions of the brain with the largest volume are shown in the table.

	Left hippocampus	Right hippocampus
Anterior		Controls
Body		Controls
Posterior	Taxi drivers	Taxi drivers

Correlations showed a significant positive correlation between the length of time as a taxi driver and the right posterior hippocampal volume, but a negative correlation for the anterior hippocampal volume.

Conclusions

There are regionally specific structural differences between the hippocampi of licensed London taxi drivers compared with those who do not drive London taxis.

The professional dependence on navigational skills in licensed London taxi drivers is associated with a relative redistribution of grey matter in the hippocampus.

It can be suggested that the changes in the arrangement of hippocampal grey matter are acquired, i.e. due to nurture.

Exam tips

Make sure you know the criteria against which the experimental and control groups were matched.

Know how the control group was selected.

Now test yourself

19 Describe voxel-based morphometry.
20 Explain why pixel counting was used in this study.

TESTED

Exam tip

Know how the data was analysed – using VBM and pixel counting.

Typical mistakes

Forgetting that the control group was not involved in the correlational analysis.

When making comparison between the experimental and control groups, forgetting to complete the comparison, for example 'Taxi drivers had greater grey matter volume in the posterior hippocampus', i.e. omitting 'compared with non-taxi drivers/controls'.

Now test yourself

21 Outline one finding from the VBM analysis.
22 Draw one conclusion from the findings of this study.

TESTED

Findings also indicate the possibility of local plasticity in the structure of a normal human brain which allows it to adapt in response to prolonged environmental stimuli.

Exam tips

Know how this study is similar to and different from the study by Blakemore and Cooper (1970).

Know how the study relates to the key theme 'Brain plasticity'.

Section A practice questions

From Blakemore and Cooper's study the impact of early visual experience:

1 Outline how this study relates to the biological area of psychology. [4]
2 Describe how the experimental method was used in this study. [2]
3 a) Outline one piece of qualitative data gathered in this study. [2]
  b) Suggest one weakness of the qualitative data gathered in this study. [2]
4 Draw one conclusion from the findings of this study. [2]

From Maguire et al.'s study on taxi drivers:

5 a) Identify the independent variable (IV) and the dependent variable (DV) in this experiment. [2]
  b) Describe one effect the independent variable (IV) had on the dependent variable (DV) in this study. [2]
6 a) Identify two controls used in this study. [2]
  b) Explain why it was important to use controls in this study. [2]
7 a) Identify the two techniques used to analyse the MRI scans. [2]
  b) Outline one difference between the MRI scans of taxi drivers and non-taxi drivers as identified through VBM analysis. [2]
8 a) Outline one strength of using a correlation in this study. [2]
  b) Outline one weakness of using a correlation in this study. [2]
9 Describe two similarities between the study by Blakemore and Cooper on the impact of early visual experience and the taxi driver study by Maguire et al. [4]
10 Explain how both Blakemore and Copper's study on the impact of early visual experience and Maguire et al.'s study on taxi drivers link to the key them of 'Brain plasticity'. [4]

For practice questions linked to Sections B and C of the exam paper turn to Chapter 15.

ONLINE

Summary

By the end of this chapter for the two AS-level studies and/or the four A-level studies you should:
- know the research method and sample
- know the key findings
- be able to suggest at least one way in which each study could be improved and possible implications of the suggestion(s) for methodology, ethics, reliability, validity, usefulness, practicality, etc.
- know how each study relates to the area of biological psychology
- know strengths/weaknesses of conducting research under controlled conditions,

laboratory experiments, snapshot versus longitudinal studies, observation and self-reports (including rating scales) as ways to gather data, the use of hypothetical scenarios, quantitative and qualitative data, the sample
- be able to consider the issues of reliability, validity and ecological validity, ethnocentrism
- understand how each study links to the psychological debates of nature/nurture, freewill/determinism, reductionism/holism, individual/situational explanations, usefulness of research, ethical considerations, conducting socially sensitive research, psychology as a science.

13 The area of the psychology of individual differences

Outline of the individual differences area

REVISED

In general terms, this approach looks at the differences between people rather than factors that are common to all people. The approach therefore covers intelligence and personality and the way these have been tested, concepts and definitions of normality and abnormality, and a huge range of descriptions and explanations of a variety of mental health issues (for example, addiction) and disorders (for example, schizophrenia).

Much of psychology is concerned with how groups of people behave and their typical or 'average' behaviour. In contrast, the study of individual differences focuses on the differences within each group, how individual people differ in their behaviour and personal qualities, and what this tells us about human behaviour.

This approach has always attracted a lot of controversy because it seems to create divisions between people – we are telling people they have more or less of a human quality than another person. The reason this results in controversy is because of the arguments about why we have individual differences – for example, if one person scores more on an IQ test than another person, is that because they are genetically different or because they have been educated differently? The questions become even more controversial when the average scores of groups of people are considered.

An assumption of the individual differences area of psychology is that every individual is unique both genetically and in their experiences, and this uniqueness is displayed through their behaviour.

An implication of the individual differences area of psychology is that if every individual is unique, everyone behaves differently and it is difficult to define 'normal' behaviour.

> ### Now test yourself
>
> 1 Outline one key feature of the area of individual differences.
>
> TESTED

Key theme: Understanding disorders

REVISED

Classic study: Freud (1909): Little Hans

Relation to the area of individual differences

The individual differences area of psychology looks at differences rather than similarities between individuals. Some individuals behave in ways other people find strange and sometimes even worrying. Some children are often afraid of things other children and adults are not and these fears are demonstrated through behaviours which other people consider abnormal. A phobia is an 'intense, persistent and irrational fear of a particular object, situation, place or activity which is accompanied by a compelling desire to avoid and escape it' (Woods, 2001). Freud believed children's fears and phobias are a physical or mental manifestation of inner conflicts relating to their psychosexual development. He believed all children pass through specific stages of psychosexual development but, because everyone is unique, any subconscious conflicts that develop as children pass through these phases are explicitly expressed differently by individual children.

This study shows that Little Hans was passing through the phallic stage of psychosexual development and the inner conflicts that arose through his experience of the **Oedipus complex** in this stage were expressed uniquely by developing a phobia of horses (Figure 13.1).

Theory/theories on which the study is based

Theory of infantile sexuality/Theory of psychosexual development

According to Freud's theory, sexuality is not confined to physically mature adults but is evident from birth. However, different parts of the body are particularly sensitive at different times during childhood.

The sequence of the psychosexual stages is determined by maturation (nature) and how the child is treated by others (nurture).

Freud's stages of psychosexual development are: oral stage: 0 to 1 year, anal stage: 1 to 3 years, phallic stage: 3 to 5/6 years, latency stage: 5/6 years to puberty, genital stage: puberty to maturity.

The Oedipus complex for boys and the **Electra complex** for girls form part of the phallic stage.

> **Exam tip**
>
> Make sure you know Freud's psychosexual stages of development.

Background to the study

Hans was described as a cheerful and straightforward child, but when he became 'ill' (developed his phobia) it was obvious that there was a difference between what he said and what he thought. Freud thought this was because things were going on in Hans' unconscious mind of which he was unaware. Freud therefore decided to help Hans by interpreting his behaviour and telling him why he was thinking and behaving as he was. This is a process known as psychoanalysis.

Freud documented the case of Little Hans to show how his fears, dreams and fantasies were symbolic of his unconscious passing through the phallic stage of psychosexual development. He used this study to support his ideas about the origins of phobias, his theory of infantile sexuality and the Oedipus complex, and his belief in the effectiveness of psychoanalytic therapy.

> **Exam tip**
>
> Be able to describe the Oedipus complex and how it relates to this study.

Research method

This was a longitudinal case study. A case study gathers detailed data of either a single individual or a very small group of individuals, an institution or an event. Here, in-depth, detailed data was gathered on one individual – Little Hans – in relation to his fantasies, fears and phobias.

Now test yourself

2 Outline how the study of Little Hans relates to the area of individual differences.

TESTED ☐

Figure 13.1 Little Hans was afraid of horses, particularly disliking their muzzles and blinkers

the **Oedipus complex** is experienced by young boys around the age of four when they are going through the phallic stage of psychosexual development. The boy has subconscious sexual feelings for his mother and fears his father as a rival for his mother's attentions. To resolve this subconscious conflict/complex the boy identifies with his father and takes on/imitates his behaviour.

the **Electra complex** is experienced by young girls around the age of four when they are going through the phallic stage of psychosexual development. The girl has subconscious sexual feelings for her father and fears her mother as a rival for her father's attentions. To resolve this subconscious conflict/complex the girl identifies with her mother and takes on/imitates her behaviour.

Now test yourself

3 List the five stages of psychosexual development.

TESTED ☐

The study is considered longitudinal as it documents developments in Hans' fears from when he was nearly three years old until he was five. This allowed Freud to link the evidence gathered to his developmental theory of sexuality.

Data was gathered by Little Hans' father (a firm believer in Freud's ideas) regularly observing and questioning Hans. He then sent records of the events and conversations to Freud, who interpreted the information and replied to Little Hans' father with advice on how to proceed.

Outline of the procedure/study

Just before he was three, Hans started to show a lively interest in his 'widdler' and the presence/absence of this organ in others – human and non-human. At this time he had a tendency to masturbate, bringing threats from his mother to send for Dr A. to cut it off.

When he was three and a half, Hans gained a baby sister, Hanna, whom he resented and subsequently, subconsciously, wished his mother would drop in the bath so she would drown.

Later Hans developed a fear of being bitten by white horses. This seemed to be linked to two incidents:
1 Overhearing a father say to a child, 'Don't put your finger to the white horse or it will bite you.'
2 Seeing a horse that was pulling a carriage fall down and kick about.

His fear was then generalised to carts and buses.

Both before and after the development of his phobia of horses, Hans was both anxious his mother would go away and prone to fantasies and daydreams. These included:
● the giraffe fantasy
● two plumber fantasies
● the parenting fantasy.

Having received 'help' from his father and Freud, after the parenting fantasy both the 'illness' and analysis came to an end.

Key findings

Freud considered Little Hans' fear of horses to be a subconscious fear of his father. This was because the dark around the mouth of a horse plus the blinkers resembled the moustache and glasses worn by his father. He was fearful of his father because he was experiencing the Oedipus complex.

Hans' fascination with his 'widdler' was because he was going through the phallic stage of psychosexual development and experiencing the Oedipus complex.

His daydream about giraffes was a representation of him trying to take his mother away from his father so he could have her to himself – another feature of the Oedipus complex.

Hans' fantasy of becoming a father again linked to his experiencing the Oedipus complex.

His fantasy about the plumber was interpreted as him now identifying with his father and having passed through the Oedipus complex.

Now test yourself

4 Explain why this is considered a longitudinal case study.

TESTED ☐

Exam tip

Refer back to your textbook and make sure you familiarise yourself with the different fantasies mentioned in Freud's study. Be able to describe at least two of Hans' fantasies and his phobia of horses.

Now test yourself

5 Describe Hans' giraffe fantasy.

TESTED ☐

Typical mistakes

Not realising or acknowledging that any behaviour linked to the Oedipus/Electra complex is as a result of subconscious forces.

Not realising that not only was Hans' father probably biased in his reporting of Hans' behaviour (because he wanted to support his friend, Freud) but that Freud himself was very likely to interpret any of the information passed to him by Hans' father in a biased way as he wanted to find evidence to support his own theories.

Now test yourself

6 Outline why Hans had a fascination for his 'widdler'.

TESTED ☐

Conclusions

Freud concluded that his study of Hans provided support for:
- his theory of psychosexual development/infant sexuality
- his suggestion that boys in the phallic stage of psychosexual development experience the Oedipus complex
- the nature of phobias and his theory that they are the product of unconscious anxiety displaced onto harmless external objects
- his concept of unconscious determinism which holds that people are not consciously aware of the causes of their behaviour
- his use of psychoanalytic therapy to treat disturbed thoughts, feelings and behaviours by first identifying the unconscious cause(s) of the disturbance and then bringing them into the conscious so that they can be discussed and resolved.

> **Exam tips**
>
> Know how this study is similar to and different from the study by Baron-Cohen *et al.* (1997).
>
> Know how the study relates to the key theme 'Understanding disorders'.
>
> Know how the study relates to the area of individual differences.

Contemporary study: Baron-Cohen *et al.* (1997): Autism in adults

Relation to the area of individual differences

The individual differences area looks at differences rather than similarities between individuals. People with autism behave in ways that others often find strange and worrying as they are different to the norm. People with autism have a cognitive disorder that develops throughout childhood, leading to them having particular difficulties in social situations, resulting in unique behaviours, generally considered outside the range of 'normal behaviour'.

Theory/theories on which the study is based

The most influential theory of autism in recent years maintains that what all autistic people have in common (the core deficit) is mind-blindness (Baron-Cohen, 1990), a severe impairment in their understanding of mental states and in their appreciation of how mental states govern behaviour. They lack a 'theory of mind' (TOM).

Individuals diagnosed with autism show a tremendous variation in the degree to which they are affected. To address this issue, a 'spectrum of autism' was devised. Difficulties experienced by children, judged in relation to set criteria, allow them to be placed within the spectrum. For example.

Classic autism	Asperger syndrome	Normality

←——————————————·····························————————————→

(Those with Asperger syndrome (AS) show the same characteristics as autism but are of average or above average intelligence and appear to have good communication skills, though this may not actually be the case.)

> **Now test yourself**
>
> 7 Explain what is meant by the term 'theory of mind'.
>
> TESTED

Background to the study

Some evidence suggests that a TOM deficit is not a core cognitive deficit in autism. But no conclusive evidence has yet shown that individuals such as adults with 'high-functioning autism' or Asperger syndrome have an intact TOM. This is because usual tests to assess TOM have a ceiling in developmental terms corresponding to a mental age of about six years. Therefore, although existing TOM tests are challenging for six year olds, they are far too easy for adults who all pass even though they may not have a fully functioning TOM.

Happé (1994) tested adults with autism or Asperger syndrome on an 'advanced' TOM task and found her participants had more difficulty with her mental state stories (Happé's Strange Stories) than matched controls.

Baron-Cohen *et al.* built on Happé's research by using an adult test to assess theory of mind competence in high-functioning adults with autism or AS.

Research method

This was a quasi/natural experiment because the independent variable – the type of person: adults with high-functioning autism/AS, normal adults and adults with Tourette syndrome (TS) – was naturally occurring so could not be manipulated or controlled by the researchers. The dependent variable was the performance – score out of 25 – on the Eyes Task (Figure 13.2), measured by showing each participant 25 black-and-white, standardised photographs of the eye region (male and female) and asking them to make a forced choice between two mental state words (target and foil) to best describe what the person in the photograph was feeling or thinking.

The study used a matched participants design because the group of normal adults and the group with TS were age-matched with the group of adults with autism/AS.

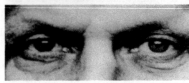

Figure 13.2 Two of the expressions used in the Eyes Task

> **Typical mistake**
>
> Not being able to describe the Eyes Task accurately.

Now test yourself

8 Describe the Eyes Task.

TESTED

Outline of the procedure/study

Three groups of participants were tested:
- Group 1: 16 individuals with high-functioning autism or Asperger syndrome (HFA = 4, AS = 12). The sex ratio was 13:3 (M:F). All were of normal intelligence and were recruited through an advert in the National Autistic Society magazine and a variety of clinical sources.
- Group 2: 50 normal age-matched adults (25M:25F), drawn from the general population of Cambridge.
- Group 3: 10 adults with Tourette syndrome, also age-matched with Groups 1 and 2. The sex ratio was 8:2 (M:F). All were of normal intelligence and were recruited from a tertiary referral centre in London.

The Eyes Task, the **Strange Stories Task** and the two control tasks (Gender Recognition Task, Basic Emotion Recognition Task) were presented in random order to all participants.

The Gender Recognition Task involved identifying the gender of the eyes used in the Eyes Task. The task controlled for face perception, perceptual discrimination and social perception. The Basic Emotion Recognition Task involved judging photographs of whole faces displaying basic emotions identified by Ekman (1992). The task was carried out to check whether difficulties on the Eyes Task were due to difficulties with basic emotional recognition. The Strange Stories Task was used to validate the results from the Eyes Task.

Participants were tested individually in a quiet room in their home, in the researchers' clinic or in the researchers' laboratory at Cambridge University.

in the **Strange Stories Task** Happé (1994) developed a theory of mind test which was considered appropriate for normal 8 to 9 year olds. The task involves story comprehension, where the key question concerns either a character's mental states (the experimental condition) or physical events (the control condition). Happé found that both adults with autism and Asperger syndrome had more difficulty with the mental state task than 'normal' control participants.

Key findings

Results of the Eyes Task (out of 25) are shown in the table.

	Mean score	Range
Autistic/AS	16.3	13–23
Normal	20.3	16–25
TS	20.4	16–25

The mean score for adults with TS (20.4) was not significantly different from normal adults (20.3), but both were significantly higher than the autism/AS mean score (16.3).

Normal females performed significantly better than normal males on the Eyes Task (mean 21.8 versus 18.8) but the normal males were significantly better than the autism/AS group (mean 18.8 versus 16.3).

The autism/AS group made significantly more errors on the Strange Stories Task than either of the other two groups.

On the Gender and Emotion control tasks, there were no differences between the groups.

Within the autism/AS group there was no significant correlation between IQ and performance on the Eyes Task.

Conclusions

Contrary to previous research with adults, these results seem to provide evidence that adults with autism/AS do possess an impaired theory of mind.

As some of the autism/AS group hold university degrees it is reasonable to suggest that TOM deficits are independent of general intelligence.

Section A practice questions

From Freud's study of Little Hans:
1 a) Outline Little Hans' parenting fantasy. [2]
   b) Give a Freudian explanation for Hans' parenting fantasy. [2]

2 a) Describe how the data was gathered. [2]
  b) Suggest one problem with the way Freud interpreted the data. [2]
3 Describe why Freud suggested that Hans' fear of horses symbolised his fear of his father. [4]
4 a) Outline one strength of the case study method as used in this study. [2]
  b) Outline one weakness of the case study method as used in this study. [2]

From the study by Baron-Cohen et al. on autism in adults:
5 Describe two of the three groups used in this study.. [4]
6 a) Outline one difference between the performance of the autistic adults and the adults with Tourette syndrome. [2]
  b) Suggest why there was a difference in performance on the Eyes Task between the autistic adults and the adults with Tourette syndrome. [2]
7 a) Identify the two control groups used in this study. [2]
  b) Explain why one of these control groups was used. [2]
8 a) Identify the independent variable (IV) and the dependent variable (DV) in the Eyes Task. [2]
  b) Explain why this study is generally considered a quasi experiment. [2]
9 Describe how the research method differed between Freud's study of Little Hans and Baron-Cohen et al.'s study of autism in adults. [4]
10 Describe how the type of data gathered differed between Freud's study of Little Hans and Baron-Cohen et al.'s study of autism in adults. [4]

For practice questions linked to Sections B and C of the exam paper turn to Chapter 15.

ONLINE

Key theme: Measuring differences

REVISED

Classic study: Gould (1982): A nation of morons – bias in IQ testing

Relation to the area of individual differences

A key issue related to intelligence is the one of nature and nurture. Is intelligence **innate** (nature) or **learned** (nurture)? If it is learned, IQ tests measure something that is a product of a person's individual experience, in which case the only point in testing would be to work out who needs more teaching. If intelligence is innate and unchanging, then testing can be to classify people in accordance with a set of predetermined physical and mental norms. Although any test will identify differences between individuals, trying to define and measure intelligence has proved problematic.

This review by Gould of Yerkes' work not only highlights individual differences in intelligence between men from a variety of social and cultural backgrounds who were recruited into the American army in the First World War, it also reveals how culturally biased and unfair IQ tests can be, suggesting that the differences in intelligence found between the army recruits and subsequent social developments were based on unfair criteria.

Theory/theories on which the study is based

Theories of **intelligence** include:
- psychometric (factor-analysis) theories, for example Spearman's two-factor theory, Burt and Vernon's hierarchical model, Thurstone's primary mental abilities

> **innate** behaviour is due to nature (what people are born with) whereas **learned** behaviour is due to nurture (what people have learned from their environment and through experiences after birth).

> **intelligence** is usually said to involve mental capabilities such as the ability to reason, plan, solve problems, think abstractly, comprehend ideas and language, and learn.

- fluid and crystallised intelligence, for example Cattell, 1963; Horn and Cattell, 1967, 1982
- information-processing approach, for example Sternberg, 1979; Fishbein, 1984
- Gardner's (1983, 1998) theory of multiple intelligences.

Trying to define intelligence has proved problematic, so researchers have tended to focus instead on testing intelligence, whatever intelligence may be!

The term 'IQ' is the usual test score given in an intelligence test. It stands for 'intelligence quotient', a quotient being the result of a division – mental age (MA, one's score on the test) divided by one's chronological age (CA). The quotient is then multiplied by 100 to get rid of decimals.

Background to the study

In 1904, Binet and Simon were commissioned by the French government to devise a test which would identify those children who would not benefit from ordinary schooling because of their inferior intelligence. The result was the Binet-Simon Scale (1905), generally accepted as the first intelligence test.

Wechsler developed the most widely used test of adult intelligence, the Wechsler Adult Intelligence Scale (WAIS), in 1944. This has also been revised numerous times since it was first used.

A major impetus to the development of group testing was America's involvement in the First World War. A quick and easy method of selecting more than one million recruits was needed and the result was the Army Alpha and Beta tests.

Yerke believed that intelligence was inherited and therefore could not be changed (i.e. due to nature). He believed that if he could show that intelligence tests were reliable and valid, then quantifiable measures would prove his point. With the outbreak of the First World War, the now Colonel Yerkes used recruits for the American army as a source of sufficient data to show that intelligence testing was scientific.

In this study Gould aimed to examine the early history of intelligence testing as conducted by Yerkes. He aimed to identify the following issues:
- the problematic nature of psychometric testing in general and the measurement of intelligence in particular
- the problem of theoretical bias influencing research in psychology, in particular how psychological theories on the inherited nature of intelligence and the prejudice of a society can dramatically distort the objectivity of intelligence testing
- the problem of the political and ethical implications of research, in this case the use of biased data to discriminate between people in suitability for occupation and even admission to a country.

Research method

This study is not a piece of empirical research. It is important to be aware that the article is an edited extract from Gould's (1981) book, *The Mismeasure of Man*, in which he traces the history of the measurement of human intelligence from nineteenth-century craniology (the measurement of skulls) to today's highly technical and sophisticated methods of IQ testing.

Now test yourself

13 Explain what is meant by the term 'intelligence quotient'.

TESTED

Exam tips

Know why this review was conducted.

Know why Yerkes wanted to test the intelligence of the American army recruits in the First World War.

Now test yourself

14 Describe why Yerkes wanted to give American army recruits intelligence tests.
15 Outline two of Gould's aims when conducting this review.

TESTED

The study is therefore a review article that looks at the history of Robert M. Yerkes' intelligence testing of recruits for the US army in the First World War and his attempt to establish psychology as a scientific discipline.

Outline of Yerkes' procedure/study

The sample consisted of 1.75 million army recruits in the USA during the First World War. The recruits included white Americans, 'Negroes' and European immigrants.

From May to July 1917, Yerkes, together with a number of colleagues who shared his views on the hereditary nature of intelligence, wrote the army mental tests. Together they developed three types of test, the first two of which could be given to large groups and took less than an hour to complete:

1 The Army Alpha Test: This was designed for literate recruits. It consisted of eight parts. It included items with which we are totally familiar as part of intelligence testing: analogies, filling in the next number in a sequence, etc. It required a good basic understanding of English language skills and literacy. Although Yerkes considered the tests to measure 'native intellectual ability (intelligence that is not influenced by education and/or culture), they were in fact extremely biased. After all, how could someone who was unfamiliar with American culture achieve a decent score? The following examples give some idea of the type of questions asked:
   ● Washington is to Adams as first is to …….
   ● Crisco is a: patient medicine, disinfectant, toothpaste, food product?
   ● The number of kaffir's legs is 2, 4, 6, 8?
2 The Army Beta Test: This was a test designed for people who were illiterate or failed the Army Alpha Test. It had seven parts and consisted of picture completion tasks (Figure 13.3). The pictures were again

Exam tip

Be able to describe features of the sample.

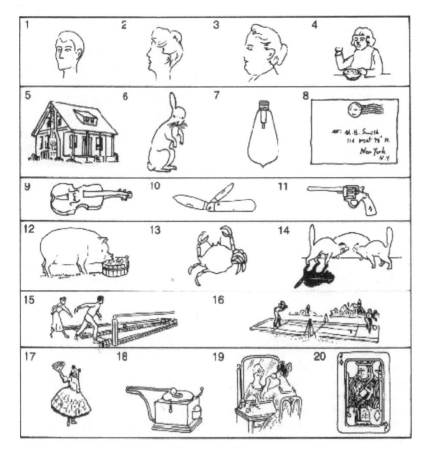

Figure 13.3 An extract from the Army Beta Test

Answers at **www.hoddereducation.co.uk/myrevisionnotes**

culturally specific and would have been extremely difficult to complete if participants had no knowledge of some of the items. There were also maze tests, counting the number of cubes, finding the next in a series of symbols and translating numerals into symbols using a code to work from. The instructions were written (in English), in three of the seven parts the answers had to be given in writing, yet this was a test for illiterates who may never have held a pencil beforehand.

3 The Individual Spoken Examination: If recruits failed on the other two tests, they were supposed to be given an individual spoken examination; however, this rarely happened. Every individual was given a grade from A to E, with plus and minus signs – for example, C− indicated a low average intelligence, suitable for the position of ordinary private in the army; D indicated a person rarely suited for tasks requiring special skill, forethought, resourcefulness or sustained alertness.

Administration of the tests caused numerous problems:

- Recruits who were illiterate should immediately have been assigned to the Beta Test, or given it if they failed the Alpha Test, but this only happened in some camps. Therefore, illiterate or immigrant recruits often sat the Alpha Test and came out scoring next to nothing.
- In fact, the levels of literacy among Americans, especially black Americans, were much lower than Yerkes anticipated and this confounded the problems further.
- Queues for the Beta Test began to build up and this led to an artificial lowering of standards by the administrators in order to reallocate more men to the Alpha Test. In some camps, the minimum level of schooling was sufficient to warrant sitting the Alpha test, whereas in others the recruits had to achieve a certain grade.
- Besides these inconsistencies in administration, further problems arose with men, especially black men, who failed the Alpha Test not being allowed to sit the Beta Test.
- Only one fifth of those who failed the Beta Test were allowed to take the individual examination.

Key findings

The data was analysed by E.G. Boring, Yerkes' lieutenant, who manipulated the results. Selected data was converted to a common standard to look for racial and national averages. The following 'facts' emerged:

- The average mental age of white, American, adult males stood just above the edge of moronity at a shocking and meagre 13.04 (Terman had previously set the standard at 16). This indicated that the country was 'a nation of morons' and as such was taken by the eugenicists to show that the poor, Negroes and feeble-minded had been interbreeding and lowering the overall intelligence of the population.
- The data also showed that European immigrants could be graded by their country of origin, with the darker people of Southern Europe and the Slavs of Eastern Europe being less intelligent than the fair people of Western and Northern Europe.
- The black man had an average mental age of 10.41. However, the lighter the skin colour, the higher the score.

Typical mistake

Not knowing how the administration of the tests caused many problems.

Exam tip

Be able to describe how the Alpha and Beta Tests and Individual Spoken Examination were conducted.

Now test yourself

16 Outline the sample used in this study.
17 Identify the three types of test used by Yerkes.

TESTED

Analysis and subsequent developments

The tests had a large impact on officer screening. By the end of the war, two thirds of the men who had been promoted were those who had taken the tests and achieved good test results. According to Yerkes, there was also a 'steady stream of requests' from commercial concerns, educational establishments and individuals for the use of army methods of psychological examining or for the adaptation of such methods for special needs.

The 'fact' that the average mental age of Americans was 13 was concerning, but the most important implication these tests had was the differences in racial and national groups. Bearing in mind that these tests were now accepted measures of innate intelligence, here was evidence (obviously distorted) that there really was a difference between racial and national groups in their levels of intelligence – for example, Nordic people from Northern Europe had been shown to be the most intelligent.

This 'evidence' was used by Carl Brigham, Assistant Professor at Princeton University, in a book which was ideal propaganda for any racists. The book noted that although some Jews were extremely accomplished scholars, statesmen and performing artists, they were noticeable only because they were unusual exceptions to the rule as the majority had been assessed as having low levels of intelligence.

Although the tests were supposed to be accurate irrespective of country of origin or first language, even Yerkes admitted the results showed that there was a problem for people who were not familiar with English. The most recent immigrants had been Latins and Slavs who spoke little English, so, naturally, they had scored the lowest scores of all.

The Immigration Restriction Act was passed in 1924 by the US Congress and was shaped by Yerkes' findings. People from Southern and Eastern Europe and from the Alpine and Mediterranean nations who had scored very poorly on the army tests were no longer welcome in the USA. The way this was controlled was by looking at data from a census of immigrants, which had been conducted in 1890 when immigration from Southern and Eastern Europe was very low. It was decided that the quota of immigrants allowed into America would be two per cent of each recorded nation taken from the 1890 figures. This obviously meant that the numbers of 'the unwanted' would be very low. Gould, in his book, makes it clear why more recent data from another census (1920) was not used as the basis – because the proportions of immigrants in 1920 were very different, i.e. there had been more southern and eastern European immigrants so working on the two per cent immigration quota would have meant more would have been allowed into America.

These immigration restrictions were to have horrendous consequences as the immigration from Southern and Eastern Europe all but ceased. The persecution of the Jews which started well before the actual beginning of the Second World War meant that many Jews tried to escape from their homeland but there was 'no admittance' to America. Calculations suggest that as many as six million people from Southern, Central and Eastern Europe were denied entry into America between 1924 and the start of the Second World War in 1939. The fate of many of them as a result of the Nazi regime is well known.

> **Typical mistake**
>
> Not knowing developments that followed once the results of the mass intelligence testing of the army recruits were published.

> **Now test yourself**
>
> 18 Outline two 'facts' that emerged from this study.
>
> TESTED

Gould's conclusions (based on Yerkes' findings)

IQ tests are culturally and historically biased.

IQ tests do not measure innate intelligence.

IQ testing is often unreliable and may not produce valid results.

Inappropriate, poorly administered IQ tests can lead to tragic consequences.

Nations can be graded by their intelligence.

Gould therefore suggested that the findings allowed Yerkes to suggest that America was a nation of morons.

Contemporary study: Hancock *et al.* (2011): Language of psychopaths

Relation to the area of individual differences

People behave in many different ways either because they choose to or because for some genetic, mental or physical reason they 'naturally' behave outside the cultural beliefs of what is generally considered normal behaviour. In some cultures, for example, boys who want to be ballet dancers, people who appear to have more than one personality and individuals who choose to live like hermits are considered 'different' because they behave outside the 'average' for their particular society. Words as well as actions can reveal significant insights about psychological functioning, which can further inform about differences between individuals as well as commonalities.

This study investigates the language of **psychopaths** and indicates that psychopaths are more likely than non-psychopaths to view their crime as a logical outcome of a plan, linguistically frame their homicide as more in the past and in more psychologically distant terms, give less emotionally intense descriptions of their crimes and use less emotionally pleasant language and focus more on physiological needs than higher-level social needs operating on a primitive but rational level: as a group they show individual differences.

Theory/theories on which the study is based

Words can reveal significant insights about psychological functioning, for example Pennebaker (2003). Underlying cognitive and emotional processes can be revealed through subtle patterns in word choice.

Quantitative word counts can be used as a tool in the identification and examination of abnormal psychological processes (Schnurr and Tucker, 1988). Psychopathy may therefore be reflected in idiosyncratic linguistic styles.

Psychopaths have specific combinations of cognitive, social and emotional characteristics that differentiate them from the general population (Hare, 2003, 2006).

Background to the study

Patrick (2006) found psychopaths exhibit no apparent deficits in intellect.

Previous studies have revealed that psychopaths' language appears to be less cohesive than that of non-psychopaths, for example Cleckley (1976), Williamson (1993).

Hancock *et al.*'s aim was to examine whether the language of psychopaths reflected (in describing their violent crime), as predicted, an instrumental/predatory world view, unique socio-emotional needs and a poverty of effect.

Now test yourself

19 Draw one conclusion from the findings of this study.

TESTED

Exam tips

Know how this study is similar to and different from the study by Hancock *et al.* (2011).

Know how the study relates to the key theme 'Measuring differences'.

a **psychopath** is a person suffering from chronic mental disorder with abnormal or violent social behaviour.

Now test yourself

20 Outline what one previous piece of research had found in relation to the behaviour of psychopaths.

TESTED

Research method

This study used semi-structured/open-ended interviews (a self-report method) which employed the Step-Wise Interview technique to gather data in relation to the language of psychopaths and non-psychopaths who had committed murder.

The Step-Wise Interview is an investigative interview, usually used with children. The procedure encourages and facilitates the individual's recall of events. Every opportunity is provided to obtain the individual's version. This is done by always beginning with the most general, open phase of the interview and proceeding to more narrow forms of questioning only when required. The less prompting the better. The interviewer must demonstrate patience and allow as much of the interview content as possible to come from the individual. The Step-Wise Interview is part of a fact-finding process. The interviewer must be alert to developmental differences in language and memory and never assume that they know what an individual means by the use of a particular word.

The narratives were subsequently transcribed and analysed through content analysis using the PCL-R and the DAL.

Outline of the procedure/study

The sample:

- 52 male murderers (14 psychopathic, 38 non-psychopathic) incarcerated in Canadian correctional facilities who admitted their crime and volunteered for the study.
- 16 per cent of convictions were for first-degree murder, 64 per cent of convictions were for second-degree murder and 20 per cent of convictions were for manslaughter.
- There were no differences between the type of crime (manslaughter, second-degree murder, first-degree murder) and psychopathy versus control (non-psychopathy).
- Mean age at the time of their current homicide was 28.9 years – range of 14 to 50 years.
- The two groups did not differ on age (psychopaths: M = 39.71 years, controls: M = 39.91 years).
- The two groups did not differ significantly in the amount of time since the homicide was committed (psychopaths: M = 11.87 years, controls: M = 9.82 years).

The procedure:

First, potential participants were asked whether they would be interested in taking part in a research study. Interested individuals underwent a psychopathy assessment:

- Psychopathy was measured using the Psychology Checklist-Revised (PCL-R). Psychopathy, as measured by the PCL-R, is characterised by 20 criteria scored from 0 to 2 for a maximum score of 40. The clinical diagnostic cut-off for psychopathy is scores of 30 or above.
- The PCL-R assessments were conducted by either extensively trained prison psychologists or by a researcher who was well trained in the coding of the PCL-R (an inter-rater reliability check showed a significant positive correlation with p ≤ .001).
- Using a cut-off score of 25 (which had previously been justified for research purposes), 14 offenders were classified as psychopathic and 38 as non-psychopathic.

Exam tip

Know the key features of the sample, how it was gathered and the criteria used to classify participants as either psychopaths or non-psychopaths.

Now test yourself

21 Identify two similar features between the psychopaths and the non-psychopaths.

TESTED

Participants were then interviewed. At the beginning of the interview, the purpose of the study (to examine the manner in which homicide offenders recall their homicide offence) and the procedure were verbally explained.

While being audio-taped, participants were asked to describe their homicide offences in as much detail as possible. In this open-ended interviewing procedure, each participant was encouraged to provide as much information about the crime as possible from the beginning to the end, omitting no details. Participants were prompted to do this using a standardised procedure known as the Step-Wise Interview.

The interviewers were two senior psychology graduate students and one research assistant, all of whom were blind to the psychopathy scores of the offenders. Interviews lasted about 25 minutes.

The narratives were subsequently transcribed, as close to verbatim as possible, and then checked to ensure spelling errors were corrected, all interviewer comments were deleted and proper nouns and abbreviations were spelled out.

Two text analysis tools were then used to analyse the transcripts:
1 The corpus analysis program Wmatrix was used to compare parts of speech and to analyse semantic concepts contained in the psychopath and control corpora.
2 The Dictionary of Affect in Language (DAL) software program was used to examine the affective tone of the words.

The interviews of the psychopaths and controls produced a total of 127,376 words. The 14 psychopath narratives contained 29,562 words and averaged 2,111.6 per participant. The 38 control narratives contained 97,814 words and averaged 2,574 per participant. Therefore there was no significant difference in the average number of words produced by psychopaths and controls.

Instrumental language analysis:

Psychopaths produced more subordinating conjunctions than controls, for example because, since, as, so that.

Hierarchy of needs analysis:

Psychopaths used approximately twice as many words related to basic physiological needs, including eating, drinking and monetary resources, when describing their murders than controls.

Controls used significantly more language related to social needs, including family, religion and spirituality, than psychopaths.

Semantic content of homicide descriptions, related to Maslow's hierarchy of needs across psychopathic and non-psychopathic offenders				
	Psychopaths	**Frequency %**	**Controls**	**Frequency %**
Physiological and safety needs				
Food	89	.30	117	.12
Drink	196	.66	370	.38
Clothing	120	.41	266	.27
Money	78	.26	160	.16
Social needs				
Family	84	.28	555	.57
Religion	36	.12	201	.21

Emotional expression of language:

The degree to which the psychopaths had physiologically distanced themselves/were simply detached from their homicide was examined through the use of the past and present form of verbs and the rate of articles.

Temporal representations of psychopathic and non-psychopathic offenders				
	Psychopaths	Frequency %	Controls	Frequency %
Temporal construal				
Lexical verbs – past tense, e.g. gave	1,798	6.08	5,466	5.59
Lexical verbs – present tense, e.g. work	727	2.46	2,853	2.92
Articles, e.g. a, the	1,281	4.33	3,877	3.96

- Psychopaths used more past tense verbs than controls, e.g. stabbed.
- Psychopaths used fewer present tense verbs than controls, e.g. stab.
- Psychopaths produced a higher rate of articles than controls, revealing that their language involved more concrete nouns.
- Psychopathic language was significantly less fluent than that of controls.
- Initially, no significant differences in the emotional content of language between the two groups in terms of pleasantness, intensity or imagery were found. However, further analysis showed psychopaths used less positive or emotionally intense language.

Conclusions

Psychopaths are more likely than non-psychopaths to describe cause-and-effect relationships when describing their murder.

Psychopaths are more likely to view their crime as a logical outcome of a plan than non-psychopaths.

Psychopaths focus more on physiological needs than higher-level social needs compared with non-psychopaths.

Psychopaths are focused on a lower level of necessities in Maslow's hierarchy of needs than non-psychopaths.

Psychopaths will linguistically frame their homicide as more in the past and in more psychologically distant terms than non-psychopaths.

Psychopaths give less emotionally intense descriptions of their crimes and use less emotionally pleasant language than non-psychopaths.

Psychopaths operate on a primitive but rational level.

Now test yourself

23 Outline one finding from the hierarchy of needs analysis.
24 Outline one finding from the analysis of emotional expression of language.

TESTED ☐

Exam tips

Know how this study is similar to and different from the study by Gould (1982).

Know how the study relates to the key theme 'Measuring differences'.

Section A practice questions

From Gould's study 'A nation of morons':
1 Describe two ways in which the IQ tests used by Yerkes were biased. [4]
2 Describe the Army Alpha Test. [4]
3 From Yerkes' findings cited in this study:
  a) Outline one difference in performance between the white Americans and the black Americans. [2]
  b) Suggest why a difference in performance was found between the white and black Americans. [2]
4 Outline how the American Immigration Restriction Act of 1924 by the US Congress and was shaped by Yerkes' findings. [4]

Answers at **www.hoddereducation.co.uk/myrevisionnotes**

From Hancock et al.'s study into the language of psychopaths:
5 Describe the sample used in this study. [4]
6 a) Identify the sampling technique used in this study. [1]
   b) Suggest one strength of using this technique in this study. [2]
7 Outline the procedure followed during the interviews. [4]
8 Draw two conclusions from the findings of this study. [4]
9 Suggest why the studies by Gould into bias in IQ testing and Hancock et al. into the language of psychopaths allow one to view psychology as a science. [4]
10 Describe how the studies by Gould into bias in IQ testing and Hancock et al. into the language of psychopaths are different in relation to measuring differences between individuals. [4]

For practice questions linked to Sections B and C of the exam paper turn to Chapter 15.

ONLINE

Summary

By the end of this chapter for the two AS-level studies and/or the four A-level studies you should:
- know the research method and sample
- know the key findings
- be able to suggest at least one way in which each study could be improved and possible implications of the suggestion(s) for methodology, ethics, reliability, validity, usefulness, practicality, etc.
- know how each study relates to the individual differences area of psychology
- know strengths/weaknesses of conducting research under controlled conditions, laboratory experiments, snapshot versus longitudinal studies, observation and self-reports (including rating scales) as ways to gather data, the use of hypothetical scenarios, quantitative and qualitative data, the sample
- be able to consider the issues of reliability, validity and ecological validity, ethnocentrism
- understand how each study links to the psychological debates of nature/nurture, freewill/determinism, reductionism/holism, individual/situational explanations, usefulness of research, ethical considerations, conducting socially sensitive research, psychology as a science.

14 Perspectives and debates

The behaviourist perspective

REVISED

Outline of the behaviourist perspective

Behaviourism ('learning theory') started in America in the early 1900s, mainly through the ideas of John Watson. Watson started the behaviourist movement in 1913 when he wrote an article entitled 'Psychology as the behaviourist views it', which set out its main principles and assumptions. Drawing on earlier work by Pavlov, behaviourists such as Watson, Thorndike and Skinner proceeded to develop theories of learning (such as classical and operant conditioning) that they attempted to use to explain virtually all behaviour. Their belief therefore was that nearly all behaviour is learned and all individuals are the products of their environments.

The behaviourists who initiated the learning theory approach were influenced by the philosophy of empiricism (which argues that knowledge comes from the environment via the senses, since humans are like a 'tabula rasa' – blank slate – at birth) and the physical sciences (which emphasise scientific and objective methods of investigation).

The behaviourist perspective dominated experimental psychology until the late 1950s, when its assumptions and methods became increasingly criticised by ethologists and cognitive psychologists. The behaviourist theories have been modified to provide more realistic explanations of how learning can occur, for example psychologists such as Bandura with his social learning theory.

Behaviourists proposed two main types of learning (conditioning):
1 Classical conditioning (Pavlov).
2 Operant conditioning (Skinner).

Bandura acknowledged the role of cognitive processes in influencing behavioural learning and proposed the social learning theory, which holds that individuals learn through observing and subsequently imitating behaviours modelled by others.

An assumption of the behaviourist perspective is that the majority of all behaviour is learned from the environment after birth.

An implication of the behaviourist perspective is that if behaviour is learned, undesirable and antisocial behaviours can be 'unlearned'.

> **behaviourism** is an approach to psychology that accounts for behaviour in terms of observable events and without reference to mental concepts such as 'mind' or 'emotion'. It is a systematic approach to the understanding of human and animal behaviour. It assumes that the behaviour of a human or an animal is a consequence of that individual's history, including especially reinforcement and punishment, together with the individual's current motivational state and controlling stimuli. Thus, although behaviourists generally accept the important role of inheritance in determining behaviour, they focus primarily on environmental factors.

Now test yourself

1 Suggest one strength of the behaviourist perspective.

TESTED

Exam tips

Know and understand the three theories linked to behaviourism, i.e. classical conditioning, operant condition, social learning theory.

Understand how social learning theory is not a pure behaviourist theory.

Know both an assumption and an implication of this perspective.

Typical mistake

Not being able to apply these theories to real-world or hypothetical scenarios.

The psychodynamic perspective

Outline of the psychodynamic perspective

'Psycho' refers to the mind and 'dynamic' refers to change of activity. The **psychodynamic** perspective therefore emphasises the active nature of mental processes and their role in shaping personality and behaviour. The perspective was developed by Sigmund Freud in the late nineteenth/ early twentieth centuries and focuses on the role of the unconscious and past experiences as the cause of current behaviours. Behaviour is therefore strongly influenced by the structure and drives of the unconscious mind.

Freud believed there were three levels of consciousness:

1 Conscious: This is what an individual is aware of at any given time, for example what they are seeing, hearing, thinking.
2 Preconscious: This is made up of memories that a person can recall when they want to, for example recalling their home address, their telephone number.
3 Unconscious: This is made up of memories, desires and fears which cause people extreme anxiety and have therefore been 'repressed' or forced out of conscious awareness. However, the unconscious still influences behaviour. This part of a person's mind can be accessed with the help of a psychoanalyst.

Freud claimed that from birth, two types of instinct motivated behaviour. The two instincts are unconsciously in constant conflict with each other and one may be dominant in a person:

1 The life instinct ('Eros'), which is needed to fulfil basic biological needs. Freud, however, also claimed that infants have the need for sexual pleasure, i.e. they obtain pleasure through erogenous zones (parts of the body that are sensitive to stimulation). Although this does not involve mature sexual needs, Freud claimed that 'infantile sexuality' is a major motivation as individuals progress through the stages of psychosexual development. The energy of the life instinct is called 'libido'.
2 The death instinct ('Thanatos'), which involves the urge to be aggressive and destructive to others and/or ourselves. This causes violence, wars and suicide.

Freud also claimed that a lot of an individual's development is determined by the three unconscious components of personality – the id, the ego and the superego:

1 The id is the basic animal part of personality that contains innate, aggressive, sexual instincts. It wants to be satisfied by whatever means possible and obeys the pleasure principle.
2 The ego is the conscious, rational mind. It negotiates between the id and the superego to work out whether an individual can actually have what they want – it works on the reality principle.
3 The superego is an individual's conscience. It is the moral part of personality and includes ideas about how to behave that were learned from parents and significant others. Psychological development is therefore strongly influenced by early experiences and relationships with parents.

An assumption of the psychodynamic perspective is that many important influences on behaviour come from a part of the mind – the unconscious – about which an individual has no direct awareness.

An implication of the psychodynamic perspective is that through the use of psychoanalysis what in an individual's unconscious mind is

psychodynamics is the interaction of various conscious and unconscious mental or emotional processes, especially as they influence personality, behaviour and attitudes.

Exam tips

Know that this perspective focuses on the role of the unconscious and past experiences as the cause of current behaviours.

Know that this perspective is concerned with the psychology of mental or emotional forces or processes developing especially in early childhood and their subconscious effects on behaviour and mental states.

Know both an assumption and an implication of this perspective.

Typical mistakes

Forgetting that the perspective focuses particularly on the role of the unconscious and past experiences as the cause of current behaviours.

Not being able to apply this perspective to real-world or hypothetical scenarios.

Now test yourself

2 Suggest one weakness of the psychodynamic perspective.

TESTED

influencing their behaviour can be brought to the conscious mind so the cause of the behaviour can be identified. Once brought to the conscious mind and identified, the behaviour, if undesirable, can be treated or managed.

Debates in psychology

Nature/nurture

Nature sees behaviour being strongly influenced by genetic, biological and physical factors.

Nurture sees behaviour being strongly influenced through learning processes and the environment.

Freewill/determinism

Freewill suggests that individuals can choose how they want to behave and so have responsibility for their own behaviour.

Determinism suggests behaviour is controlled by genes and past experiences so an individual has little or no control over their behaviour.

Reductionism/holism

Reductionism breaks down behaviour into its constituent parts and focuses on a single factor as being the main influence on behaviour, for example an individual's biological make-up.

Holism takes a wider view on behaviour and sees it as too complex to be broken down into individual constituents. It is a more Gestaltist view which sees behaviour as more than the mere sum of its individual parts.

Individual/situational explanations

An individual explanation for behaviour sees the personal characteristics and traits of an individual to be the main cause of their behaviour.

A situational explanation for behaviour sees the surrounding environment, including other people in that environment, as being the main cause of an individual's behaviour.

Usefulness of research

Any research that enhances a person's understanding and which can be applied to real-life situations can be considered useful.

Ethical considerations

These are based on BPS guidelines and include respect, informed consent, right to withdraw, confidentiality, competence, responsibility, protection of participants, debriefing, integrity and deception. These issues have already been covered in Chapter 4.

Conducting socially sensitive research

Researchers should be mindful when conducting psychological research that could in any way cause individuals harm or distress, have political or social consequences or stigmatise either an individual or a particular group of people.

Now test yourself

3 Briefly explain the nature/ nurture debate.
4 Outline one advantage of taking a reductionist view of behaviour.
5 Explain why the study by Loftus and Palmer on eyewitness testimony can be considered useful.
6 Describe the following ethical considerations:
   ● Informed consent.
   ● Right to withdraw.
   ● Confidentiality.
   ● Debriefing.
   ● Deception.
7 Explain how one of the core studies can be considered socially sensitive research.

TESTED

Psychology as a science

The nature and principles of scientific enquiry include an understanding of the following concepts: cause and effect, falsification, replicability, objectivity, induction, deduction, hypothesis testing, manipulation of variables, control of variables, standardisation and quantifiable measures. These issues have already been covered in Chapter 6.

Exam tip

It is important to have a good understanding of psychological debates and issues as aspects of these may be raised in any of the AS level and/or A level modules.

Summary

By the end of this chapter you should:
- know and understand the behaviourist perspective
- know and understand the psychodynamic perspective
- know, understand and be able to consider debates in psychology.

Now test yourself

8 Define the following concepts:
- Cause and effect.
- Replicability.
- Control of variables.
- Standardisation.

TESTED

14 Perspectives and debates

15 Practice questions on psychological themes through core studies – Sections B and C

Having completed Component 2, you should now be able to attempt the following examination-style practice questions.

Section B: Areas, perspectives and debates

REVISED

1 a) Briefly outline the developmental area. [2]

b) Suggest one implication of the developmental area. [2]

c) Describe how one core study links to the developmental area. [4]

d) Describe how any one core study may either be placed in the developmental area or be viewed from the behaviourist perspective. [4]

e) Outline the nature/nurture debate in relation to the developmental area. Support your answer with evidence from appropriate core studies. [6]

f) Suggest one strength and one weakness of conducting socially sensitive research. Support your answer with evidence from appropriate core studies. [12]

Total marks [30]

2 a) Outline one assumption of the area of individual differences. [2]

b) Explain why any one core study can be placed in the area of individual differences. [4]

c) Suggest one strength of the area of individual differences. Support your answer with evidence from any of the core studies that can be placed in this area. [4]

d) Describe the difference between the behaviourist perspective and the psychodynamic perspective. Support your answer with evidence from any appropriate core studies. [6]

e) Discuss strengths and weaknesses of the behaviourist perspective. Support your answer with evidence from any of the core studies that can be viewed from this perspective. [12]

Total marks [28]

3 a) Outline how the social area explains behaviour. [2]

b) Describe how one core study can be considered as providing a social explanation for behaviour. [4]

c) Suggest why studies placed in the biological area are generally considered to be low in ecological validity. Support your answer with evidence from any of the core studies placed in this area. [6]

d) Discuss ethical considerations in relation to the biological area. Support your answer with evidence from any of the core studies placed in this area. [20]

Total marks [32]

4 a) Describe the difference between freewill and determinism. [2]

b) Explain how one core study shows that individuals have freewill. [4]

c) Describe one similarity and one difference between the cognitive and social areas. Support your answer with evidence from core studies placed in these areas. [10]

d) Describe how the cognitive area allows psychological research to be considered scientific. Support your answer with evidence from any core studies placed in this area. [15]

Total marks [31]

Section C: Practical applications

1 'I don't like swimming.'

Jane was terrified of water and would always try to find an excuse for not participating in swimming lessons at school. After several weeks her teacher drew her to one side and asked her why she persistently failed to take part. Jane replied, 'I just don't like swimming.' The teacher then asked if there was any particular reason why she didn't like swimming, to which Jane replied, 'No. I just don't like it.'

Fortunately, the swimming teacher was able to speak to Jane's mother during a parents' evening at school the following week. She said, 'I'm afraid Jane has failed to participate in any swimming lessons so far this term. Are you aware of any reason why she doesn't want to take part?' Jane's mother replied, 'She never goes into a swimming pool. She won't even go paddling or swimming in the sea when we go on holiday. At home, she will only have a shower. I can't get her to have a bath, even if she's really cold. I think she has a phobia of water and is frightened her head will go under the water and she will drown.' 'I see,' said the teacher. 'Can you think of any reason why she may feel this way?' Jane's mother replied, 'Well, when she was very little – about two years old – her older brother pushed her right under the water when they were playing in the paddling pool. I don't think she really remembers the incident but it could be buried somewhere in her unconscious mind.' 'You may be right,' replied the teacher. 'I think this unconscious fear of drowning is being shown through her avoidance of swimming lessons.'

a) Identify one psychological concern raised by the source above. Support your answer with evidence from the source. [4]
b) Explain why the source above can be placed in the area of individual differences. [4]
c) Briefly outline one core study and explain how it could relate to Jane's phobia of water. [6]
d) Use your psychological knowledge to suggest a programme that could be developed to manage Jane's phobia of water so she takes part in swimming lessons. [10]
e) Evaluate the programme you have suggested in part (d). [10]

Total marks [34]

2 'There's always someone worse off than me!'

Inspired by a friend's successful battle against leukaemia, university student Simon Ford decided to donate stem cells to save the life of a stranger. When asked why he had been prepared to inconvenience himself by going to the university's hospital and giving up valuable study time to help someone he didn't even know, Simon said, 'Victims of any sort need help.'

Simon's generous behaviour was reported in the university's monthly magazine. Another student read the article and decided to follow Simon's example. Lucy Armstrong signed up to be a donor and was soon notified that she was a perfect match for an unknown patient who urgently needed a bone marrow transplant. Lucy had no second thoughts about donating and although she felt tired and bruised after the procedure, she said, 'It was a small price to pay for what could save another person's life.'

a) Explain why this report can be placed in the social area. Support your answer with evidence from the source. [4]

b) Briefly outline one core study and explain how it could relate to the helping behaviours described in the source. [8]

c) Use your psychological knowledge to suggest a programme to encourage helping behaviours within universities. [10]

d) Evaluate the programme you have suggested. [12]

Total marks [34]

3 Pay attention!

The first member of the Smith family home in the evenings always switches on the television. All, except Mr Smith, a policeman, were home by 6 p.m. on Wednesday 25 November 2015. Mr Smith's son had switched to BBC so he could watch 'Pointless', followed by the six o'clock news and 'The One Show'. Mr Smith was late leaving his office at the local police station so did not get home until 7 p.m. As he walked in the door, he called out, 'Did you all hear the news? The Chancellor announced in his Autumn Statement that he is going to protect the police budget. Isn't that great?'

No one in the family responded, so Mr Smith repeated his question, 'Did you hear the news?'

These are the answers given by family members:

Mrs Smith: 'I know the news was on but I didn't hear it as I was on the telephone at the time.'

Mr Smith's son: 'I didn't hear the announcement. I was listening to a podcast.'

Mr Smith's daughter: 'I didn't hear what he (the Chancellor) said as my friend, Sally, called round and we were talking about what had gone on in school today.'

'You are all hopeless,' said Mr Smith. 'None of you can listen to more than one thing at a time.'

a) Identify one psychological concern raised by the source above. Support your answer with evidence from the source. [4]

b) Explain why the source above can be placed in the cognitive area. [4]

c) Briefly outline one core study and explain how it could relate to the auditory inattention shown by Mr Smith's family. [5]

d) Use your psychological knowledge to suggest how teachers could improve auditory attention in young children. [10]

e) Evaluate your suggestions. [10]

Total marks [33]

4 Is television teaching children to be aggressive?

Discussions during a Parent–Teacher Association meeting revealed that teachers were very concerned about increased aggression shown by boys in particular while playing at break and lunchtime. Parents also expressed concern over increased aggression shown by their children at home. One parent said, 'My boys always seem to be fighting.' A teacher, who had a child of their own in the school and who had also noticed increased aggression in their child, suggested that a new television programme called 'Venus Attack', which her son loved to watch, although broadcast on a children's television channel seemed to contain a lot of violent behaviour. Other parents then made similar suggestions, saying that their children liked to watch programmes like 'Action Hero', 'War Planets' and 'Super Power Fighters'. Some also said their children enjoyed watching professional wrestling and martial arts programmes but that after seeing the programmes charged around the house rather like the Karate Kid!

The chairman of the meeting suggested that perhaps the children were learning new ways of being aggressive from their observation of models.

a) Identify one psychological concern raised by the above source. Support your answer with examples from the source. [6]

b) Outline one piece of psychological research and explain how it relates to the source above. [8]

c) Use your psychological knowledge to suggest how the issue you identified in part (a) could be managed. [10]

d) Evaluate how you would manage the issue you have identified. [10]

Total marks [34]

16 Component content and exam format

Component content

This component consists of one compulsory section: Issues in mental health.

Students will also choose to study two of the following applied psychology options:
- Child psychology
- Criminal psychology
- Environmental psychology
- Sport and exercise psychology.

Each topic contains the following:
- **Background:** with reference to psychology, students should be able to explain and exemplify the background and consider relevant issues and debates in relation to the topic area.
- **Key research:** students should be able to describe the key research and appreciate how it relates to the topic area.
- **Application:** students should be able to relate the application to a novel situation.

Section A: Issues in mental health

When approaching the exam questions, make sure you have detailed descriptions using psychological terminology and can evaluate them using the issues and debates in Component 2.

Topic	Background	Key research	Application
The historical context of mental health	Historical views of mental illness *You need to be able to describe and evaluate at least two historical views of mental illness for the exam.* Defining abnormal *You need to be able to describe and evaluate at least one definition of abnormality for the exam.* Categorising mental disorders *You need to be able to describe and evaluate at least one method of categorising mental disorders for the exam.*	Rosenhan (1973) On being sane in insane places	Characteristics of an affective disorder, a psychotic disorder and an anxiety disorder

Topic	Background	Key research	Application
The medical model	The biochemical explanation of mental illness The genetic explanation of mental illness Brain abnormality as an explanation of mental illness *You need to be able to describe and evaluate at least one biochemical explanation of mental illness, one genetic explanation of mental illness and one area of brain abnormality as an explanation of mental illness for the exam.*	Gottesman *et al.* (2010) Disorders in offspring with two psychiatrically ill parents	Biological treatment of one specific disorder
Alternatives to the medical model	The behaviourist explanation of mental illness The cognitive explanation of mental illness *You need to be able to describe and evaluate at least one behaviourist explanation and one cognitive explanation of mental illness for the exam.* One from: ● the humanistic explanation of mental illness ● the psychodynamic explanation of mental illness ● the cognitive neuroscience explanation of mental illness. *You need to be able to describe and evaluate at least one other non-biological explanation of mental illness.*	Szasz (2011) The myth of mental illness: 50 years later	Non-biological treatment of one specific disorder

Section B: Option 1 – Child psychology

When approaching the exam questions, make sure you have detailed descriptions using psychological terminology and can evaluate them using the issues and debates in Component 2.

Topic	Background	Key research	Application
Intelligence (Biological)	What psychologists mean by intelligence and what biological factors could affect intelligence. *You need to be able to describe at least one psychological definition of intelligence and at least two biological factors which could affect intelligence.*	van Leeuwen *et al.* (2008) A twin-family study of general IQ	At least one method of assessing intelligence

Topic	Background	Key research	Application
Pre-adult brain development (Biological)	Brain development and the impact of this on risk taking behaviour. *You need to be able to describe at least one area of brain development in pre-adults and at least one way this might impact on risk taking behaviour.*	Barkley-Levenson and Galván (2014) Neural representation of expected value in the adolescent brain	At least one strategy to reduce risk-taking behaviours using knowledge of brain development
Perceptual development (Cognitive)	Perceptual development in children and how this can be studied in babies and animals. *You need to be able to describe at least one area of perceptual development in children and at least one way this might be studied in babies and one way in which it might be studied in animals.*	Gibson and Walk (1960) The visual cliff	At least one play strategy to develop perception in young children
Cognitive development and education (Cognitive)	Cognitive development in children and the impact of this on education. *You need to be able to describe at least one theory of cognitive development in children and at least one way this might impact on educational practice.*	Wood et al. (1976) The role of tutoring in problem-solving	At least one cognitive strategy to improve revision or learning
Development of attachment (Social)	The development of attachment in babies and the impact of failure to develop attachments. *You need to be able to describe at least one theory of the development of attachment in babies and one impact of the failure to develop attachment.*	Ainsworth and Bell (1970) Attachment, exploration and separation: illustrated by the behaviour of one-year-olds in a Strange Situation	At least one strategy to develop an attachment-friendly environment
Impact of advertising on children (Social)	The influence of television advertising on children and the stereotyping in such advertising. *You need to be able to describe at least one influence of television advertising on children and at least one way in which stereotyping occurs.*	Johnson and Young (2002) Gendered voices in children's advertising	At least one strategy to reduce the impact of advertising which is aimed at children

Section B: Option 2 – Criminal psychology

When approaching the exam questions, make sure you have detailed descriptions using psychological terminology and can evaluate them using the issues and debates in Component 2.

Topic	Background	Key research	Application
What makes a criminal? (Biological)	Physiological and non-physiological explanations of criminal behaviour. *You need to be able to describe at least one physiological and one non-physiological explanation of criminal behaviour.*	Raine et al. (1997) Brain abnormalities in murderers indicated by positron emission tomography	At least one biological strategy for preventing criminal behaviour

Topic	Background	Key research	Application
The collection and processing of forensic evidence (Biological)	Motivating factors and bias in the collection and processing of forensic evidence. *You need to be able to describe at least two motivating factors and at least one bias in the collection and least two motivating factors and at least one bias in the processing of forensic evidence.*	Hall and Player (2008) Will the introduction of an emotional context affect fingerprint analysis and decision-making?	At least one strategy for reducing bias in the collection and processing of forensic evidence
The collection of evidence (Cognitive)	Collection and use of evidence from witnesses and suspects. *You need to be able to describe at least one way of collecting and using evidence from witnesses and at least one way of collecting and using evidence from suspects.*	Memon and Higham (1999) A review of the cognitive interview	At least one strategy for police interviews
Psychology and the courtroom (Cognitive)	How juries can be persuaded by the characteristics of witnesses and defendants. *You need to be able to describe at least one way characteristics of witnesses and at least on way characteristics of defendants can persuade juries.*	Dixon et al. (2002) The role of accent and context in perceptions of guilt	At least one strategy to influence jury decision making
Crime prevention (Social)	How the features of neighbourhoods and a zero tolerance policy can influence crime. *You need to be able to describe at least two features of neighbourhoods which can influence crime and at least one way in which a zero tolerance policy can influence crime.*	Wilson and Kelling (1982) The police and neighbourhood safety: Broken windows	At least one strategy for crime prevention
Effect of punishment (Social)	Punishment and reform as responses to criminal behaviour. *You need to be able to describe at least one way criminals are punished and at least one method used to reform criminals.*	Haney et al. (1973) Study of prisoners and guards in a simulated prison	At least one strategy for reducing reoffending

Section B: Option 3 – Environmental psychology

When approaching the exam questions, make sure you have detailed descriptions using psychological terminology and can evaluate them using the issues and debates in Component 2.

Topic	Background	Key research	Application
Stressors in the environment (Biological)	Environmental stressors and their impact on our biological responses. *You need to be able to describe at least two environmental stressors and at least one impact of each of them on our biological responses.*	Black and Black (2007) Aircraft noise exposure and residents' stress and hypertension	At least one strategy for managing environmental stress

Topic	Background	Key research	Application
Biological rhythms (Biological)	Biological rhythms and the impact of their disruption on our behaviour. *You need to be able to describe at least two biological rhythms and at least one impact of the disruption of each of them on our behaviour.*	Czeisler *et al.* (1982) Rotating shift work schedules that disrupt sleep are improved by applying circadian principles	At least one strategy for reducing the effects of jetlag or shift work
Recycling and other conservation behaviours (Cognitive)	Conservation behaviours and the factors which influence the tendency to conserve or recycle. *You need to be able to describe at least two conservation behaviours and at least two factors which will influence our tendency to conserve or recycle.*	Lord (1994) Motivating recycling behaviour: a quasi-experimental investigation of message and source strategies	At least one technique used to increase recycling or other conservation behaviour
Ergonomics – human factors (Cognitive)	Cognitive overload and the impact of observation in the workplace environment. *You need to be able to describe cognitive overload and at least one impact of observation in the workplace.*	Drews and Doig (2014) Evaluation of a configural vital signs display for intensive care unit nurses	At least one workplace design based on ergonomic research
Psychological effects of built environment (Social)	The impact of the built environment and urban renewal on our wellbeing. *You need to be able to describe the impact of the built environment on our wellbeing and the impact of urban renewal on our wellbeing.*	Ulrich (1984) View through a window may influence recovery from surgery	At least one example of environmental design used to improve health/well-being
Territory and personal space (Social)	Territory and personal space in the workplace. *You need to be able to describe territory and personal space in the workplace.*	Wells (2000) Office clutter or meaningful personal displays: the role of office personalisation in employee and organisational well-being	At least one office design strategy based on research into territory or personal space

Section B: Option 4 – Sport and exercise psychology

When approaching the exam questions, make sure you have detailed descriptions using psychological terminology and can evaluate them using the issues and debates in Component 2.

Topic	Background	Key research	Application
Arousal and anxiety (Biological)	Optimising arousal, controlling anxiety and measuring anxiety in sport. *You need to be able to describe at least one method of optimising arousal, at least one method of controlling anxiety in sport and at least one method of measuring anxiety in sport.*	Fazey and Hardy (1988) The inverted-U hypothesis: a catastrophe for sport psychology	At least one technique for managing arousal and anxiety in sport

Topic	Background	Key research	Application
Exercise and mental health (Biological)	Benefits of exercise to mental health. *You need to be able to describe at least two benefits of exercise to mental health.*	Lewis *et al.* (2014) Mood changes following social dance sessions in people with Parkinson's	At least one exercise strategy to improve mental health
Motivation (Cognitive)	Self-efficacy and sports confidence, including imagery and sports orientation. *You need to be able to describe self-efficacy, sports confidence, the use of imagery in sports and sports orientation.*	Munroe-Chandler *et al.* (2008) Playing with confidence: the relationship between imagery use and self-confidence and self-efficacy in youth soccer players	At least one strategy for motivating athletes
Personality (Cognitive)	Personality, its measurement and its relationship to sport. *You need to be able describe at least one psychological theory of personality and its measurement, and at least one way in which it relates to sport.*	Kroll and Crenshaw (1970) Multivariate personality profile analysis of four athletic groups	At least one strategy for using knowledge of personality to improve sports performance
Performing with others (Social)	Teams, coaching and leadership. *You need to be able describe at least one psychological theory of teams related to sport, at least one theory of coaching related to sport and one theory of leadership related to sport.*	Smith *et al.* (1979) Coach effectiveness training: a cognitive–behavioural approach to enhancing relationship skills in youth sports coaches	At least one strategy for improving team performance
Audience effects (Social)	How an audience can facilitate or inhibit sports performance; home advantage. *You need to be able describe at least one way an audience can facilitate sports performance and one way in which an audience can inhibit sports performance, plus a psychological explanation of home advantage.*	Zajonc *et al.* (1969) Social enhancement and impairment of performance in the cockroach	At least one strategy for training for and playing spectator sports

Exam format

REVISED

Exam facts

H567 (A level):
- This paper counts as 35 per cent of total A level.
- It is a written paper of TWO hours.
- A total of 105 marks are available for the paper.

Exam structure

The paper has TWO sections:
- Section A: Issues in mental health

○ This is a compulsory section and candidates are required to answer ALL questions.

○ Questions will range from short answer to extended response.

● Section B: Options

○ Candidates answer **one** question from each of the **two** options they have studied.

○ Each question will have three parts.

○ Section B has **four** options:

a) Child psychology

b) Criminal psychology

c) Environmental psychology

d) Sport and exercise psychology.

What could I be asked?

The examination will require candidates to apply the methodological issues and debates across a range of topics, further developing material in the specification and making links between the issues and debates and the content of this component.

Methodological issues and debates:

● Nature/nurture
● Freewill/determinism
● Reductionism/holism
● Individual/situational explanations
● Usefulness of research
● Ethical considerations
● Conducting socially sensitive research
● Psychology as a science
● Ethnocentrism
● Validity
● Reliability
● Sampling bias.

Content:

● Descriptions of concepts, theories and studies specified by the indicative content
● Application of methodological issues and debates in psychology
● Recognition of the contribution the key research has made to the topic
● Application of the background, key research and application to novel situations with which psychologists might be concerned
● Consideration of ways in which different areas of psychology can inform our understanding of applied psychology
● Exploration of social, moral, cultural and spiritual issues where applicable
● Recognition of how the key research contributes to an understanding of individual, social and cultural diversity
● Recognition of how society makes decisions about scientific issues and how psychology contributes to the success of the economy and society.

Answers at **www.hoddereducation.co.uk/myrevisionnotes**

17 Section A: Issues in mental health

The historical context of mental health

Historical views of mental health: for example, **trepanning** of skulls, **prefrontal lobotomy**, ancient Chinese, Egyptian, Roman and Greek views on mental health, changes in British views of mental health over time.

Defining abnormality: for example, statistical infrequency, deviation from social norms, maladaptiveness, deviation from ideal mental health; the effects and implications of being diagnosed as mentally ill.

Categorising mental disorders: the *Diagnostic and Statistical Manual of Mental Disorders (DSM)*, particularly the 5th edition predominantly used in the USA; the *International Classification of Disorders (ICD)* – predominantly used throughout the rest of the world; issues relating to their validity and reliability.

> **Exam tip**
>
> Be able to provide a clear description of one definition of abnormality.

Key research: Rosenhan (1973): On being sane in insane places

Theory/theories on which the study is based

Benedict (1934) suggested that normality and abnormality are not universal. What is viewed as normal in one culture may be seen as quite aberrant in another.

Abnormality can be seen as any of: a deviation from the average, a deviation from the norm, a deviation from ideal mental health, personal distress, others' distress, maladaptiveness, unexpected behaviour, highly unpredictable behaviour, mental illness (Gross, 2010).

The belief has been strong that patients present symptoms, that those symptoms can be categorised and, implicitly, that the sane are distinguishable from the insane. In 1886 Emil Kraepelin developed the first comprehensive classification system for mental disorders, believing they could be diagnosed from observable symptoms, just like physical illnesses.

Two major Western classification systems exist today – the American Psychiatric Association's *DSM* and the World Health Organization's *ICD*. The two systems in use at the time of this study were the *DSM IV* and the *ICD-10*.

Background to the study

Research has shown that the reliability of early classification systems such as the *DSM* were very poor. Beck *et al.* (1962) found that agreement on diagnosis for 153 patients (where each patient was assessed by two psychiatrists from a group of four) was only 54 per cent. This was said to be due to vague criteria for diagnosis and inconsistencies in the techniques used to gather data.

Now test yourself

1 Describe the term 'trepanning'.

TESTED

trepanning of skulls in the historical context of mental health referred to the act of drilling holes in the skull to let the 'demon' out.

prefrontal lobotomy is a procedure that was once used to reduce uncontrollably violent or emotional people. Technically this is a type of psychosurgery (surgery for psychological purpose that destroys brain tissue to change a person's behaviour) in which the nerves that connect the frontal lobes to the parts of the brain that control emotions are severed. Used in the 1930s, the patient would be shocked into a coma, then the surgeon would drive a big pick-like tool through the person's eye socket and move it around to cut the nerves. Nasty!

OCR A Level Psychology 121

Other studies have also shown that the belief that symptoms can be easily categorised to allow a diagnosis of 'sane or insane' may be questioned, for example Szasz (1961), Grove (1970), Sarbin (1972).

Rosenhan believed that gains could be made in deciding which of these (the individual's disposition or the situation he is placed in) is the best explanation by getting normal people (that is, people who do not have, and have never suffered, symptoms of serious psychiatric disorders) admitted to psychiatric hospitals and then determining whether they were discovered to be sane and if so, how. If the sanity of such **pseudopatients** was always detected, there would be prima facie evidence that a sane individual can be distinguished from the insane context in which he is found. Normality (and presumably abnormality) is distinct enough that it can be recognised wherever it occurs, for it is carried within the person. If, however, the pseudopatient's sanity was never discovered, serious difficulties would arise for those who support traditional modes of psychiatric diagnosis. Given that the hospital staff were not incompetent, that the pseudopatient had been behaving as sanely as he had been outside of the hospital, and that it had never been previously suggested that he belonged in a psychiatric hospital, such an unlikely outcome would support the view that psychiatric diagnosis betrays little about the patient but much about the environment in which an observer finds him.

> a **pseudopatient** is a researcher who poses as a patient.

Rosenhan's study had three main aims:
- to extend the efforts of previous researchers who had submitted themselves to psychiatric hospitalisation but who had commonly remained in hospitals for only short periods of time, often with the knowledge of hospital staff
- to test the diagnostic system in use at the time of the study (*DSM IV*) to see whether it was valid and reliable. To do this he and seven other individuals got themselves admitted to psychiatric hospitals
- to observe and report on the experience of being a patient in a psychiatric hospital.

> ## Now test yourself
> 2 Outline why this study was conducted.
>
> TESTED ☐

Research method

This is a field study in which Rosenhan uses a field experiment, participant observation and self-report. It is sometimes also considered a field experiment, with the independent variable being the 12 different hospitals and the dependent variable being the treatment and experiences of the pseudopatients.

> ### Exam tip
> Know the research method and sample.

Outline of the procedure/study

The pseudopatients were eight sane people (five men, three women) who were a psychology graduate in his twenties, three psychologists, a paediatrician, a psychiatrist, a painter and a housewife.

Once in the hospitals, the pseudopatients became participant observers, with the psychiatrists, doctors, nurses and other members of staff at the hospitals, together with the genuine patients, also becoming participants.

> ### Exam tip
> It is important to know all four parts of the procedure.

Part (a)

The eight pseudopatients all used fake names and those in mental health professions also used fake occupations. No other alterations of person, history or circumstances were made. The significant events of the pseudopatient's life history were presented as they had actually occurred. Relationships with parents and siblings, with spouse and children, with people at work and in school, consistent with the aforementioned exceptions, were described as they were or had been. Frustrations and upsets were described along with joys and satisfactions. These facts are important to remember because, if anything, they strongly biased the subsequent results in favour of detecting sanity, since none of their histories or current behaviours was seriously pathological in any way.

With the exception of Rosenhan, who was one of the pseudopatients, the presence of pseudopatients and the nature of the research programme were not known to hospital staff. Rosenhan's presence was known to the hospital administrator and chief psychologist and, so far as he knew, to them alone.

They sought admission to 12 hospitals (of varying ages, resources and staff ratios) across five states in the USA. Pseudopatients called the hospital and arranged an appointment. On arrival they reported they had been hearing voices which were unclear, unfamiliar, of the same sex as themselves, and said, 'empty', 'hollow' and 'thud'.

Once admitted, pseudopatients immediately behaved normally. They interacted with staff and patients and participated in ward activities. When asked by staff how they were feeling, they indicated that they were fine, that they no longer experienced symptoms. They responded to instructions from attendants, to calls for medication (only two tablets were swallowed) and to dining hall instructions. Beyond such activities as were available to them on the admissions ward they observed the behaviour of staff and genuine patients and recorded their observations in a notebook. Initially these notes were written 'secretly,' but as it soon became clear that no one much cared, they were subsequently written on standard tablets of paper in such public places as the dayroom. No secret was made of these activities.

Pseudopatients had the responsibility of persuading hospital staff that they were sane and could therefore be discharged.

Part (b)

In four of the hospitals pseudopatients approached members of staff and asked, 'Pardon me Mr/Dr/Mrs X, could you tell me when I will be eligible for grounds privileges/when I will be presented at the staff meeting/when I am likely to be discharged?'

While the content of the question varied according to the appropriateness of the target and the pseudopatient's (apparent) current needs, the form was always a courteous and relevant request for information. Care was taken never to approach a particular member of staff more than once a day, lest the staff member become suspicious or irritated.

Pseudopatients observed the responses and recorded them in their notebooks.

Part (c)

A young lady approached individual faculty members at Stanford University who seemed to be walking purposefully to some meeting or teaching engagement and asked them the following six questions:
1 'Pardon me, could you direct me to Encina Hall?' (At the medical school: 'to the Clinical Research Center?')
2 'Do you know where Fish Annex is?' (There is no Fish Annex at Stanford.)
3 'Do you teach here?'

Now test yourself

3 Outline the procedure followed by the pseudopatients to gain admittance to hospital.

TESTED

Now test yourself

4 Identify two questions the pseudopatients asked hospital staff.

TESTED

4 'How does one apply for admission to the college?' (At the medical school: 'to the medical school?')

5 'Is it difficult to get in?'

6 'Is there financial aid?'

Part (d)

Staff at a research and teaching hospital who were aware of the findings of the first study but doubted that such an error could occur in their hospital were warned that one or more pseudopatients would present themselves over the next three months attempting to be admitted to the psychiatric hospital. None actually did so.

Each member of staff was asked to rate each patient who arrived at admissions/the ward according to the likelihood that they were a pseudopatient. A 10-point scale was used, with 1 and 2 reflecting high confidence that the patient was not genuine.

Key findings

Part (a)

All the pseudopatients were admitted to the hospitals where they remained for between seven and 52 days (mean length of stay = 19 days). Seven out of the eight pseudopatients were diagnosed as schizophrenic, and when they were finally discharged, they left with the diagnosis of 'schizophrenia in remission'. The other pseudopatient was diagnosed as having manic-depressive psychosis.

None of the staff asked the pseudopatients what the notes were, they just assumed the behaviour was part of their illness and made comments in their records, such as 'Patient engages in writing behaviour'. Other normal behaviours were also misinterpreted, for example pacing the hospital corridors through boredom was a sign of anxiety, queuing early for lunch was observed by one psychiatrist as a characteristic of the oral-acquisitive nature of their syndrome.

If anything went wrong and a patient became upset or distressed by the staff's behaviour, the response was seen to be because of their illness, not due to the situation (an extreme case of making dispositional not institutional attributions).

Pseudopatients' visitors said they saw no changes in their behaviour as a result of being hospitalised.

Many real patients detected the pseudopatients' sanity – 35 out of 118 genuine patients voiced their suspicions in the first three hospitalisations, recognising they were fakes, making such comments as, 'You're not crazy, you're a journalist or a professor. You're checking up on the hospital,' probably as a result of the fact that they were making notes.

Rosenhan reports that 2,100 pills were handed out to the pseudopatients during their stay in the hospitals, although all but two were flushed down the toilet. As long as the patients' behaviour was acceptable while on the wards, such actions were not noticed.

The staff tended to keep themselves away from the patients except for administrative or practical duties (inside the glass quarters, which the pseudopatients called 'the cage'). On average attendants spent

11.3 per cent (range 3 to 52 per cent) of their time outside the cage. Daytime nurses emerged from the cage on average 11.5 times per shift, while late afternoon and night nurses emerged on average 9.4 times per shift.

The doctors were even more remote and seemed to maintain the greatest distance, except on admission and discharge. On average, physicians emerged on the ward 6.7 (range 1 to 17) times per day. Surely it should have been the other way round, with those senior members of staff who wield the most power being the most familiar with the patients' case histories, and yet those doctors tended to see the patients on arrival and departure only.

The other major impact on the pseudopatients was their complete lack of power in the psychiatric wards. Their movements were watched and restricted, they had virtually no contact with staff, any staff member could enter their quarters and examine their possessions, for whatever reason, and their notes were available to all members of staff. Patients also suffered from a minimum of personal privacy – for example, personal hygiene and waste evacuation were often monitored, some hospitals had no toilet doors, examinations were conducted in semi-public rooms and on one occasion a nurse was observed adjusting her bra in full view of the patients. It was also found that there were instances of serious physical abuse to patients. Sometimes these were observed by other patients, who were presumably considered to be irrelevant, but such instances of abuse of power stopped immediately when another member of staff appeared.

All pseudopatients experienced powerlessness and depersonalisation.

Now test yourself

7 Outline four findings from part (a) of the study.

TESTED

Parts (b) and (c)

Responses received by the pseudopatients versus a young female student asking simple questions are shown in Table 17.1.

Table 17.1 Responses: pseudopatients (psychiatric hospital) versus a young female student (university) asking simple questions

Responses (per cent)	Psychiatric hospital Psychiatrists	Psychiatric hospital Nurses	University campus (non-medical) Faculty	University medical centre (physicians) 'Looking for a psychiatrist'	University medical centre (physicians) 'Looking for an internist (doctor)'
Moves on, head averted	71	88	0	0	0
Makes eye contact	23	10	0	11	0
Pauses and chats	2	2	0	11	0
Stops and talks	4	0.5	100	78	100
Mean number of questions answered (out of six)	*	*	6	3.8	4.8
No. of respondents	13	47	14	18	15
No. of attempts	185	1283	14	18	15

*The researchers did not ask a set number of questions in the hospital so the data is not applicable

The most common response was either a brief response offered while they were 'on the move', with head averted, or no response at all. Few staff made eye contact with the pseudopatients.

Note also the lack of responses towards the pseudopatients compared with controls in both eye contact and conversation. Students were talked to 100 per cent of the time whereas the pseudopatients were only talked to 4 per cent of the time by psychiatrists and 0.5 per cent by nurses. Another notable thing about these findings is that when the student asked where she could find a psychiatrist, the response she received decreased to 78 per cent, indicating that people in general find mental illness quite hard to deal with.

Part (d)

Although no pseudopatients actually presented themselves, out of 193 genuine patients who attended for psychiatric treatment, 41 were judged, with high confidence, to be pseudopatients by at least one member of staff. At least one psychiatrist considered 23 to be suspect and one psychiatrist and one other staff member considered 19 to be suspect.

Conclusions

Psychiatric diagnosis is extremely inaccurate and Rosenhan's claim that 'we cannot distinguish the sane from the insane in psychiatric hospitals' is actually given considerable support.

Hospitals seem to be special environments where behaviour becomes distorted easily and patients are treated in such a way as to perpetuate any problems they may have rather than being provided with the kind of environment that would help and support them.

Patients in psychiatric hospitals experience powerlessness and depersonalisation.

Once a patient has been labelled 'insane', all subsequent behaviour is seen in the light of the label given.

Institutionalisation in psychiatric hospitals has negative effects on interred patients.

Mental health workers are insensitive to the feelings and emotions of psychiatric patients.

The *DSM IV* had poor reliability.

The diagnosis of mental illness can be influenced by the situation an individual finds themselves in.

Exam tips

Know how the study relates to the component 'Issues in mental health'.

Know how the study relates to the topic 'The historical context of mental health'.

Know how the study relates to defining abnormality, categorising mental disorders and how the classification of mental illness can result in the 'stickiness of labels'.

Application

Characteristics of an affective disorder, for example depression.

Characteristics of a psychotic disorder, for example schizophrenia.

Characteristics of an anxiety disorder, for example specific phobias such as agoraphobia, arachnophobia, claustrophobia.

Now test yourself

8 Use Table 17.1 on page 125 to identify two findings in relation to the way nurses responded to questions asked by pseudopatients.
9 Use Table 17.1 to identify one finding in relation to the way physicians in the university medical centre responded to the remark, 'I'm looking for a psychiatrist'.
10 Outline two findings from part (d) of the study.

TESTED

Exam tip

Know the key findings and be able to draw conclusions from them.

Now test yourself

11 Suggest one conclusion that can be drawn from the findings of this study.

TESTED

Now test yourself

12 What is a phobia?

TESTED

The medical model

REVISED

The biochemical explanation of mental illness: for example, the role of neurotransmitters such as serotonin, dopamine, norepinephrine/noradrenaline.

The genetic explanation of mental illness: for example, the concept of genetic transmission of mental illness/genetic vulnerability to mental illness.

Brain abnormality as an explanation for mental illness: for example, in relation to depression, schizophrenia, bipolar disorder; the use of brain-scanning techniques such as positron emission tomography (PET) to identify brain abnormalities.

> **Exam tips**
>
> Be able to give a clear description of each of the biological explanations of mental illness.
>
> Read the question carefully as it may focus on one particular biological explanation only.

Key research: Gottesman *et al.* (2010): Disorders in offspring with two psychiatrically ill parents

Theory/theories on which the study is based

Signs and symptoms of mental illness can vary, depending on the particular disorder, circumstances and other factors. Mental illness symptoms can affect emotions, thoughts and behaviours.

Schizophrenia is a severe mental disorder, characterised by profound disruptions in thinking, affecting language, perception and the sense of self. It often includes psychotic experiences, such as hearing voices or delusions. Schizophrenia typically begins in late adolescence or early adulthood.

Bipolar disorder is a chronic episodic illness associated with behavioural disturbances. It is characterised by episodes of mania and depression.

Background to the study

Gottesman *et al.* proposed that studies of the outcome in the offspring of parents with homotypic disorders, for example schizophrenia and bipolar affective disorder, may show that they have also been diagnosed with a mental disorder, in particular the one that their parents have, suggesting a genetic or hereditary basis for mental health disorders.

This study aimed to build on previous research and, in an attempt to have a large sample size, was conducted using all register-based diagnoses for each patient reported in the nationwide Danish Psychiatric Central Register.

> **Now test yourself**
>
> 13 Explain why the Danish Psychiatric Central Register was used in this study.
>
> TESTED

Research method

This was a national register-based cohort study conducted in Denmark. The study therefore used secondary data.

Outline of the procedure/study

The sample was a population-based cohort of over 2.6 million persons (actual number = 2, 685,301) born in Denmark, alive in 1968 or born later than 1968, and with a link to their mother and father established from the Civil Registration System. The investigation was restricted to persons aged ten years or over before 1 January 2007.

Those who had ever received diagnoses of schizophrenia, bipolar affective disorder or unipolar depressive disorder were identified from the Psychiatric Central Register among a group of parent couples with both parents ever having been admitted to a psychiatric facility from 1 April 1970 to 1 January 2007. For each of these groups of parent couples, their offspring, the eldest reaching age 52 years at follow-up, were checked in the register for admissions with similar or related diagnoses, and cumulative incidences were calculated.

> **Exam tip**
>
> Know the research method, sample and procedure for the study.

For comparison, cumulative incidences were also calculated in the offspring of couples with only one parent ever having been admitted to a psychiatric facility for the selected diagnoses and the other parent never having been admitted.

To create a base rate from the general population for comparison, cumulative incidences were calculated in the offspring of parent couples with neither parent ever having been admitted (cleaned population) and parent couples with no restrictions on parent diagnoses (uncleaned population).

Cumulative incidences of schizophrenia and bipolar disorder in offspring of both parents with heterotypic disorders were calculated in parent couples in which one parent was admitted for schizophrenia and the other parent was admitted for bipolar disorder to inform discussions about genetic overlap between schizophrenia and bipolar disorder. To get an estimate or impression of normality in the offspring of the various groups of parent couples, the cumulative incidences of any psychiatric diagnosis in the offspring were calculated.

Because both the parents and their offspring might have been admitted more than once with different diagnoses, they might appear in more than one of the groups of parent couples or offspring; thus the groups were not mutually exclusive. Furthermore, some of the offspring might have their own children in this longitudinal design; therefore, the same person might have dual status as both offspring and in one of the groups of parent couples.

Parents and offspring were classified according to their diagnoses at discharge from admissions to inpatient or outpatient treatment facilities. Each admissions diagnosis was defined by the corresponding codes from *ICD-8* and *ICD-10*, the first time the parents and offspring were recorded with that diagnosis in the Danish Psychiatric Central Register.

Disorders were categorised as schizophrenia, schizophrenia–related disorders, bipolar affective disorder, unipolar depressive disorder and 'a psychiatric disorder' as defined by numerous codes from the *ICD-8* and *ICD-10*.

The study was approved by the Danish Data Protection Agency. Because data available for register-based research does not include information that can lead to the identification of individuals, approval from the National Scientific Ethical Committee was not required.

Key findings

The risk of schizophrenia in 270 offspring of 196 parent couples who were both admitted to a psychiatric facility with a diagnosis of schizophrenia was 27.3 per cent (increasing to 39.2 per cent when schizophrenia–related disorders were included) compared with 7.0 per cent in 13,878 offspring from 8,006 couples with only one parent ever admitted for schizophrenia and 0.86 per cent in 2,239,553 offspring of 1,080,030 couples with neither parent ever admitted.

The risk of bipolar disorder was 24.9 per cent in 146 offspring of 83 parent couples who were ever admitted with bipolar disorder (increasing to 36.0 per cent when unipolar depressive disorder was included) compared with 4.4 per cent in 23,152 offspring from 11,995 couples with only one parent ever admitted and 0.48 per cent in 2,239,553 offspring of 1,080,030 couples with neither parent ever admitted.

Risks of schizophrenia and bipolar disorder in offspring of couples with one parent with schizophrenia and the other with bipolar disorder were 15.6 per cent and 11.7 per cent, respectively.

Now test yourself

14 Describe the sample used in this study.
15 Describe one way in which this study can be considered ethical.

TESTED

Exam tip

Know the key findings and be able to draw conclusions from them.

Now test yourself

16 Outline two findings from this study.
17 Draw one conclusion from the findings of this study.

TESTED

The maximal risks of any psychiatric disorders in the offspring of parents both with schizophrenia or both with bipolar disorder were 67.5 per cent and 44.2 per cent, respectively.

For the general population with no restrictions on parents' psychiatric admissions, the uncleaned control group of parents, the cumulative incidence was 14.1 per cent. Therefore, in the study population of offspring, only one in seven had been admitted by age 52 years.

Conclusions

The offspring of dual matings diagnosed with psychosis constitute a super-high-risk sample of psychosis.

The risk of offspring being admitted to hospital with a diagnosis of schizophrenia is higher if both parents have been admitted with the same diagnosis than for offspring who have either had just one parent admitted with the diagnosis or neither parent ever having been admitted with the diagnosis.

The risk of offspring being admitted to hospital with a diagnosis of either bipolar disorder or unipolar depressive disorder is higher if both parents have been admitted with the same diagnosis than for offspring who have either had just one parent admitted with the diagnosis or neither parent ever having been admitted with the diagnosis.

Application

A biological treatment of one specific disorder, for example depression – antidepressant drugs such as MAOIs, SSRIs, NRIs, electroconvulsive therapy (ECT), transcranial magnetic stimulation (TMS); schizophrenia – antipsychotic drugs.

> **Exam tips**
>
> Know how the study relates to the component 'Issues in mental health'.
>
> Know how the study relates to the topic 'The medical model'.
>
> Know how the study can be seen as a biological explanation of mental disorders.

> **Now test yourself**
>
> 18 Describe electroconvulsive therapy (ECT).
>
> TESTED

> **Exam tips**
>
> Know how biological treatment can be used to treat one specific disorder.
>
> The question is likely to be worded generically so focus on the specific disorder selected.

Alternatives to the medical model

REVISED

The behaviourist explanation of mental illness: how learning processes can be used to explain the origin of mental illness, for example classical conditioning (the case of Little Albert), operant conditioning, social learning theory.

The cognitive explanation of mental illness: how individuals with a mental illness are considered to have faulty thought processes, for example the negative cognitive triad proposed by Beck, the link between irrational thoughts and mental illness as proposed by Ellis.

One from:
a) The humanistic explanation of mental illness, for example Carl Rogers' theory involving the actualising tendency and the self-concept, Maslow's hierarchy of needs.
b) The psychodynamic explanation of mental illness, for example Freud's hydraulic model, the roles of the id, ego and superego in explaining schizophrenia, Freud's theory of depression.
c) The cognitive neuroscience explanation of mental illness, for example the increasing use of brain-imaging techniques (MRI, PET, etc.) to

> **Exam tips**
>
> Be able to give a clear description of the behaviourist, cognitive and one from the humanistic, psychodynamic and cognitive neuroscience explanations for mental illness.
>
> Read the question carefully as it may focus on one particular explanation only.

investigate the relationship between cognitive function and brain function as a way to identify mental illness.

Key research: Szasz (2011): The myth of mental illness: 50 years later

Theory/theories on which the study is based

The idea of mental illness may be closely related to the social values of individual societies. In the West, it is generally held that changes in descriptions and treatments of mental illness are the result of increasing knowledge and understanding. We now accept that mental illness exists but acknowledge that there is a great deal of research still to be done on its causes and treatments.

Psychiatrist Thomas Szasz holds a more extreme view and claims that there is no such thing as mental illness. He argues that, by definition, 'disease means bodily disease' and, given that the mind is not literally part of the body, disease is a concept that should not be applied to the mind. Although Szasz's position has not gained widespread credence, his writings have generated debate over questions such as whether disease must, by definition, refer to bodily disease.

Background to the study

In his essay 'The myth of mental illness', published in 1960, and in his book of the same title which appeared in 1961, Szasz stated that his aim was to challenge the medical character of the concept of mental illness and to reject the moral legitimacy of the involuntary psychiatric interventions it justifies. He proposed that the phenomena formerly called 'psychoses' and 'neuroses', now simply called 'mental illnesses', should be viewed as behaviours that disturb or disorient others or the self; we should reject the image of the patients as the helpless victims of pathobiological events outside their control; and withdraw from participating in coercive psychiatric practices as incompatible with the foundational moral ideals of free societies.

Szasz noted that modern psychiatry rests on a basic conceptual error – the systematic misinterpretation of unwanted behaviours as the diagnoses of mental illnesses pointing to underlying neurological diseases susceptible to pharmacological treatments. Instead he proposed that people called 'mental patients' should be viewed as active players in real-life dramas, not passive victims of pathophysiological processes outside their control.

In this essay, Szasz reviews the recent history of the culturally validated medicalisation of (mis)behaviours and the social consequences in light of his earlier arguments. The article offers an alternative to the medical model for an explanation for mental illness.

Research method

This article critiques (reviews) changes in the beliefs and concepts surrounding mental health and changes in mental healthcare in the USA over the 50 years since 1960. As such it is not a study and does not involve participants or a specific procedure.

The article has four main sections:
1 Fifty years of change in US mental healthcare.
2 Mental illness – a medical or legal concept?
3 'Mental illness' is a metaphor.
4 Revisiting 'The myth of mental illness.'

Now test yourself

19 Outline how a phobia could develop through classical conditioning.
20 Outline a cognitive explanation for depression.

TESTED

Now test yourself

21 Outline the aim of Szasz's study.

TESTED

Answers at **www.hoddereducation.co.uk/myrevisionnotes**

Outline of the article

Section 1: Fifty years of change in US mental healthcare

In the 1950s, according to Szasz, the notion that the responsibility for the healthcare of the American people should lie with the federal government had not yet entered national consciousness. Most people called 'mental patients' were considered incurable and were confined in state mental hospitals. The physicians who cared for them were employees of the state governments. Non-psychiatric physicians in the private sector treated voluntary patients and were paid by their clients or the clients' families.

Since that time, the formerly sharp distinctions between medical hospitals and mental hospitals, voluntary and involuntary patients, private and public psychiatry have blurred into non-existence. Now, virtually all mental health care is the responsibility of the government and it is regulated and paid for by public money.

Everyone defined as a mental health professional is now legally responsible for preventing their patient from being 'dangerous to himself or others', i.e. psychiatry is thoroughly medicalised and politicised. There is therefore no legally valid non-medical approach to mental illness, just as there is no legally valid non-medical approach to measles or melanoma.

Section 2: Mental illness – a medical or legal concept?

Debate about what counts as mental illness has been replaced by political-judicial decrees and economic criteria: old diseases such as homosexuality disappear, whereas new diseases such as attention-deficit hyperactivity disorder appear.

Fifty years ago, the question 'What is mental illness?' was of interest to physicians, philosophers and sociologists as well as the general public. This question has now been settled by the holders of political power: they have decreed that mental illness is a disease like any other. In 1999, US President Bill Clinton declared: 'Mental illness can be accurately diagnosed, successfully treated, just as physical illness.' Surgeon general, David Satcher, agreed: 'Just as things go wrong with the heart and kidneys and liver, so things go wrong with the brain.' Thus have political power and professional self-interest united in turning a false belief into a 'lying fact'.

According to Szasz, 'the claim that mental illnesses are diagnosable disorders of the brain is not based on scientific research; it is an error, or a deception, or a naive revival of the somatic premise of the long-discredited humoral theory of disease.' His claim that mental illnesses are fictitious illnesses is not based on scientific research, but rests on the pathologist's materialist-scientific definition of illness as the structural or functional alteration of cells, tissues and organs. If this definition of disease is accepted, Szasz claims that mental illness is a **metaphor**.

In his essay/book 'The myth of mental illness', Szasz called public attention to the linguistic pretensions of psychiatry and its pre-emptive rhetoric. He insisted that mental hospitals are like prisons, not hospitals, that involuntary mental hospitalisation is a type of imprisonment, not medical care, and that coercive psychiatrists function as judges and jailers, not physicians and healers. He also suggested that the traditional psychiatric perspective of interpreting mental illnesses and psychiatric responses to them as matters of medicine, treatment and science should be discarded, instead being interpreted as matters of morals, law and rhetoric.

> **Now test yourself**
>
> 22 Outline two changes observed by Szasz that have occurred since he wrote 'The myth of mental illness' 50 years earlier.
>
> TESTED ☐

> a **metaphor** is a figure of speech in which a word or phrase is applied to an object or action that it does not literally denote in order to imply a resemblance – *Collins English Dictionary*.

> **Now test yourself**
>
> 23 According to Szasz, why is mental illness considered a medical concept?
>
> TESTED ☐

Section 3: 'Mental illness' is a metaphor

The proposition that mental illness is not a medical problem runs counter to public opinion and psychiatric dogma. Szasz illustrates his contention that mental illness is a metaphor through the following example: 'The physician who concludes that a person diagnosed with a mental illness suffers from a brain disease discovers that the person was misdiagnosed: he did not have a mental illness, he had an undiagnosed bodily illness. The physician's erroneous diagnosis is not proof that the term 'mental illness' refers to a class of brain diseases (p.180 of original article).

The process of biological discovery has characterised some of the history of medicine, with one form of 'madness' after another being identified as the manifestation of one or another somatic disease, for example beriberi. The result is that the illness ceases to be a form of psychopathology and becomes classified and treated as a form of neuropathology. Szasz therefore argues that if all the conditions now called mental illnesses proved to be brain diseases, there would be no need for the notion of mental illness and the term would become devoid of meaning. However, because the term refers to the judgements of some persons about the (bad) behaviours of other persons, what actually happens is precisely the opposite – an ever-expanding list of mental disorders.

Changing perspectives on human life (and illness)

According to Szasz, the old religious-humanistic perspective on the tragic nature of life has been replaced with a modern, dehumanised, pseudomedical one. The secularisation of everyday life, and thus the medicalisation of the soul and of personal suffering, began in late sixteenth-century England. Szasz illustrates this point through a reference to Shakespeare's *Macbeth*. Overcome by guilt for her murderous deeds, Lady Macbeth 'goes mad': she feels agitated, is anxious, unable to eat, rest or sleep. Her behaviour disturbs Macbeth, who sends for a doctor and demands that he cure his wife. The doctor says that he cannot cure her but that 'the patient must minister to himself' (Act V, Scene 3).

Today, however, the role of the physician as curer of the soul is uncontested. Today, people like Lady Macbeth would be considered a mentally ill patient who, like other humans, is inherently healthy/good but whose mental illness makes her sick/ill-behaved.

Mental illness is in the eye of the beholder

Szasz claims that all the behaviours we call mental diseases are in fact the products of the medicalisation of disturbing or disturbed behaviours, i.e. the observer's construction and definition of the behaviour of the people he observes as medically disabled individuals needing medical treatment. He claims that this cultural transformation has been driven mainly by the modern therapeutic ideology that has replaced the old theological world view and the political and professional interests it sets in motion. Medical practice has always rested on patient consent. An individual with a bodily illness is therefore not deprived of his liberty (unless he is legally incompetent or demonstrates dangerous behaviour towards others because of a contagious disease). However, individuals categorised as mentally ill rather than sick are deprived of their liberty and responsibility, which is a violation of their human rights.

Szasz holds that mental illness is a myth. Diseases of the body have causes, such as infectious agents or nutritional deficiencies, and often can be prevented or cured by dealing with these causes. He believes that individuals said to have mental diseases have reasons for their actions that must be understood. They cannot be treated or cured by drugs or other medical interventions, but may be helped by people who respect them, understand their predicament and help them to help themselves overcome the obstacles they face. The practice of Western medicine rests on the premise that the patient is free to seek, accept or reject diagnosis and treatment. Psychiatric practice, however, rests on the premise that the patient may be a danger to either themselves or others and that the moral and professional duty of the psychiatrist is to protect the patient from themselves and society from the patient. Yet the diagnosis of a patient's illness is in the hands of a licensed physician and therefore mental illness is in the eye of the beholder.

Section 4: Revisiting 'The myth of mental illness'

Szasz claims that many critics misread his book. He says it was not a book on psychiatry but a book about psychiatry, but that many critics have overlooked the fact that it is supposed to be a radical effort to recast mental illness from a medical problem into a linguistic-rhetorical phenomenon. He is therefore not surprised that most sympathetic appraisals of his text have come from non-psychiatrists who have not felt threatened by his re-visioning of psychiatry, for example the essay, 'The rhetorical paradigm in psychiatric history: Thomas Szasz and the myth of mental illness', by professor of communication Richard E. Vatz and law professor Lee S. Weinberg.

Having an illness does not make an individual into a patient

One of the most illicit assumptions inherent in the standard psychiatric approach to insanity is treating people called mentally ill as sick patients needing psychiatric treatment, regardless of whether they seek or reject such help. This accounts for an obvious but often overlooked difficulty peculiar to psychiatry, namely that the term refers to two radically different kinds of practices: curing/healing souls by conversation and coercing/controlling people by force, authorised and mandated by the state. Critics of psychiatry, journalists and the public alike regularly fail to distinguish between counselling voluntary clients and coercing and excusing captives of the psychiatric system.

Formerly, when church and state were allied, people accepted theological justifications for state-sanctioned coercion. Today, when medicine and the state are allied, people accept therapeutic justifications for state-sanctioned coercion. This is how, 200 years ago, psychiatry became an arm of the coercive apparatus of the state. And this is why today all of medicine threatens to become transformed from personal care into political control.

These issues are not new. Bleuler (1911) said: 'The most serious of all schizophrenic symptoms is the suicidal drive. I am even taking this opportunity to state clearly that our present-day social system demands a great and entirely inappropriate cruelty from the psychiatrist in this respect. People are being forced to continue to live a life that has become unbearable for them for valid reasons . . . Most of our worst restraining measures would be unnecessary, if we were not duty-bound to preserve the patients' lives which, for them as well as for others, are only of negative value. If all this would, at least, serve some purpose! . . . At the present time, we psychiatrists are burdened with the tragic responsibility of obeying the cruel views of society; but it is our responsibility to do our utmost to bring about a change in these views in the near future.' Here Bleuler was pleading for the recognition of the rights of 'schizophrenics' to define and control their own lives and that psychiatrists not deprive them of their liberty to take their own lives. Unfortunately, in Szasz's view, Bleuler's plea to resist 'obeying the cruel views of society' have been ignored by psychiatrists. Instead, Bleuler's invention of schizophrenia lent impetus to the medicalisation of the longing for non-existence, led to the creation of the pseudoscience of 'suicidology' and contributed to landing psychiatry in the moral morass in which it now finds itself (p.182 of the original article).

Conclusions

According to Szasz:
- psychiatry is a pseudoscience
- mental illness is a myth/mental illnesses are fictitious illnesses/mental illness is a metaphor
- mental illness is now considered a legal concept and no longer a medical concept
- the old religious-humanistic perspective on the tragic nature of life has been replaced with a modern, dehumanised, pseudomedical one
- mental illness is in the eye of the beholder
- it is wrong to treat individuals called mentally ill as sick patients needing psychiatric treatment, regardless of whether they seek or reject such help. These individuals should have the right and liberty to define and control their own lives.

Over the past 50 years, psychiatry (in the USA) has become thoroughly medicalised and politicised.

Mental illness is now considered a legal concept and no longer a medical concept.

There are alternatives to the medical model for an explanation for mental illness.

Now test yourself

25 Outline two conclusions drawn by Szasz in his review of the changes in the beliefs and concepts surrounding mental health and changes in mental healthcare in the USA over the 50 years since 1960.

TESTED ☐

Exam tips

Be able to outline the four sections of the article and draw conclusions from them.

Be able to compare points made by Szasz in his 1960 essay 'The myth of mental illness' with points made in his 2010 article in relation to validity.

Know how the article relates to the component 'Issues in mental health'.

Know how the article relates to the topic 'Alternatives to the medical model'.

Understand how the article can be seen to challenge the concept of mental illness.

Application

A non-biological treatment of one specific disorder: for example, anxiety disorders – systematic desensitisation, flooding, aversion therapy; depression – cognitive behavioural therapy (CBT), rational emotive behavioural therapy (REBT), rational therapy (RT), psychoanalysis/psychoanalytic psychotherapy; schizophrenia – psychoanalysis (dream analysis, free association)/psychoanalytic psychotherapy.

Now test yourself

26 Describe a non-biological treatment for one specific disorder.

TESTED ☐

Practice questions

Issues in mental health

1. a) Outline how mental disorders can be categorised. [3]
   b) Suggest one limitation of categorising mental disorders. [2]
2. Rosenhan (1973) found that pseudopatients once labelled 'insane' and hospitalised felt depersonalised. With reference to this key research, discuss why individuals admitted to psychiatric hospitals may develop feelings of depersonalisation. [6]
3. Suggest how a non-biological treatment can be used to treat any one specific disorder. [6]
4. Compare the behaviourist explanation for mental illness with the cognitive explanation for mental illness. [8]
5. Discuss the nature/nurture debate in relation to mental illness. [10]

ONLINE

Summary

By the end of this chapter you should:
- know and understand some historical views of mental illness, Rosenhan's study and the characteristics of an affective disorder, a psychotic disorder and an anxiety disorder
- know and understand the biochemical, genetic and brain abnormality explanations of mental illness, Gottesman *et al.*'s study and

a biological treatment of one specific mental disorder
- know and understand the behaviourist and cognitive explanations of mental illness, one explanation from the humanistic, psychodynamic and cognitive neuroscience explanations of mental illness, Szasz's study and a non-biological treatment of one specific mental disorder.

Generic exam tips for this and your two optional topics

You should:
- be able to explain and exemplify the background and consider relevant issues and debates in relation to the topic areas of 'Issues in mental health', and two from 'Child psychology', Criminal psychology' 'Environmental psychology or 'Sport and exercise psychology'.
- be able to describe and evaluate the key research and appreciate how it relates to the topic areas of 'Issues in mental health', and two from 'Child psychology', Criminal psychology' 'Environmental psychology or 'Sport and exercise psychology' through the consideration of such issues as: strengths/weaknesses of the sample, strengths/weaknesses of the methodology, strengths/weaknesses of observation as a way to gather data, strengths/weaknesses of self-reports, quantitative versus qualitative data, reliability, validity and ecological validity, ethnocentrism.

- be able to apply the following methodological issues and debates in relation to the content of the topic area 'Issues in mental health', and two from 'Child psychology', Criminal psychology' 'Environmental psychology or 'Sport and exercise psychology': nature/nurture, freewill/determinism, individual/situational explanations, usefulness of research, ethical considerations, conducting socially sensitive research, psychology as a science, ethnocentrism, validity, reliability, sampling bias.
- be able to apply knowledge and understanding of the topic areas of 'Issues in mental health', and two from 'Child psychology', Criminal psychology' 'Environmental psychology or 'Sport and exercise psychology' to a novel situation.
- remember that Section B of the exam paper will focus on this topic and will contain a range from short answers to extended response questions.

Intelligence (Biological)

What psychologists mean by intelligence: for example, factor models of intelligence (e.g. Spearman, Carroll's three-stratum model, Thurstone, Cattell – fluid intelligence and crystallised intelligence, Sternberg's triarchic theory of intelligence, Gardner's concept of multiple intelligences, Goleman).

What biological factors could affect intelligence: for example, the relationship between sex and intelligence in relation to neural anatomy and hormones, sex differences in brain structure and brain activity, the genetic transference of intelligence.

Key research: Van Leeuwen *et al.* (2008): A twin-family study of general IQ

Theory/theories on which the study is based

Individual differences in intelligence tend to cluster in families (Bouchard and McGue, 2003, 1981; Boomsma, 1993; Deary, Spinath and Bates, 2006). The resemblance (in intelligence) between relatives can be due to genetic relatedness, environmental similarities, cultural transmission from one generation to the next, social interactions between family members, or a combination of these mechanisms. The hypothesis of marital interaction or convergence states that spousal correlations arise because spouses spend time together. Spouses would tend to become more similar the longer they are together either because they influence each other or because they share similar experiences. However, the few studies that tested this hypothesis found no indications of convergence for intelligence (Gilger, 1991; Mascie-Taylor, 1989; Watson *et al.*, 2004).

Phenotypic assortment assumes that spouses choose each other based on observable characteristics (Reynolds, Baker and Pederson, 1996), in this case on intelligence or a trait related to it, i.e. individuals will tend to mate with partners of a similar intelligence level.

Social homogamy refers to assortment based on solely environmental similarities. Spousal phenotypes therefore become correlated because spouses meet each other within a particular environment. In the case of intelligence, the social homogamy hypothesis states that people with the same intelligence level live in the same social environment. Within a particular social environment, partners do not choose each other on the basis of intelligence, but since they live in the same environment, they tend to mate with people with a similar general intelligence (IQ).

The causes in this resemblance (in intelligence) are best studied using a twin-family study. This is because monozygotic (MZ; identical) twins share all, or nearly all of their DNA and dizygotic (DZ; fraternal) twins share on average 50 per cent of their segregating genes (Boomsma, Busjahn and Peltonen, 2002; Plomin *et al.*, 2002). This larger resemblance in MZ than DZ twins is therefore suggestive of genetic influences on twin resemblance, rather than environmental influences.

Exam tips

Be able to provide a clear description of the term 'intelligence'.

Be able to describe how biological factors could affect intelligence.

phenotypic assortment is a mating pattern and a form of sexual selection based on the concept that individuals with similar observable physical or biochemical characteristics will be attracted towards each other.

Including parents in a twin design adds extra information about the origins of individual differences. The resemblance between parents and offspring may reflect genetic transmission, cultural transmission, or both.

Background to the study

Previous twin studies have estimated the contribution of genetic effects to the variability in intelligence at 25 to 50 per cent.

Previous spouse and family studies have shown that spouses resemble each other in IQ scores and traits correlated to IQ, such as educational attainment (Watkins and Meredith, 1981; Mascie-Taylor, 1989; Watson et al., 2004).

Previous research has shown that the environment might have a greater influence in less intelligent people than in more intelligent people, for example Finkel and Perderson, 2001.

This article builds on previous research. It uses an extended twin design which includes MZ (see Figure 18.1) and DZ twins, their siblings and their parents, to study to what extent assortative mating, cultural inheritance and GE (genotype–environment) interaction and correlation are present for IQ. Data on general IQ was collected in both generations with the **Raven's Progressive Matrices test**.

Until this study only the CAP (Colorado Adoption Project) study had examined the genetic and environmental transmission of intelligence from parents to their children in the presence of spousal resemblance.

The study investigates whether biological factors and/or environmental factors might affect intelligence. Van Leeuwen et al. expected additive genetic effects would explain a large part of any individual differences in intelligence.

Research method

This research article/paper assesses the presence of assortative mating, gene–environment interaction and the heritability of intelligence in childhood using a twin-family design with twins, their siblings and parents from 112 families. Two competing hypotheses about the cause of assortative mating in intelligence – social homogamy and phenotypic assortment – are evaluated and their implications for the heritability estimate of intelligence considered. The researchers also assessed GE interaction by testing to see whether there was an association between absolute difference scores in MZ twins (reflecting non-shared environmental effects) and average scores (reflecting familial effects).

This study could also be viewed as a collection of (mini) case studies, the findings of which were collated and analysed in order to compare the two hypotheses about the cause of assortative mating in intelligence.

In addition, the study may be viewed as a correlational study as the researchers were looking for relationships between such factors as intelligence and biological factors, intelligence and environmental factors.

The study was approved by the Central Committee on Research Involving Human Subjects (CCMO).

Outline of the procedure/study

Twins were recruited from the Netherlands Twin Registry (NTR) and therefore came from all over the Netherlands. Twin families with an extra sibling between nine and 14 years were selected from two birth cohorts (1995–1996). Because the twins and siblings also took part in an

Now test yourself

2 Outline what previous research has shown in relation to genetic effects on intelligence.

TESTED

Raven's Progressive Matrices test is a non-verbal test often used in educational settings. It is usually a 60-item test which measures abstract reasoning and allows a non-verbal estimate of fluid intelligence to be made.

Figure 18.1 MZ twins

Now test yourself

3 Explain why this study may be viewed as a correlational study.

TESTED

MRI study, there were several exclusion criteria such as a pacemaker and metal materials in the head. Families with children with a major medical history, psychiatric problems (as reported by the parents), participation in special education, or physical or sensory disabilities were also excluded.

A total of 214 families were invited by letter, which was sent out one to two months before the twins' ninth birthday. Two weeks after receiving the letter, the families were contacted by phone. Of these families 52 per cent (112) agreed to participate. There was no significant difference between the educational level of mothers who did participate and who did not participate in the study.

Of the 112 families, 103 had full siblings (siblings with the same mother and father) who wanted to participate. Mean age of the twins at time of cognitive assessment was 9.1 years, ranging from 8.9 to 9.5 years. There were 23 MZ male, 23 DZ male, 25 MZ female, 21 DZ female and 20 DZ pairs of opposite sex. Zygosity was based on DNA tests and questionnaire items.

Mean age of the siblings was 11.9 years, ranging from 9.9 to 14.9. Mean age of the biological fathers was 43.7 and of the biological mothers was 41.9.

Parents signed informed consent forms for their children and themselves. Children also signed their own consent forms. Parents were compensated for their travel expenses and children received a present.

Testing procedures

The study collected cognitive, behavioural and hormonal data, pubertal status and structural MRI brain data. Data collection took place on two different days. Cheek swabs, for DNA isolation, were collected at home by parents and children.

For cognitive testing, families arrived between 9 a.m. and 11 a.m. Children were tested in separate rooms with a cognitive test battery, including the Raven's Standard Progressive Matrices (SPM; Raven, 1960). Parents completed the Raven's Advanced Progressive Matrices (APM; Raven et al., 1998). The whole protocol took approximately five hours, including two short breaks and one longer lunch break.

Materials

Children were individually tested with the SPM, which they completed at their own pace after verbal instruction. The test consists of 60 problems divided into five sets of 12. In each set the first problem is as nearly as possible self-evident. The problems within a set become progressively more difficult. The test is intended to cover the whole range of intellectual development from the time a child is able to grasp the idea of finding a missing piece to complete a pattern, and to be sufficiently long to assess a child's maximum capacity to form comparisons and reason by analogy. The test provides an index of general intelligence. For children, retest reliability is .88 (Raven, 1960).

Parents were given the APM since the SPM is too easy for most adults. They received written instructions and completed the test at their own pace. The APM is comparable to the SPM, with the main difference being the level of difficulty. The APM consists of two sets. The first set contains 12 practice items, to familiarise participants with the test. The second set consists of 36 items, which are identical in presentation and

zygosity refers to the degree of similarity between twins.

Exam tip
Ensure you know the research method and details of the sample.

Now test yourself
4 Outline the sample used in this study.
TESTED

Exam tip
Know the procedure – for both the children and the adults.

Now test yourself
5 Outline the procedure followed for the cognitive tests.
TESTED

argument to those in Set I. They only increase in difficulty more steadily and become considerably more complex. Reported retest reliability for adults is .91 (Raven et al., 1998).

Key findings

Descriptive statistics of the Raven IQ scores are shown in Table 18.1. Parents received the APM (maximum achievable score = 36), offspring received the SPM (maximum achievable score = 60).

Table 18.1 The Raven IQ scores

	N	Minimum	Maximum	Mean	SD
Fathers	94	4	36	27.0	6.5
Mothers	95	9	36	25.9	6.0
Male siblings	44	24	56	43.8	7.8
Female siblings	57	30	49	46.4	6.5
Male twins	114	13	50	36.7	8.6
Female twins	110	19	50	36.6	7.1

For the estimated IQ measures (based on the Rasch scaling), no significant sex differences were observed: neither in the total group, nor within groups (parents, siblings, twins). Correlations were higher in MZ twins than in first-degree relatives (siblings, DZ twins and parent–offspring pairs).

The mean IQ score was higher in the older siblings than the younger and there was more variance in siblings than in twins, even though the same test was used. This could not be fully explained by age differences among the siblings.

The spousal (parental) correlation for the Rasch IQ estimates was significant and moderately high (0.33). A model assuming that this correlation is due to phenotypic assortment proved superior to a model assuming that the correlation was due to purely environmental factors that are transmitted from generation to generation.

The distribution of Rasch IQ scores looked more or less normal, though the distribution of the estimated measures in twins showed a slight negative skew and the sibling and parental data a slight positive skew.

Corrected for scale unreliability effects, additive genetic effects account for 67 per cent of the variation in intelligence and the remainder is explained by random environmental factors, including measurement error, indicating that inherited genetic factors influence children's intelligence.

Non-additive genetic effects and cultural transmission effects were not significant.

Findings in relation to GE interaction suggested that the environment is relatively more important in explaining individual differences for low IQ groups than for high IQ groups.

Conclusions

Variability in fluid intelligence as measured by the Raven's Progressive Matrices test is largely explained by additive genetic effects that are transmitted from parents to offspring.

Individual differences in intelligence are largely accounted for by genetic differences.

Now test yourself

6 From Table 18.1:
   a) Identify the maximum IQ score achieved by the fathers.
   b) Identify the mean IQ score of the male twins.
   c) Identify the minimum IQ score achieved by the male siblings.
   d) Identify the standard deviation on IQ scores for the mothers.

TESTED ☐

Exam tip

Know the key findings and be able to draw conclusions from them.

Now test yourself

7 Outline the results of the correlational analysis between the IQ of the parents.

TESTED ☐

Exam tips

Know how the study relates to the component 'Child psychology'.

Know how the study relates to the topic 'Intelligence (biological)' – viewing intelligence from the biological area.

Know how the study relates to what biological factors could affect intelligence.

Parental influence on their children's IQ can be explained by the transmission of genes. Cultural transmission from parents does not influence their children's IQ.

Environmental factors are significantly more important in children with a genetic predisposition for low IQ than in children with a genetic predisposition for high IQ.

Environmental factors influencing IQ are generally not shared among siblings.

Application

At least one method of assessing intelligence: examples include IQ tests (such as the Raven's Progressive Matrices, the Wechsler intelligence tests, the Woodcock–Johnson IQ test), human figure drawing tests, using questions and answers to measure crystallised intelligence, puzzles and pictures to assess fluid intelligence, building and drawing-type tasks to assess visual-spatial intelligence.

Pre-adult brain development (Biological)

REVISED

Brain development: for example, early and adolescent brain development and the impact on behavioural development; ways in which psychologists can study brain development (such as studying the development of the structure of the nervous system and then correlating this with the emergence of specific behaviours, studying neural structures in areas of the brain in relation to behavioural disorders).

The impact of brain development on risk-taking behaviour: for example, the way in which adolescents' brains develop and hormonal changes in puberty can impact on decision making and risk-taking behaviours; the influence of the prefrontal cortex, the limbic system and the maturation of the ventral striatum on risk-taking behaviours in adolescents.

Key research: Barkley-Levenson and Galván (2014): Neural representation of expected value in the adolescent brain

Theory/theories on which the study is based

Adolescence is characterised by heightened sensitivity to rewards (Galván, 2013). **Subjective value** (SV) is defined as the value that an individual places on a stimulus (Knutson *et al.*, 2008). To make a choice, an organism determines the SV of each alternative and then selects the one with the greatest SV (for example, Bartra *et al.*, 2013).

Research has found that the ventromedial prefrontal cortex (VMPFC) and the ventral striatum (VS) regions represent SV during choice for monetary stimuli, charitable donations, consumer goods and food.

It is currently unknown whether there are **ontogenetic differences** in how EV is represented in the brain and whether these differences confer a greater influence in value-based choices in adolescents versus adults (Barkley-Levenson and Galván, 2014).

Background to the study

Previous work shows that the adolescent reward system is hyperactive, but this finding may be confounded by differences in how teens value money.

Now test yourself

8 Outline one way of assessing intelligence.

TESTED

Exam tips

The question is likely to be worded generically so focus on the specific method selected for describing how intelligence can be assessed.

Be able to apply at least one method of assessing intelligence to a novel situation.

Now test yourself

9 Outline how the maturation of the ventral striatum can influence risk-taking behaviour.

TESTED

Exam tip

Be able to outline how brain development may impact on risk-taking behaviour.

subjective value is defined as the value an individual places on a stimulus. Expected value (EV) is defined as the sum of all the possible outcomes of a particular choice.

ontogentic differences refer to differences in biological development.

Answers at **www.hoddereducation.co.uk/myrevisionnotes**

To address this, Barkley-Levenson and Galván examined the neural ontogeny of objective value representation.

Until this study, it was not clear whether the adolescent brain attributes greater value to available rewards or whether the effect is driven by adolescents valuing money to a greater extent than adults because they typically have less access to and experience with it. The goal of this study was to disentangle these possibilities by examining subjective valuation (indexed by behaviour) of objectively valued choices.

Barkley-Levenson and Galván had three hypotheses:
1 Adolescents will exhibit greater behavioural sensitivity (accept more gambles) to increasing EV than adults.
2 Neurobiologically VS activation will modulate in proportion to increasing EV more for adolescents than for adults.
3 Adults who behave like adolescents in terms of gambling behaviour will not exhibit hyperactive striatal activation.

Research method

This was a quasi experiment using an independent measures design, conducted under laboratory conditions. The independent variable was whether the participant was an adult or an adolescent. This was naturally occurring and could not be manipulated. The dependent variable was neural activation in the brain measured using fMRI while participants performed a simple mixed gambles game.

A secondary analysis was conducted to test the hypothesis that an exaggerated VS activation in adolescents would be observed even after matching adolescents and adults on subjective valuation (acceptance of gambles).

Outline of the procedure/study

Participants were 19 healthy, right-handed adults (ages 25 to 30, mean age 27.9 years; 11 female and therefore eight male) and 22 healthy, right-handed adolescents (ages 13 to 17, mean age 15.6 years; 11 female and therefore 11 male).

All participants were recruited through poster and internet advertisements approved through the Institutional Review Board at the University of California, Los Angeles (UCLA), and through a database of prior research participants. All participants reported no prior diagnosis of psychiatric or neurologic illness or development delays, had no metal in their bodies and were not taking psychoactive medication.

Participants visited the laboratory for an intake session and for the neuro-imaging session. At the intake session, all participants provided informed consent and participants under the age of 18 provided assent while their parents/guardians completed the informed consent form.

Each participant was also asked to provide the primary source and amount of spending money per month. This was because the valuation of monetary rewards might be influenced by available spending money/income. There was a significant effect of age on spending money each month: mean for adolescents = $52.50, mean for adults = $467.11.

Finally, at the intake session, participants were familiarised with an MRI environment with a mock scanner.

Now test yourself

10 Outline Barkley-Levenson and Galván's three hypotheses.
11 Explain why this study is considered a quasi experiment.

TESTED

Exam tip

Know the research method and sample.

Participants were given $20 for completing the intake session and were informed that they would use the $20 as 'playing' money during the fMRI task on the subsequent laboratory session. They were also informed that there was an opportunity to win up to $20 more in addition to their playing money (for a total of $40) but that there was a possibility that they would lose the $20 during the gambling fMRI task. Allowing them to feel ownership of the $20 earned during the intake session helped preclude the 'house money effect' (increased risk-taking behaviour that is observed when the money at stake is not the participant's own). In actuality, all participants were assigned a payment of between $5 and $10 corresponding to a trial that they accepted, to ensure that no participants were required to return money to the experimenters.

Approximately one week after the intake session, participants returned to the laboratory for the fMRI session. During the fMRI scan (see Figure 18.2), participants completed a gambling task. In this task, participants were presented with a series of gambles with a 50 per cent probability of gaining the amount shown on one side of a 'spinner' and a 50 per cent probability of losing the amount shown on the other side. The gain and loss amounts were independently manipulated, with gain amounts selected from the range of whole-dollar values between +$5 and +$20 and loss amounts selected from the range of whole-dollar values between −$5 and −$20, for a total of 144 trials. Randomly interspersed within these trials were 24 gain-only trials and 24 loss-only trials, with values drawn from the same range, for a total of 192 trials across four runs. These gain-only and loss-only trials allowed for a broader range of EVs within the task than mixed gambles alone would provide. The EVs of the mixed gambles ranged from −$7.50 to +$7.50, whereas the EVs of the gain-only gambles ranged from +$6 to +$19 and the EVs of the loss-only gambles ranged from −$6 to −$19. The side of the spinner in which the gain and loss appeared and the order of the stimuli were counterbalanced across participants.

For each trial, participants decided whether or not they would be willing to play that gamble for real money. Participants were informed that one of the trials that they chose to accept would be selected at the end of the scan and played for real money, with that amount of money added to or subtracted from their overall payment for taking part. This procedure was designed to encourage a choice on each trial that was consistent with the participant's actual feelings about that gamble.

Participants were extensively trained before the scan to make sure they understood all aspects of the gambling task.

Key findings

There were 20 adolescent and 17 adult participants in the final sample as the others did not provide any useful data. Results showed that acceptance rates did not change in either adolescents or adults when there was no risk involved in both gain-only and loss-only trials, suggesting that adolescents behave similarly to adults when there is no risk involved.

Across all participants, trials with positive EV were accepted significantly more than trials with EV of zero, which were accepted significantly more than trials with negative EV. No significant differences were observed between adolescent and adult participants in the percentage of EV+ trials accepted, the percentage of EVo trials accepted, or the percentage of EV− trials accepted.

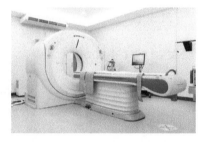

Figure 18.2 An fMRI scanner

> **Exam tip**
>
> Be able to outline the procedure.

> **Now test yourself**
>
> 12 Outline the sample used in this study.
> 13 Outline the gambling task used in this study.
>
> TESTED

> **Exam tip**
>
> Know the key findings and be able to draw conclusions from them.

Increasing EV increased the likelihood of an accept response. There was more activation in the VS in adolescents than adults as EV increased.

The amount of disposable income did not have an effect on the relationship between EV and acceptance rates.

No significant differences were observed between adolescent and adult participants in reaction time.

Increasing EV had a stronger influence over gambling choices in adolescents relative to adults. Activation in some brain areas increased with increasing EV activation while activation in other brain areas decreased with increasing EV. This unique adolescent ventral striatum response remained even after matching groups on acceptance behaviour.

Conclusions

The value of available options has a greater influence in adolescent versus adult choices, even when objective value and subjective choice are held constant.

Maturational changes in neural representation of valuation during adolescence are most robust in the VS.

Neural differences in sensitivity to EV change across development.

Hyperactivation of reward circuitry in adolescence may be a normative ontogenetic shift that is due to greater valuation in the adolescent brain/ the unique adolescent response to rewards is mediated by ontogenetic differences in valuation and is not simply a methodological consequence of using money as the rewarding stimulus.

Neural representations of value in adolescents are linked to increased risk-taking behaviour.

Adolescents behave similarly to adults when there is no risk involved (in gambling).

Application

At least one strategy to reduce risk-taking behaviours using knowledge of brain development: examples include changing the context – graduated driver licensing schemes, educating parents and providing them with more support to reduce neglect/maltreatment in childhood to prevent risk taking or impulsivity, encouraging discourse between adolescents and their parents to learn to assess risk, ensuring the adolescent has positive social networks to reduce risky behaviours, harm-reduction programmes.

Perceptual development (Cognitive)

REVISED

Perceptual development in children: for example, know what is meant by the term '**perception**'/the process of perception; cultural differences in perception; the development of perception in children, including the development of visual perception, pattern perception, face perception, constancies, depth perception.

How perceptual development can be studied in babies and animals: for example, studying the development of infant perception through habituation, preferential looking (for instance, the work by Fantz); studying perceptual development in animals using 'selective rearing' – raising an animal from birth under controlled conditions to observe the outcome (such as the work with kittens by Blakemore and Cooper, the

> **Exam tips**
>
> Know how the study relates to the component 'Child psychology'.
>
> Know how the study relates to the topic 'Pre-adult brain development (biological)'.
>
> Know how the study relates to brain development and the impact of this on risk-taking behaviour.

> **Now test yourself**
>
> 14 Outline one finding in relation to the activation of the ventral striatum.
> 15 Draw one conclusion from the findings of this study.
>
> TESTED

> **Exam tips**
>
> The question is likely to be worded generically so focus on the specific strategy selected to reduce risk-taking behaviours using knowledge of brain development.
>
> Be able to apply at least one strategy to reduce risk-taking behaviours using knowledge of brain development to a novel situation.

> **perception** is the process by which information in the environment is transformed into an experience of objects, sounds, events, etc. It is a combination of both the physical processes involved with the senses and the processes within the brain which integrate and interpret the sensory inputs.

work with chimps by Riesen, 1965), studying the development of depth perception in both children and animals using the 'visual cliff'.

Key research: Gibson and Walk (1960): The visual cliff

Theory/theories on which the study is based

Height perception is a form of distance perception: information in the light reaching the eye provides stimuli that can be utilised for the discrimination both of depth and of receding distance on the level.

With both eyes open, the brain receives and integrates information from both eyes to allow objects to be perceived in three dimensions.

Depth cues (which are two-dimensional) allow for three-dimensional perception. These cues include overlap, height in visual field, relative size, linear perspective and texture gradient.

Depth perception is the visual ability to perceive the world in three dimensions (3D) and the distance of an object.

When an observer moves, the apparent relative motion of several stationary objects against a background gives hints about their relative distance. If information about the direction and velocity of movement is known, motion parallax can provide absolute depth information (Ferris, 1972). This effect can be seen clearly when driving in a car – nearby things pass quickly, while far-off objects appear stationary.

Human infants at the creeping and toddling stage are prone to falls from more or less high places. They must be kept from going over the brink by side panels on their cots, gates on stairways and the vigilance of adults. As their muscular co-ordination matures they begin to avoid such accidents on their own.

The effects of early experience and of such deprivations as dark-rearing represent important cues to the relative roles of maturation and learning in animal behaviour.

Background to the study

This study investigated the age at which infants start to show the ability to utilise visual stimuli for the discrimination of depth and the recording of receding distance on the level. The study's main aim, however, was to show support for the suggestion that both humans' and other species' depth perception and thus avoidance of falling from such things as steep cliffs is innate. This was studied by observing the behaviour of chicks, turtles, rats, lambs, kids, pigs, kittens and dogs, as well as human infants on the visual cliff apparatus.

In addition, the study aimed to determine which of two visual cues plays the decisive role in depth perception – (a) the fact that distance decreases the size and spacing of pattern elements projected on the retina, or (b) motion parallax, which causes the pattern elements on the shallow side to move more rapidly across the field of vision when the animal moves its position (on the board) or moves its head.

Research method

The main study was a laboratory experiment that used a repeated measures design. The IV was whether the infant was called by its mother

Answers at **www.hoddereducation.co.uk/myrevisionnotes**

from the cliff side or the shallow side (of the visual cliff apparatus). The DV was whether or not the child would crawl to its mother.

This was a repeated measures design because the infant was called from both the cliff side and the shallow side of the apparatus.

The studies using other species are quasi (laboratory) experiments. The naturally occurring IV was the animal species, such as rat/chick/lamb/kitten. The DV was whether the animal preferred the shallow side or the deep side of the visual cliff apparatus.

Outline of the procedure/study

Participants were 36 infants ranging in age from six months to 14 months. Their mothers also participated in the experiment, which meant that parental consent must have been given. The behaviour of chicks, turtles, rats, lambs, kids, pigs, kittens and dogs on the visual cliff apparatus was also observed.

The visual cliff apparatus

The apparatus consisted of a board laid across a large sheet of heavy glass which was supported a foot or more above the floor. On one side of the board a sheet of patterned material was placed flush against the under-surface of the glass, giving the glass the appearance as well as the state of solidity. On the other side a sheet of the same material was laid on the floor; this side of the board thus became the visual cliff.

Each child was placed on the centre board and his mother called him from the cliff side and the shallow side successively. Similarly, chicks, turtles, rats, lambs, kids, pigs, kittens and dogs were placed on the visual cliff apparatus and their subsequent behaviour was observed.

The visual cliff experiment was then further developed at the Cornell Behavior Farm. The patterned material was fixed to a sheet of plywood so that the 'depth' of the deep side could be adjusted. A number of control experiments were conducted (using animals) to ensure the design of the visual cliff apparatus had no hidden bias:

a) In one of these experiments, reflections from the glass were eliminated by lighting the patterned surfaces from below the glass.

b) In some experiments the patterned surface was replaced with a homogeneous grey surface.

c) To eliminate the optical difference between the two sides of the board, in some experiments the patterned surface was placed directly against the under-surface of the glass on each side.

When trying to determine which of two visual cues plays the decisive role in depth perception – (a) the fact that distance decreases the size and spacing of pattern elements projected on the retina, or (b) motion parallax, which causes the pattern elements on the shallow side to move more rapidly across the field of vision when the animal moves its position (on the board) or moves its head:

a) the potential distance cue provided by pattern density was removed by increasing the size and spacing of the pattern elements on the deep side in proportion to its distance from the eye

b) the cue of motion parallax was removed by placing the patterned material directly against the glass on either side of the board but smaller and more densely spaced pattern elements on the cliff side were used.

Now test yourself

18 Explain why the main part of this study is said to use a repeated measures design.

TESTED ☐

Exam tip

Know the research method and samples.

To determine whether depth perception in rats and kittens is innate, groups of light-reared and dark-reared rats were tested using the visual cliff experiment because it requires no re-training.

Key findings

All of the 27 infants (100 per cent) who crawled off the board crawled out on the shallow side at least once. Only three of the 27 children (11 per cent) who moved off the board crawled off the brink onto the glass suspended above the pattern on the floor. Many of the infants crawled away from the mother when she called to them from the cliff side.

Some of the infants cried when their mother stood on the cliff side because they could not get to her without crossing the apparent chasm. Often the infants would peer down through the glass on the deep side and then back away.

Some infants patted the glass with their hands, yet despite this tactual assurance of solidity would refuse to cross the apparent chasm.

Many infants supported themselves on the glass over the deep side as they manoeuvred awkwardly on the board.

At an age of less than 24 hours a chick was found to never make a 'mistake' and always hopped off the board on the shallow side.

Kids and lambs were tested on the visual cliff as soon as they could stand. No goat or lamb ever stepped onto the glass of the deep side, even at one day old. When one of these animals was placed on the glass of the deep side, it refused to put its feet down and backed up into a defensive posture. If it was then pushed across the glass until its head and field of vision crossed the edge of the surrounding solid surface, it would relax from its defensive posture and spring forward on the surface.

When kids and goats were tested on the moderated version of the visual cliff:
a) when the pattern was immediately beneath the glass, the animal would move about freely
b) when the optical floor was dropped more than a foot below the glass, the animal froze into its defensive posture
c) despite repeated experience of the tactual solidity of the glass, the animals never learned to function without optical support, i.e. their sense of security or danger continued to depend upon the visual cues that gave them their perception of depth.

Hooded rats when tested on the visual cliff:
- showed little preference for the shallow side as long as they could feel the glass with their vibrissae (whiskers)
- moved about normally when placed upon the glass over the deep side
- showed good visual depth-discrimination when the centre board was raised several inches so that the glass was out of reach of their whiskers – 95 to 100 per cent of them descended on the shallow side
- still consistently chose the shallow side when tested using the patterned surface lit from below to eliminate reflections from the glass
- showed no preference for either the shallow or the deep side when the patterned surface was replaced with a grey surface
- descended without preference to either side when the patterned surface was placed directly against the under-surface of the glass on each side, but when the pattern was lowered 10 inches below the glass on each side, they stayed on the board.

Now test yourself

19 Describe the visual cliff apparatus.

TESTED

Exam tip

Know the procedure followed in the visual cliff situation.

Now test yourself

20 Outline the findings when the infant was called to from the shallow side of the cliff.
21 Outline the findings when the infant was called to from the deep side of the cliff.

TESTED

Kittens proved to have excellent depth discrimination. At four weeks – about the earliest age a kitten can move about easily – they were found to invariably choose the shallow side of the cliff. On the glass over the deep side they either froze or circled aimlessly backwards until they reached the centre board.

The poorest performance on the visual cliff was shown by turtles – 76 per cent of the aquatic turtles crawled off the board to the shallow side.

With only the cue of motion parallax to guide them:
● adult rats still preferred the shallow side, though not as strongly as in the standard experiment
● infant rats and chicks chose the shallow side nearly 100 per cent of the time under both conditions
● both light-reared and dark-reared rats preferred the shallow side.

Without the potential distance cue provided by pattern density:
● both young and adult hooded rats preferred the side with the larger pattern
● day-old chicks showed no preference for the larger pattern – these results suggest that learning played some part in the preference exhibited by the rats as they were tested at a somewhat older age than the chicks
● dark-reared rats, like the day-old chicks, showed no significant preference for either the shallow or steep side.

When the visual cliff experiment was used to determine whether depth perception was innate in rats:
● at the age of 90 days both light-reared and dark-reared rats showed the same preference for the shallow side of the apparatus. These results support Lashley and Russell's conclusion that depth perception in rats is innate.

When the visual cliff experiment was used to determine whether depth perception was innate in kittens:
● dark-reared kittens at the age of 27 days at first crawled or fell off the centreboard equally often on both the deep and shallow sides
● when placed on glass over the deep side, they did not back in a circle like light-reared (normal) kitten but showed the same behaviour that they had exhibited on the shallow side
● once exposed to the light the dark-reared kittens were tested daily. After a week they were performing in every respect like normal, light-reared kittens, i.e. they showed the same unanimous preference for the shallow side.

Now test yourself

22 Outline two findings in relation to depth perception in young animals.

TESTED ☐

Conclusions

Most human infants can discriminate depth as soon as they can crawl.

A seeing animal can discriminate depth when its locomotion is adequate, even when locomotion begins at birth.

Depth perception in humans develops before many locomotor abilities.

Infants should not be left close to a brink.

Depth perception in chicks, kids and goats and kittens manifests itself rapidly. Hooded rats and kittens use tactile cues from their whiskers to help their depth perception.

The survival of any species requires that its members develop depth discrimination by the time they take up independent locomotion,

Now test yourself

23 Suggest one conclusion that can be drawn from the findings of this study in relation to depth perception in young children.

TESTED ☐

whether this be at one day (the chick and the goat), three to four weeks (the rat and the cat) or six to ten months (the human infant).

Both infant rats and chicks can discriminate depth by differential motion alone, with no aid from texture density.

Depth perception in rats is innate.

Depth perception in kittens is maturational.

In some animals, only motion parallax is an innate cue for depth discrimination.

Application

At least one play strategy to develop perception in young children: examples include sensory integrative (SI) therapy, games to develop aural perception such as sound bingo, tactile toys to develop touch perception, shape sorter toys, jigsaws to develop visual and shape perception.

> **Exam tips**
>
> The question is likely to be worded generically so focus on the specific strategy selected to develop perception in young children.
>
> Be able to apply at least one play strategy to develop perception in young children to a novel situation.

> **Exam tips**
>
> Know how the study relates to the component 'Child psychology'.
>
> Know how the study relates to the topic 'Perceptual development (cognitive)'.
>
> Know how the study relates to how perceptual development can be studied in babies and animals.

> **Now test yourself**
>
> 24 Describe one play strategy to develop perception in young children.
>
> TESTED ☐

Cognitive development and education (Cognitive)

REVISED ☐

Cognitive development in children: for example, Piaget's theory of cognitive development, including the sensorimotor stage, pre-operational stage, concrete operational stage, formal operational stage, the role of schema; Vygotsky's theory of cognitive development, including the concepts of zone of proximal development (ZPD) and the role of a more knowledgeable other (MKO); Bruner's stage theory of cognitive development, including the enactive stage, the iconic stage, the symbolic stage; Perry's nine-point scheme of intellectual development, including dualism, multiplicity, relativism, commitment.

How cognitive development in children impacts on education: for example, the implementation of the spiral curriculum to reflect Bruner's three stages of cognitive development; the use of scaffolding to reflect Vygotsky's concept of the zone of proximal development; the use of discovery learning to reflect Piaget's belief that children will interact with their environment and so construct their own meaning rather than simply memorising something; the use of a staged curriculum to reflect Piaget's theory of cognitive development.

> **Now test yourself**
>
> 25 Outline Piaget's four stages of cognitive development.
>
> TESTED ☐

> **Exam tips**
>
> Be able to describe Piaget's stage theory of cognitive development.
>
> Be able to describe at least one way in which cognitive development in children impacts on education.

Key research: Wood *et al.* (1976): The role of tutoring in problem solving

Theory/theories on which the study is based

The usual type of tutoring situation is where one individual (the tutor) 'knows the answer', while the other (the child) does not. Tutorial interactions are therefore a crucial feature of infancy and childhood (Woods *et al.*, 1976).

Problem-solving is the mastery of 'lower-order' or constituent problems that are absolutely necessary for success with a larger problem, each level influencing the other, for example reading, where the deciphering of words makes possible the deciphering of sentences, and sentences then aid in the deciphering of particular words (Smith, F., 1971). The process of skill acquisition is therefore analogous to problem-solving.

The intervention of a tutor involves a kind of 'scaffolding' process that enables a child or novice to solve a problem, carry out a task or achieve a goal which would be beyond his unassisted efforts. Scaffolding consists essentially of the adult 'controlling' the elements of the task that are initially beyond the learner's capacity, so he can concentrate on and complete only those elements that are within his range of competence.

Well-executed scaffolding begins by luring the child into actions that produce recognisable-for-him solutions. Once that is achieved, the tutor can interpret discrepancies to the child. Finally, the tutor stands in a confirmatory role until the tutee is checked out to fly on his own (Woods *et al.*, 1976).

Comprehension of a solution must precede production because without comprehension there can be no effective feedback.

Background to the study

Woods *et al.* contended that a learner cannot benefit from any assistance in the processes of problem-solving or skill acquisition unless the learner is able to recognise a solution to a particular class of problems before he is himself able to produce the steps leading to it without assistance, i.e. comprehension of the solution must precede production (Woods *et al.*, 1976).

Woods *et al.* wanted to examine a 'natural' tutorial in the hope of gaining knowledge about natural as well as automated teaching tasks.

The main aim of this study was therefore to examine some of the major implications of the interactive, instructional relationship between the developing child and his elders for the study of skill acquisition and problem solving. The changing interaction of tutor and children provided the data for this study.

Research method

This was a controlled observation in which participants were observed as they tried to complete a predetermined building task with appropriate intervention and guidance from a tutor. Participants were observed in individual sessions lasting from 20 minutes to one hour. The observed and recorded interactions between the tutor and the child as the task was attempted provided the data.

Outline of the procedure/study

The sample consisted of 30 children (accompanied by their parents) who lived within a five-mile radius of Cambridge, Massachusetts, i.e. within easy reach of Harvard University where the research was conducted. Their parents had replied to advertisements for 'subject volunteers'. The children, who were from predominantly middle-class or lower

> **Exam tip**
>
> Know the research method.

> **Now test yourself**
>
> 26 Outline the main aim of this study.
> 27 Describe the research method used in this study.
>
> TESTED ☐

middle-class families, were equally divided into three, four and five year olds, with each age group being equally divided between girls and boys, i.e. there were 10 × three year olds, 10 × four year olds and 10 × five year olds, with five girls and five boys in each group.

The task

The toy designed for the task consisted of 21 blocks that combined to form a pyramid standing about nine inches high with a nine inch square base. The pyramid had six levels, with the top block being a solid square with a circular depression in its bottom. Each remaining layer was composed of four equal-sized blocks made up of two locking pairs. Each pair fitted together with a hole and peg arrangement. When one pair was fitted in the correct orientation, two other half pegs were brought together, the other pair bringing together two half-holes. These formed the means for connecting the two pairs to form the four-piece layer. The blocks were designed so that all pegs would fit into all holes. In addition to pegs and holes, each four-block layer had a shallow round depression in its base and a matched elevation on top. These could be formed only by putting the appropriate pairs together in the correct orientation, since each block possessed one quarter of each of the larger connectives.

The tutoring procedure

The tutor's procedure was agreed upon in advance. The tutor (a woman) endeavoured to gear her behaviour to the needs of each individual child while following as closely as possible a standardised procedure to maintain reasonable comparability between each child and age group.

The aim was to allow each child to do as much as possible for themselves. The tutor always tried to instruct verbally before intervening more directly, the latter being done only when the child failed to follow verbal instructions. The child's success or failure at any point in time thus determined the tutor's next level of instruction.

When the child entered the experimental room they were seated at a small table with the 21 blocks of various shapes and sizes spread out in a jumble. The child was invited to play with the blocks. The child could have no idea what the blocks might look like when put together.

The child was left to their own devices for about five minutes so that they could become familiar with both the blocks and the situation. The tutor would then usually take up two of the smallest blocks and show the child how they could be joined together to make a connected pair. If the child had already discovered how to do this during the free-play time, the tutor would use it as an example and ask the child to 'make some more like that one'.

The tutor then recognised and responded systematically to three types of response from the child:
1 **If the child ignored her and continued with his play:** the tutor would again present suitable and constrained material already assembled, perhaps simply joining and positioning two blocks to form a correct pair.
2 **If the child took up the blocks which the tutor had just assembled and manipulated them and then tried to assemble pieces for himself but overlooked a key feature:** the tutor would

verbally draw the child's attention to the fact that the construction was not completed – for example, if they had selected pieces themselves and put them together wrongly, the tutor would ask the child to compare their construction with hers and to make theirs similar.

3 **If the child tried to make something with blocks presented for construction by the tutor in a way more or less similar to her own method, for instance by putting pegs into holes:** the tutor would correct any errors that resulted.

Where possible, the child was left to their own devices so that they could pace the task for themselves as far as possible. The tutor intervened only if the child stopped constructing or got into difficulty. The tutor brought to the task a gentle, appreciative approach to the children.

System of scoring

a) The child was scored as either manipulating separate pieces which they were seeking to assemble or as assembling pieces previously made up.

b) The assembly operations were further subdivided into two categories:
   i) assisted, in which the tutor either presented or specifically indicated the materials for assembly
   ii) unassisted, where the child themselves selected material.
   In both cases, the constructions created might or might not meet all task constraints.

c) When the constructions did not meet the task constraints, i.e. were mismatched, the researchers (observers) noted whether the child rejected them or simply laid them down as assembled (wrongly).

d) When the child picked up and disassembled previous constructions, it was noted whether or not they went on to reassemble them again.

Every intervention by the tutor was noted. These were classified into one of three categories:

1 Direct assistance (in which the tutor either presented or specifically indicated the materials for assembly).

2 A verbal error prompt (which characteristically took the form, 'Does this (a mismatched construction) look like this one (a matched one)?').

3 A straightforward verbal attempt to get the child to make more constructions, for example: 'Can you make more like this?'

In each case, the child's subsequent behaviours were scored into the categories identified in a) to d) above. Two scorers, working independently, achieved 94 per cent agreement on a pool of 594 events scored directly from video tape.

> **Exam tip**
>
> Know the procedure in relation to the task, the tutoring procedure and the scoring system.

Key findings

The children enjoyed playing with the blocks during the initial five-minute free-play period but did not always enjoy giving up their imaginative play for the more constrained task of building a pyramid. Imaginative free play was often followed by a rather uninspired performance of the presented task.

Observations on tutorials

The total number of acts (whenever a child picked up blocks and put them together or when they selected previous constructions and took them

> **Now test yourself**
>
> 28 Identify the three types of response from the child to which the tutor responded.
>
> TESTED ☐

> **Now test yourself**
>
> 29 Identify the three categories of assistance noted by the tutor.
>
> TESTED ☐

apart) was roughly similar for all ages: median for the three year olds = 39, for the four year olds = 41 and for the five year olds = 32. The difference between the four and five year olds was not significant. Therefore, in terms of overall task activity, there were no significant differences between the groups.

The composition of the activities differed markedly from age group to age group. Older children did better than younger children in the tasks producing a larger number of correct constructions in which they actually put self-made pieces of the puzzle together correctly themselves. The ratio of incorrect to correct solutions progressed from 9 : 0 (three year olds) to 2 : 8 (four year olds) to 1 : 2 (five year olds). It took 15 acts of pair construction to make a correct pyramid. More than 75 per cent of those acts were unassisted among the five year olds compared with 50 per cent and 10 per cent among the four year olds and three year olds respectively.

None of the three year olds could put four blocks together correctly, while all the four and five year olds did so at least once.

Older children frequently picked up matching pieces for construction with no prior 'trial and error': a median of seven such 'quick' constructions being made by each five year old compared with three per four year old and less than one per three year old.

The youngest children took apart almost as many constructions as they put together: median for three year olds = 13.0. Older children were less likely to 'deconstruct' their assemblies: median for four year olds = 5.0, for five year olds = 4.0.

When a three year old took up and disassembled a correct construction he put it back together again on average two-thirds of the time (without the tutor's intervention). In contrast, having picked up an incorrect construction, he would restore it only 14 per cent of the time. The five year olds reconstructed nine out of ten correct constructions they had disassembled and only two in ten of the incorrect ones they had disassembled. The difference was not very great between them and the younger groups, however.

Three year olds were just as sensitive as four year olds to the difference between acceptable and unacceptable constructions. The two were equally likely to reassemble appropriate constructions and to leave scattered those that had previously been inappropriately constructed.

The tutorial relationship

The younger children needed the greatest amount of help. For three year olds the proportion of totally unassisted constructions was 64.5 per cent, for the four year olds 79.3 per cent and for the five year olds 87.5 per cent.

The median instances per child for constructions carried out with pieces offered by the tutor as compared with self-selected pieces was 9.0 for the three year olds, 6.5 for the four year olds and 3.0 for the five year olds.

Three year olds usually ignored the tutor's suggestions, paying little heed, particularly to her verbal comments. This is illustrated by the disparity between the median figure of 112 tutor rejections by the three year olds in contrast to virtually none by the older children.

Now test yourself

30 Outline two ways in which age influenced the children's behaviour.

TESTED

The tutor intervened directly twice as often with the three year olds as with the four year olds and four times more often than with the eldest group. These figures are shown in Table 18.2.

Table 18.2 **Median instances of direct interventions, verbal corrections and general verbal directions (reminding subjects of task requirements)**

	Age		
	3	**4**	**5**
Direct intervention (showing)	12.0	6.0	3.0
Verbal correction (telling)	3.0	5.0	3.5
Verbal direction and reminder (telling)	5.0	8.0	3.0
Total verbal intervention	8.0	13.0	7.5
Total help received	20.0	19.0	10.5
Ratio: $\dfrac{\text{show}}{\text{tell}}$	$\dfrac{12.0}{8.0}$ $= 1.5$	$\dfrac{6.0}{13.0}$ $= 0.46$	$\dfrac{3.0}{7.5}$ $= 0.40$

Total help received

The five year olds received significantly less help than both the four year olds and the three year olds. The three and four year olds did not differ significantly.

Both the five year olds and the four year olds received a significantly higher proportion of verbal assistance than the three year olds; four and five year olds did not differ in this respect (figures shown in Table 18.2).

The predominant mode of interaction between the tutor and the four-year-old tutee has become verbal and the principal form of that verbal interaction is a combination of reminding the child of the task requirements and correcting their efforts as they seek to carry on.

The number of direct interventions drops by half from the three year olds to the four year olds and drops again by half with the five year olds. The balance shifts from showing to telling as the age increases from three to four years (see Table 18.3).

Table 18.3 **Relative successes of each age group with 'showing' and 'telling'**

	Age		
	3	**4**	**5**
Success rates of showing interventions	40%	63%	80%
Success rates of telling interventions	18%	40%	57%

The number of acts the child could sustain between tutorial interventions rose steadily with age and experience, as shown in Table 18.4.

Table 18.4 **Relative frequency of interventions by the tutor expressed as interventions per number of construction operations (both assisted and unassisted) performance by each child**

	Age		
	3	**4**	**5**
Total construction operations	262	352	280
Total interventions	201	198	112
Operations per intervention	1.3	1.8	2.5

Now test yourself

31 From Table 18.2, outline the findings in relation to the median total amount of help received by the children in the different age groups.

TESTED ☐

Now test yourself

32 From Table 18.3, identify the percentage success rate when showing the four-year-old children what to do.

TESTED ☐

The five year olds performed significantly more operations per intervention than the four year olds (U = 12, $p < 0.02$) who performed more than the three olds (U = 10, $p < 0.002$).

Analysis of tutoring

In 478 opportunities the tutor conformed to the pre-set rules/procedure 86 per cent of the time. She did so most frequently with the youngest children (92 per cent) and less frequently with the four year olds (86 per cent). With the five year olds her behaviour fell midway (86 per cent), though the difference between this group and the others was not statistically different.

The majority of her 'errors' with the four year olds was due to a tendency to offer more help than was allowed by the rules. The fact that she committed most violations with the middle age group suggests that a tutor is faced with a great deal of relatively unstructured behaviour from a child who initiates most of the task activity themselves. These are the ones most difficult to accommodate within a fixed set of tutorial rules. Though she often had difficulty getting the three year olds to engage and stay focused on the task, the tutor was seldom left in doubt as to what the child had done in response to her instructions, and when tutoring the five year olds she found the child soon learned the task constraints and conducted their efforts in an appropriate serial order, making it easy for her to follow the set procedure.

The 'scaffolding' process

The functions of the tutor were seen to include:
● recruitment
● reduction in degrees of freedom
● direction maintenance
● marking critical features
● frustration control
● demonstration.

Conclusions

Increasing age is marked by success (in problem-solving abilities) and by the emergence of more complex, interlocking sequences of operations (demonstrating increased problem-solving capability).

Increasing age is marked by the development of more accurate, intuitive techniques of fitting blocks together (development of more advanced problem-solving capability).

Young children (aged three years) are just as adept as four year olds at recognising an appropriate construction (i.e. they can recognise when a problem has been solved correctly). Comprehension precedes production in problem-solving – for example, a three year old can recognise what is appropriate before they can produce a sequence of operations to achieve it.

Older children are more prepared to accept and act on advice from tutors than younger children are. A tutor both intervenes more and is ignored more when working with three year olds than with either four or five-year-old children.

A tutor acts as a prodder and corrector for four year olds but is principally a confirmer or checker of instructions when interacting with five year olds.

> **Exam tips**
>
> Know the key findings in relation to the performance of the children, the tutorial relationship and the scaffolding process.
>
> Be able to draw conclusions from the findings.

> **Now test yourself**
>
> 33 Outline the 'direction maintenance' and 'frustration control' aspects of the scaffolding process.
>
> TESTED ☐

Formal programmes of 'individualised' teaching may be most difficult to realise at the most crucial point – the mid-phase of learning.

In tutoring, effectiveness depends upon the tutor and tutee modifying their behaviour over time to fit the perceived requirements and/or suggestions of the other.

The effective tutor must have at least two theoretical models to which they must attend. One is the theory of the task or problem and how it may be completed, the other a theory of the performance characteristics of the tutee. The actual pattern of effective instruction is therefore both task and tutee dependent, the requirements of the tutorial being generated by the interaction of the tutor's two theories.

The tutor operates with an implicit theory of the learner's acts in order to recruit their attention, reduce degrees of freedom in the task to manageable limits, maintain 'direction' in the problem-solving process, mark critical features, control frustration and demonstrate solutions when the learner can recognise them.

> **Now test yourself**
>
> 34 Draw one conclusion from the findings of this study.
>
> TESTED ☐

Exam tips

Know how the study relates to the component 'Child psychology'.

Know how the study relates to the topic 'Cognitive development and education (cognitive)'.

Know how the study relates to the cognitive development of children and its impact on education.

Application

At least one cognitive strategy to improve revision or learning: examples include the use of mnemonics, such as acronyms, scaffolding, rehearsal, semantic processing and cognitive organisers such as mind maps.

> **Now test yourself**
>
> 35 What is an acronym?
> 36 Give an example of an acronym.
>
> TESTED ☐

Exam tips

The question is likely to be worded generically so focus on the specific cognitive strategy selected to improve revision or learning.

Be able to apply at least one cognitive strategy to improve revision or learning to a novel situation.

Development of attachment (Social)   REVISED ☐

The development of attachment in children: for example, the behavourist theory of attachment; the humanistic theory of attachment; Bowlby's theory of attachment, including the importance of the 'critical period'; Bowlby's four stages of attachment (pre-attachment, attachment in the making, clear-cut attachment, formation of reciprocal attachment); Ainsworth's four types of parent–infant attachment (secure, insecure avoidant, insecure resistant, insecure disorganised); Schaffer and Emerson's stages of attachment development (indiscriminate attachments, specific attachments, single attachment figure, multiple attachments); how individual differences in attachment type can be identified using the Strange Situation.

> **Now test yourself**
>
> 37 Describe what is meant by the term 'attachment'.
> 38 Describe what is meant by the 'critical period'.
>
> TESTED ☐

The impact of failure to develop attachments: for example, Bowlby's concept of an internal working model for attachment; Bowlby's maternal deprivation hypothesis; the short- and long-term effects of maternal deprivation; Bowlby's '44 juvenile thieves' research; Rutter's ideas about the consequences of privation and the difference between deprivation and privation; Robertson's three stages of separation behaviour (protesting, desperation, detachment).

Key research: Ainsworth and Bell (1970): Attachment, exploration and separation: illustrated by the behaviour of one year olds in a Strange Situation

Theory/theories on which the study is based

Infant–mother attachment has been conceived as related to separation anxiety (see Bowlby, 1960), fear of the strange and strangers (see Morgan and Ricciuti, 1969; Schaffer, 1966) and exploration (see Ainsworth, 1967; Ainsworth and Wittig, 1969). It is believed that the interrelationships between these behaviours throw light upon the biological function of infant–mother attachment.

Key concepts as proposed by Bowlby (1958, 1969) and Ainsworth (1964, 1967, 1969) are as follows:

a) An attachment may be defined as an affectional tie that one person or animal forms between themselves and another specific one – a tie that binds them together in space and endures over time. The behavioural hallmark of attachment is seeking to gain and to maintain a certain degree of proximity to the object of attachment, which ranges from close physical contact under some circumstances to inter-action or communication across some distance under other circumstances.

b) Attachment behaviours are those which promote proximity or contact. In the human infant these include active proximity- and contact-seeking behaviours such as approaching, following and clinging, and signalling behaviours such as smiling, crying and calling.

c) The very young infant displays attachment (proximity-promoting) behaviours such as crying, sucking, rooting and smiling, despite the fact that they are insufficiently discriminating to direct them differentially to a specific person. When these behaviours, supplemented by other active proximity-seeking behaviours which emerge later – presumably through a process of learning in the course of mother–infant interaction – become organised hierarchically and directed actively and specifically towards the mother, the infant may be described as having become attached to her.

d) The intensity of attachment behaviour may be heightened or diminished by situational conditions, but once an attachment has been formed, it cannot be viewed as vanishing during periods when attachment behaviour is not evident.

e) Viewed in the context of evolutionary theory, infant–mother attachment may be seen to fulfil significant biological functions, that is, functions that promote species survival. For the human species to have survived, the infant has required protection during their period of helplessness and defencelessness.

f) Exploratory behaviour is equally significant from an evolutionary point of view. The genetic biases in a species which can adapt to a wide range of environmental variations provide for a balance in infant behaviours (and in reciprocal maternal behaviours) between those which lead the infant away from the mother and promote exploration and acquisition of knowledge of the proper ties of the physical and social environment, and those which draw mother and infant together and promote the protection and nurturance that the mother can provide.

Background to the study

Up to the time of this study, only two Strange Situation studies had been guided by an ethological–evolutionary point of view. Harlow (1961) used a Strange Situation to demonstrate the security function of surrogate cloth mothers for infant rhesus macaques. Ainsworth and Wittig (1969) made a preliminary report of the attachment–exploration balance in human one year olds. Other studies, such as Rheingold (1969), focused on exploratory behaviour and reported that the presence of the mother supports it, but paid scant attention to attachment behaviour and its hierarchical manifestations in reunion episodes as well as during separation.

The purpose of this study was to highlight some distinctive features of the ethological–evolutionary concept of attachment by citing reports of the interactions between the infant's attachment behaviour and other behaviours, i.e. exploration, separation anxiety and fear of the strange; by illustrating these interactions through a report of the behaviour of one year olds in a strange situation; noting parallels between strange-situation behaviour and behaviour reported in other relevant observational, clinical and experimental contexts.

Now test yourself

39 Explain why Ainsworth and Bell decided to use the Strange Situation to test attachment-exploration.

TESTED ☐

Research method

This was a controlled observation in which participants were observed (from an adjoining room through a one-way mirror) as they participated in the Strange Situation. The observed and recorded interactions between the infant and its mother during the enactment of the Strange Situation provided the data.

Outline of the procedure/study

The participants were 56 family-reared infants of white, middle-class parents, who were originally contacted through paediatricians in private practice. Twenty-three of the infants, who had been observed longitudinally from birth onwards, were observed in the Strange Situation when they were 51 weeks old. Thirty-three of the infants were studied in the context of an independent project (Bell, in press at the time this study was published) and were observed when 49 weeks old.

The mothers of the 56 children also participated by enacting the standardised procedure pertaining to the Strange Situation.

Exam tip

Know the research method and sample.

The procedure

The Strange Situation was comprised of eight episodes which followed in a standard order for all participants. The situation was designed to be novel enough to elicit exploratory behaviour, yet not so strange that it would evoke fear and heighten attachment behaviour at the outset. The approach of the stranger was gradual, so that any fear of her could be attributed to unfamiliarity rather than abrupt, alarming behaviour. The episodes were arranged so that the less disturbing ones came first. Finally, the situation as a whole was intended to be no more disturbing than those an infant was likely to encounter in their ordinary life experience.

A room was arranged so that there was a nine by nine foot square of clear floor space, marked off into 16 squares to facilitate recording of location and locomotion. At one end of the room was a child's chair heaped with and surrounded by toys. Near the other end of the room on one side was a chair for the mother and on the opposite side, near the door, a chair for the stranger. The baby was put down in the middle of the base of the triangle formed by the three chairs and left free to move where they wished. Both the mother and the female stranger were instructed in advance as to the roles they were to play.

The Strange Situation was composed of eight discrete episodes:
- **Episode 1 (M, B, O):** mother (M), accompanied by an observer (O), carried the baby (B) into the room, and then O left.
- **Episode 2 (M, B):** M put B down in the specified place, then sat quietly in her chair, participating only if B sought her attention. Duration: three minutes.
- **Episode 3 (S, M, B):** A stranger (S) entered, sat quietly for one minute, conversed with M for one minute, then gradually approached B, showing him a toy. At the end of the third minute M left the room unobtrusively.
- **Episode 4 (S, B):** if B was happily engaged in play, S was non-participant. If he was inactive, she tried to interest him in the toys. If he was distressed, she tried to distract him or to comfort him. If he could not be comforted, the episode was curtailed; otherwise it lasted three minutes.
- **Episode 5 (M, B):** M entered, paused in the doorway to give B an opportunity to mobilise a spontaneous response to her. S then left unobtrusively. What M did next was not specified – except that she was told that after B was again settled in play with the toys she was to leave again, after pausing to say 'bye bye'. Duration of episode: undetermined.
- **Episode 6 (B alone):** B was left alone for three minutes, unless he was so distressed that the episode had to be curtailed.
- **Episode 7 (S, B):** S entered and behaved as in episode 4 for three minutes, unless distress prompted curtailment. (Ainsworth and Wittig (1969) planned a somewhat different procedure for episode 7, which was attempted for the first 14 Ss but, as it turned out, approximated the simpler procedure reported here, which was used for the remaining Ss.)
- **Episode 8 (M, B):** M returned, S left and after the reunion had been observed, the situation was terminated.

The behaviour of the participants (infants) was observed from an adjoining room through a one-way vision window. Two observers dictated continuous narrative accounts into a dual-channel tape recorder, which also picked up the click of a timer every 15 seconds. (This represents the procedure now considered standard. For the first 14 participants, however, the dual-channel recorder was not available, so one observer dictated while the other made written notes. For the second 33 participants, the author, Bell, was the sole observer.) The protocols were subsequently transcribed and consolidated, then coded.

Reliability of observation was checked by separate codings of the dictated reports made by the two authors in four cases observed by both. Product-moment coefficients of 0.99 were found for each of locomotor, manipulatory and visual exploration, and one of 0.98 for crying.

The narrative record yielded two types of measure. A frequency measure was used for three forms of exploratory behaviour – locomotor, manipulatory and visual – and for crying. A score of one was given for each 15-second interval in which the behaviour occurred. The maximum

Answers at www.hoddereducation.co.uk/myrevisionnotes

was 12 for an episode, since the standard length of an episode was three minutes. Frequency measures were obtained for episodes 2 to 7. The second measure was based upon detailed coding of behaviours in which the contingencies of the mother's or the stranger's behaviour had to be taken into consideration. The codings were then ordered into seven-point scales on the assumption that not only could the same behaviour be manifested in different degrees of intensity but different behaviours could serve the same end under different intensities of activation. There were five classes of behaviour thus scored:

1 Proximity- and contact-seeking behaviours include active, effective behaviours such as approaching and clambering up, active gestures such as reaching or leaning, intention movements such as partial approaches, and vocal signals including 'directed' cries.

2 Contact-maintaining behaviours pertain to the situation after the baby has gained contact, either through his own initiative or otherwise. They include clinging, embracing, clutching and holding on; resisting release by intensified clinging or, if contact is lost, by turning back and reaching, or clambering back up; and protesting release vocally.

3 Proximity- and interaction-avoiding behaviours pertain to a situation which ordinarily elicits approach, greeting, or at least watching or interaction across a distance, as when an adult entered, or tried to engage the baby's attention. Such behaviours include ignoring the adult, pointedly avoiding looking at her, looking away, turning away or moving away.

4 Contact- and interaction-resisting behaviours include angry, ambivalent attempts to push away, hit or kick the adult who seeks to make contact, squirming to get down having been picked up, or throwing away or pushing away the toys through which the adult attempts to mediate her interventions. More diffuse manifestations are angry screaming, throwing self about, throwing self down, kicking the floor, pouting, cranky fussing or petulance.

These four classes of behaviour were scored for interaction with the mother in episodes 2, 3, 5 and 8, and for interaction with the stranger in episodes 3, 4 and 7.

5 Search behaviour was scored for the separation episodes 4, 6 and 7. These behaviours included following the mother to the door, trying to open the door, banging on the door, remaining oriented to the door or glancing at it, going to the mother's empty chair or simply looking at it. Such behaviours implied that the infant was searching for the absent mother either actively or by orienting to the last place in which she was seen (the door in most cases) or to the place associated with her in the Strange Situation (her chair).

The score was influenced by the following features: the strength of the behaviour, its frequency, duration and latency, and by the type of behaviour itself – with active behaviour being considered stronger than signalling.

Key findings

Overall, the infants of the present sample showed little alarm in the pre-separation episodes of the Strange Situation. Their attachment behaviour was not activated; they tended not to cling to the mother or even to approach her. They used her as a secure base from which to explore the Strange Situation.

Exam tip

Know the procedure, the scoring system and the classes of behaviour scored.

Now test yourself

40 Outline the eight episodes of the Strange Situation.
41 Identify the five classes of behaviour scored.

TESTED

There was a sharp decline in all forms of exploratory behaviour from episode 2 when the baby was alone with his mother to episode 3 when the stranger was present also. Exploration remained depressed throughout episode 4 when the baby was left with the stranger.

Visual and manipulatory exploration recovered significantly in episode 5, aided by the mother's attempts to interest the baby in play again, although similar efforts by the stranger in episodes 4 and 7 were ineffective. Visual and manipulatory exploration declined again in episode 6 after the mother departed for a second time, leaving the baby alone.

All forms of exploratory behaviour declined to their lowest point in episode 7 after the stranger had returned but while the mother was still absent.

To supplement the visual exploration score, which measured visual orientation to the physical environment, visual orientation to the mother and to the stranger were also coded. The only noteworthy findings were:

- In episode 2, the baby looked at the toys and other aspects of the physical environment much more frequently than at the mother, at whom he glanced only now and then, keeping visual tabs on her.
- In episode 3, the stranger, the most novel feature of the environment, was looked at more than the toys and the mother was looked at no more frequently than before.

Crying

Findings suggested that the Strange Situation does not in itself cause alarm or distress as crying was minimal in episode 2. Crying did not increase significantly in episode 3, which suggested that the stranger was not in herself alarming for most participants, at least not when the mother was also present. The incidence of crying rose in episode 4 with the mother's first departure, but declined upon her return in episode 5. It then increased sharply in episode 6 when the mother departed a second time, leaving the baby alone. It did not decrease significantly when the stranger returned in episode 7, which suggested that it was the mother's absence rather than mere aloneness that was distressing to most of the babies, and that the greater incidence of crying in episode 6 than in episode 4 was largely due to a cumulative effect.

Search behaviour during separation

The mean strength of search behaviour was moderate in episode 4, significantly stronger in episode 6 and moderate again in episode 7. Some infants (37 per cent) cried minimally if at all in episode 6, yet searched strongly. Some (20 per cent) cried desperately but searched weakly or not at all. Some (32 per cent) both cried and searched. All but four participants reacted to being left alone with either one or other of these attachment behaviours.

Proximity-seeking and contact-maintaining behaviours

Efforts to regain contact, proximity or interaction with the mother occurred only weakly in episodes 2 and 3 but were greatly intensified by brief separation experiences. Contact-maintaining behaviour was negligible in episodes 2 and 3, but rose in the first reunion episode (5), and rose even more sharply in the second reunion episode (8). In the case of both classes of behaviour the increase from episodes 2 through 5 to 8 was highly significant. Some participants showed these behaviours in relation to the stranger as well. Some infants were picked up by the stranger in episodes 4 and 7 – in an attempt to comfort them – and some of these did cling to her and/or resist being put down again. However, proximity-seeking and contact-maintaining behaviours were displayed much less frequently and less strongly to the stranger than to the mother.

Contact-resisting and proximity-avoiding behaviours

Contact-resisting behaviour directed towards the mother occurred rarely in the pre-separation episodes because the mother had been instructed not to intervene except in response to the baby's demands, In the reunion episodes, some participants resisted contact with the mother, but many did not. About one third of the sample avoided the stranger at some time in episode 3 – ignoring her, avoiding meeting her eyes or moving further away from her. The incidence of those behaviours declined in episode 4, and even in episode 7 remained less than in episode 3. About half the sample avoided neither mother nor stranger, but those who showed this behaviour in any strength to one did not show it to the other.

Conclusions

One of the conditions which facilitates approach and exploration of a novel or unfamiliar situation is the presence, in reasonable but not necessarily close proximity, of an infant's mother – the object of attachment. The presence of the mother (or attachment figure) can tip the balance in favour of exploring the novel or unfamiliar situation rather than avoiding it or withdrawing from it. Absence of the mother (or attachment figure) tends to heighten attachment behaviour and lessens exploration of a novel or unfamiliar situation.

Based on the findings of this and other studies, including naturalistic studies of mother–infant interaction, and studies of mother–child separation and reunion in both human and non-human primates, Ainsworth and Bell made the following propositions for a comprehensive concept of attachment:

1 Attachment does not correspond exactly with attachment behaviour. Attachment behaviour may be heightened or diminished by conditions – environmental and intra-organismic – which may be specified empirically.
2 Attachment behaviour is heightened in situations perceived as threatening, whether it is an external danger or an actual or impending separation from the attachment object that constitutes the threat.
3 When strongly activated, attachment behaviour is incompatible with exploratory behaviour. Yet the state of being attached, together with the presence of the attachment object, may support and facilitate exploratory behaviours. Provided that there is no threat of separation, the infant is likely to be able to use his mother as a secure base from which to explore, manifesting no alarm in even a strange situation as long as she is present.
4 Although attachment behaviour may diminish or even disappear in the course of a prolonged absence from the object of attachment, the attachment is not necessarily diminished; attachment behaviour is likely to re-emerge in full or heightened strength upon reunion, with or without delay.
5 The incidence of ambivalent (contact-resisting) and probably defensive (proximity-avoiding) patterns of behaviour in the reunion episodes of the Strange Situation is a reflection of the fact that attachment relations are qualitatively different from one attached pair to another, i.e. there are individual differences in the quality of attachment.

Exam tip

Know the key findings and be able to draw conclusions from the findings.

Now test yourself

42 Outline how the babies in this study behaved in the pre-separation episodes of the Strange Situation.
43 Outline the findings in relation to 'search behaviour during separation'.

TESTED

Exam tips

Know how the study relates to the component 'Child psychology'.

Know how the study relates to the topic 'Development of attachment (social)'.

Know how the study relates to the development of attachment in babies.

Now test yourself

44 Outline two of Ainsworth and Bell's propositions for a comprehensive concept of attachment.

TESTED

Application

At least one strategy to develop an attachment-friendly environment: for example, improving children's experiences of hospitalisation through attachment and family-centred care, the use of a 'key person approach' to enhance a baby's experience in day/nursery care.

Exam tips

The question is likely to be worded generically so focus on the specific strategy selected to develop an attachment-friendly environment.

Be able to apply at least one strategy to develop an attachment-friendly environment to a novel situation.

Now test yourself

45 Describe one strategy to develop an attachment-friendly environment.

TESTED

Impact of advertising on children (Social)

REVISED

The influence of television on children: for example, the recognition that children are consumers and can therefore be considered an acceptable target audience for products such as toys, holidays, food and beverages; the influence of role models such as celebrities, sports stars, pop stars used in television adverts on children's subsequent behaviour; the key features of television that seem to encourage imitative behaviour in children (easy to copy, similar to other acceptable behaviours, wicked or forbidden, appealing to a child, simple scenarios, humorous, people 'getting away with it', role models, shown at appropriate times for age group, high production values – music, colour, action).

Exam tips

Be able to describe how television advertising can influence children.

Be able to describe how stereotyping can be reinforced through television advertising aimed at children.

Stereotyping in advertising aimed at children: for example, ways in which television advertising promotes gender-stereotypical behaviour – girls nurturing and passive, boys action-oriented and powerful – which, in turn, helps to perpetuate stereotypical views of gender.

Now test yourself

46 Describe the term 'stereotype'.
47 Outline a stereotypical view of boys.

TESTED

Key research: Johnson and Young (2002): Gendered voices in children's advertising

Theory/theories on which the study is based

Advertising – on television, billboards, public transport, the internet, in newspapers, magazines and cinemas – invades the consciousness of almost everyone. Sponsors pay large amounts to place adverts in locations where the largest segment of the target audience is likely to see and hear them, and they rely on new, creative approaches both to instil and to fuel the desire for more and more consumption.

The vast array of ever-interesting adverts can, however, simultaneously be short blasts of new representational forms and depictions of dominant ideology, especially in their representations of identity possibilities. Since the middle of the twentieth century, adverts have been increasingly targeted to special audiences, each of which is a 'segment' for potential profitability through consumption. Children are one of those special audiences.

Along with being cultivated as consumers, children are also the targets of what Jhally (1995) terms 'image-based influence'. One main type of image-based influence targets gender identity and uses it to link products to their consumers.

Television as a cultural resource for children

Adverts for children serve as training for consumer culture; hence, their role in enculturation and socialisation should not be underestimated (Alexander and Morrison, 1995). Through adverts, children learn that products for sale offer lifestyle enhancements, fun, peer group status and up-to-date coolness, i.e. children's viewing of adverts prepares them well for their roles as capitalist consumers.

Advertisers target children by appealing to their distinctiveness from adults and their power as 'sovereign, playful, thinking consumers' (Kapur, 1999). For today's children, advertisements are formative in their cultural environment more intensely and pervasively than ever before. Adverts offer children models for how to act, interact and speak (refer back to the core study by Bandura *et al.*). Children extrapolate commercials' content into other situations and play venues.

Some of the models used in commercials for children map onto the significant foci of dominant ideology – gender, race, ethnicity, class. Adverts are therefore part of each child's learning about gender.

Gender codes in children's advertising

Past research on television commercials directed at children has shown that conventional sex roles underlie the content of many adverts. For example, Thompson and Zerbinos (1995) in their study of 175 episodes from 41 different cartoon programmes found both that male leads significantly outnumbered female leads (99 per cent to 55 per cent) and that male and female characters portrayed gender-stereotypical roles.

Research by Welch *et al.* (1979) found that girls in adverts talked less than boys if the advert targeted both genders but talked a lot more in commercials targeted at just girls.

Television advertisements as a cultural environment

It has long been established that television contributes to the cultural environment of children. 'Young children get exposed to many ideas about social life for specifically child-oriented programming and advertising' (Kline, 1993).

Commercials comprise an alarming amount of viewing time. Research conducted on more than 10,000 adverts taken from seven television programme sources in early 1990 in the USA (Kunkel and Gantz, 1992) showed a range of 10:24 minutes (Nickelodeon) to 13:26 advertising per hour of children's programming. The 1990 Children's Television Act (USA) regulated the amount of air-time that can be devoted to commercials: 12 minutes per hour on weekdays and 10.5 minutes per hour on weekends. Most adverts run for 30 seconds, with a few 15-second spots appearing also. This equates to 24 adverts per hour on weekdays and 21 per hour on weekend days.

Now test yourself

48 Outline how television serves to reinforce gender stereotypes.

TESTED

Background to the study

Research (for example, Jhally, 1995) has shown that television commercials directed at children use gender images as a source of meaning (see Figure 18.3). Those gender images display appearances and activities linked with gender. Based on their examination of child-focused TV commercials, Johnson and Young suggest that they also present an array of linguistic markers that bolster the more visually obvious gender representations, some of which can be heard easily while others are more subtle.

Children play with a vast array of toys and eat trendy foods and snacks, many of which are introduced to them through advertising. This non-adult market was the focus of this study. The aim of this study was to provide a critical examination of discourse in television commercials made for and marketed to children in order to determine the degree to which the language codes that are used call upon gender as a meaningful cultural category for selling.

Research method

This was a content analysis, a research method in which observations of human behaviour are often made indirectly by looking at the content of communications produced by those involved. Johnson and Young coded filmed material shown in television adverts relating to boys' and girls' toys in an attempt to address two research questions:

1 Do advertisers script language differently for males and females in adverts directed at pre-school and early elementary school boys and girls?
2 How is gender used as a discourse code to link products to gender roles?

Outline of the procedure/study

As this was a content analysis study, there were no direct participants per se. Samples of children's television programmes in the cartoon genre were video recorded from commercial networks, regional independent New England stations and Nickelodeon in the fall (autumn) of 1996 and 1997 and again in the fall of 1999.

Three different programme sources, accessible to all television viewers, were used to ensure that the sample included advertisements from a broad range of cartoon programmes. The 1999 sample was added to the original two-year sample so any differences that might have occurred in the gender targeting of commercials could be checked.

Fifteen half-hour programmes were taped for fall 1996 and fall 1997, and 24 half-hour programmes were taped in the fall of 1999 (actual time for each programme was approximately 27 minutes because of commercial and station content between programmes). The total number of commercials included within the time boundaries marking the beginning and ending of the programmes, exclusive of network and station promotions, was 478 (149 for the 1996 programmes, 133 for the 1997 programmes, 196 for the 1999 programmes). The range of commercials per programme was 8.2 to 8.9 (commercials aired between programmes were not included in the analysis).

To learn more about the broad themes and more specific discourse style relevant to what children might be learning about gender from televised

Figure 18.3 A toy that is aimed at a particular gender

Now test yourself

49 Outline the aim of this study.
50 Identify the research method used in this study.

TESTED

commercials, adverts broadcast on different types of television channels were collected for analysis. Emphasis was placed on elements of the gendered voice, specifically on four aspects:

1 Voice-overs.
2 Verb elements.
3 Speaking lines given to girls and boys.
4 The conspicuous use of the word power in a number of adverts oriented to boys.

The adverts were classified in one of five product categories:

1 Food items, mainly breakfast cereals, snacks and drinks.
2 Toys.
3 Educational and public service announcements, for example anti-drug messages.
4 Recreational facilities or locales, such as Water Country, Chuck E. Cheese's and fast-food restaurants such as McDonald's.
5 Video and movie promotions.

The commercials for toys were selected as the focus for analysis. Of the 188 such adverts broadcast during the sample period, there were 147 different adverts (i.e. 22 per cent were repeats). The toy adverts were transcribed by their gender target audience using three categories:

1 Adverts targeted to boys in which boys were depicted.
2 Adverts targeted to girls in which girls were depicted.
3 Adverts targeted to both boys and girls either because both genders were featured or because there was no gender content.

NB: the coding was guided by the gender of the children portrayed rather than by the nature of the toy itself, and adverts explicitly oriented to one gender rather than the other were coded as such even if a child of the other gender could be seen either in the background or for a few seconds. Nine of the adverts (4.8 per cent) in which girls could be seen were classified as 'boy oriented' because the girls were either completely in the background or were hard to detect without replaying the adverts.

Two attributes were considered to determine the particular patterns in gendered aspects of voice-overs in adverts:

● the gender of the voice-over
● whether the voice-over was gender-exaggerated. (Male voice exaggeration was typified by masculine, aggressive voice qualities and for girls by feminine, high-pitched and/or sing-song voice qualities.)

Five categories were established to distinguish particular types of verb elements that might be relevant for gender imaging:

1 Action verb elements, e.g. crawl, fly, jump, race, ram, throw.
2 Competition/destruction verb elements, e.g. crush, fire on, knocked out, pounce, slam, stomp.
3 Agency/control verb elements, e.g. control, defeat, rule, take.
4 Limited activity verb elements, e.g. beware, get, go, know, look, talk, wait, watch.
5 Feeling and nurturing verb elements, e.g. cuddle, loves, taking care of, tuck you in.

Key findings

Results showed a greater proportion of toy adverts in 1996 and 1997 (42.3 per cent and 42.9 per cent respectively) compared with

Exam tip

Know the procedure for gathering and analysing the data.

Now test yourself

51 Describe why three different programme resources were used.
52 Identify the five categories into which the adverts were classified.
53 Identify the three categories into which the adverts were transcribed in relation to gender.
54 Identify the five categories used to distinguish particular verb elements that might have been relevant for gender imaging.

TESTED

34.7 per cent in the 1999 adverts. Commercials promoting toys made up 39.3 per cent of the sample. The distribution of commercials is shown in Table 18.5.

Table 18.5 Distribution of toy commercials

Category	Sample 1 – 1996	Sample 2 – 1997	Sample 3 – 1999	Combined
Food, drinks, snacks	47.7% (71)	41.4% (55)	45.9% (90)	45.2% (216)
Toys	42.3% (63)	42.9% (57)	34.7% (68)	39.3% (188)
Educational and public service	3.4% (5)	7.5% (10)	3.1% (6)	4.3% (21)
Recreation	2.7% (4)	2.3% (3)	6.1% (12)	4.0% (19)
Video and movie promotions	4.0% (6)	6.0% (8)	3.1% (6)	4.2% (20)
Other	NA	NA	7.1% (14)	2.9% (14)
Total	149	133	196	478

Overall, boy-oriented adverts exceeded girl-oriented adverts and there were relatively few adverts directed to both boys and girls, as shown in Table 18.6.

Now test yourself

From Table 18.5 identify:
55 The total number of toy commercials.
56 The total percentage of commercials that were categorised as 'recreation'.

TESTED ☐

Table 18.6 Gender orientation in toy commercials

Gender orientation	1996	1997	1999	Combined
Boy oriented	47.6% (30)	42.1% (24)	70.6% (48)	54.8% (103)
Girl oriented	30.2% (19)	49.1% (28)	23.5% (16)	33.0% (62)
Boy and girl	22.2% (14)	8.8% (5)	5.9% (4)	12.2% (23)
Total	$n = 63$	$n = 57$	$n = 68$	$n = 188$

Differences in gender orientation did appear for the three years sampled, however: for 1996, boy-oriented adverts outnumbered girl-oriented and boy/girl-oriented adverts; for 1997 the boy-oriented and girl-oriented adverts were similar in number but greater than boy/girl-oriented adverts; for 1999, boy-oriented adverts heavily dominated the sample.

All commercials were grouped together for the analysis of gender representations in language.

The names of many of the advertised toys vividly positioned verbal images of boys and girls in their cultural context. For example, 'Big Time Action Hero' and 'Tonka Magna Crew' stressed size as critical in male-oriented toys while 'Juice 'n Cookies Baby Alive' and 'Bedtime Bottle Baby' signified parenting as a female-linked quality. For further examples see Table 18.7, which gives sample toy names by gender orientation.

Now test yourself

57 Using Table 18.6, outline the overall difference between the boy: girl orientation of toy commercials.

TESTED ☐

Table 18.7 Sample toy names by gender orientation

Boy-oriented toys	Girl-oriented toys
Dragon Flyz	Take Care of Me Twins
Big Time Action Hero	Fluffy My Come Here Puppy
Electronic Karate Fighters	Juice 'n Cookies Baby Alive
Beast Wars Transformers	Girl Talk
Mars Attack Action Figures	Star Fairies
Total Justice Super Heroes	California Roller Girl
Super Man – The New Adventures Video Game	Clueless Fashion and Makeup Dear Diary
Tonka Magna Crew	Tea Bunnies
Play Doh Demolition Derby	Fashion Magic Fingernail Fun Salon Set
War Planets	Bedtime Bottle Baby
Super Soaker Extra Power Water Gun	Star Castles Light Up Gem Stone and
Anamorphs Transformers	Seashell Castles
Vortex Power Bat	Bowling Party Stacie
Super Sonic Power Crash Pit Racers	Friend Link
	Potty Dotty

In relation to the types of toys advertised: for boys, action figures such as Karate Fighters and Star Wars characters were most common (37 per cent of boy-oriented toys); for girls, the most common categories were 'posable figures', such as Barbie Dolls and animal figures (44 per cent of girl-oriented toys).

There was a distinct rise in the emphasis on hand-held electronic games by 1999: there were 16 such adverts in 1999 compared with just one in 1997 and none in 1996.

A male voice-over was heard in every one of the boy-oriented and boy/girl-oriented adverts. The vast majority (89 per cent) of the voice-overs in girl-oriented adverts contained female voices, though there were some with male voices. In all but 12 commercials, the voices heard were those of adults. In those a girl's voice was heard in eight girl-oriented adverts and a boy's voice in only one boy-oriented advert.

Exaggerated gender stylisation was prevalent in the voice-overs used in commercials for both boy-oriented and girl-oriented toys (80 per cent and 87 per cent respectively), though this was not common in adverts for boy/girl-oriented toys.

Table 18.8 shows frequency of verb element type by gender orientation of commercial. There were clear gender-linked patterns in the identified verb elements – for example, there was a large difference in feelings/nurturing verb elements between boy-oriented and girl-oriented adverts, and verb elements related to competition/destruction were heard frequently in boy-oriented adverts but rarely in girl-oriented adverts.

Now test yourself

58 Outline one difference in the focus of toy adverts in 1999 and 1996.

TESTED ☐

Table 18.8 Verb element type by gender orientation of toy commercial

Verb element type	Boy-oriented	Girl-oriented
Action	68	51
Competition/destruction	113	9
Agency and control	103	24
Limited activity	151	268
Feelings/nurturing	0	66

Of the 188 adverts, 41 per cent (78) included speaking in turns. More than half of the girl-oriented and boy/girl-oriented adverts contained speaking in turns (55 per cent and 53 per cent respectively) compared with the boy-oriented adverts where only 26 per cent included speaking lines.

In commercials where boys and girls appeared together there were many instances of scripted elements of gender relations – boys dominant, girls subservient; boys strong and powerful, girls weak, gossipy, powerless.

The use of the word 'power' in adverts oriented to boys was extremely conspicuous. One fifth (21 per cent) of the adverts for boy-oriented toys contained the words 'power' or 'powerful'. Of 45 power words, 28 were nouns, such as 'more power than before', 'pump up the power', and 'power' was used 17 times as an adjective, for example 'power pack', 'power base'. 'Power' was heard only once in girl-oriented toy adverts.

Conclusions

The sharply polarised gender models shown in television adverts, coupled with the verbal images created for boys and girls, recycle conventional gender ideology rather than minimising or challenging gender stereotyping.

The type of toys advertised for boys and girls reinforces traditionally polarised ideas about the play activities of boys and girls.

The use of voice-overs in television commercials generally matches the toy's targeted gender. Advertisers, when constructing voice-overs for TV toy commercials, strive to accentuate gender.

When watching television commercials, children are presented with verbal models that reinforce the language stereotype that girls (and women) engage in talk while boys (and men) prefer action to words.

Polarised patterns of language continue to be modelled in consumer advertisements directed at children.

Toy makers and their advertisers either make no effort to associate or may consciously avoid associating girl toys with power or their potential to transfer power to their users.

Application

At least one strategy to reduce the impact of advertising which is aimed at children: for example, educating parents/carers as to how they can limit/control the amount of television their children watch; developing 'media literacy' through such programmes as 'Media Smart' and 'Be AdWise'; encouraging television advertisers (possibly through the publication of further Ofcom guidelines) to both 'de-stereotype' adverts and reduce the features that have been found to encourage imitative behaviours in children.

Now test yourself

59 Use table 18.8 to outline the difference between the frequency of 'limited activity' verbs used in boy-oriented and girl-oriented adverts.

TESTED

Exam tip

Know the key findings of the study and be able to draw conclusions from them.

Exam tips

Know how the study relates to the component 'Child psychology'.

Know how the study relates to the topic 'Impact of advertising on children (Social)'.

Know how the study relates to the influence of television advertising on children and the stereotyping in such advertising.

Now test yourself

60 Draw one conclusion from the findings of this study.

TESTED

Exam tips

The question is likely to be worded generically so focus on the specific strategy selected to reduce the impact of advertising aimed at children.

Be able to apply at least one strategy to reduce the impact of advertising which is aimed at children to a novel situation.

Answers at www.hoddereducation.co.uk/myrevisionnotes

Practice questions

Child psychology

1 Outline how Barkley-Levenson and Galván's (2014) study shows how brain development may impact on risk-taking behaviour.   [10]
2 Discuss the issue of psychology as a science in relation to biological aspects of pre-adult brain development.   [15]
3 One in four 18 to 24 year olds (23 per cent) in the UK is involved in a car crash within two years of passing their driving tests (UK Department for Transport, 2014). Suggest a strategy the UK government could introduce to reduce risk taking which may lead to a reduction in traffic accidents involving young drivers.   [10]

ONLINE

Summary

By the end of this chapter you should:
- know and understand what is meant by intelligence, biological factors that could affect intelligence, Van Leeuwen *et al.*'s study and at least one method of assessing intelligence
- know and understand how brain development may impact on risk-taking behaviour, Barkley-Levenson and Galván's study, at least one strategy to reduce risk taking using knowledge of brain development
- know and understand how perceptual development can be studied in babies and animals, Gibson and Walk's study, at least one play strategy to develop perception in young children

- know and understand how cognitive development in children may impact on education, Wood *et al.*'s study, at least one cognitive strategy to improve revision or learning
- know and understand how attachment develops in babies and the impact of failure to develop attachments, Ainsworth and Bell's study, at least one strategy to develop an attachment-friendly environment
- know and understand how stereotyping in television advertising may influence children, Johnson and Young's study, at least one strategy to reduce the impact of advertising aimed at children.

What makes a criminal? (Biological)

Physiological explanations of criminal behaviour: for example, Lombroso's criminal characteristics; Sheldon's three criminal body types (endomorph, mesomorph, ectomorph); hereditary factors (genes) that may predispose individuals to the risk of criminal behaviour; low activity in the prefrontal cortex and the link to criminal behaviour, for example research by Adrian Raine; the role of twin and adoption studies.

Non-physiological explanations of criminal behaviour: for example, social explanations such as upbringing, parenting, poverty; learning explanations such as operant conditioning, social learning, Sutherland's differential association hypothesis; cognitive explanations such as moral development (for instance, Kohlberg).

Key research: Raine *et al.* (1997): Brain abnormalities in murderers indicated by positron emission tomography

Theory/theories on which the study is based

It has long been thought that damage to or dysfunction of the pre-frontal cortex of the brain may result in impulsivity, immaturity, altered emotionality, loss of self-control and the inability to modify behaviour. All of these may increase the likelihood of aggressive acts.

The **amygdala** is associated with aggressive behaviour and also the recognition of emotional stimuli such as a fearful expression on someone's face. Damage to the amygdala is associated with 'fearlessness'. The part of the limbic system made up of the amygdala, hippocampus and pre-frontal cortex governs the expression of emotion. Together with the thalamus, these areas are important in learning, memory and attention and it has been suggested that abnormal functioning may lead to problems such as not being able to form conditioned emotional responses and the failure to learn from experiences.

Background to the study

One particular group of violent offenders are those who plead not guilty by reason of insanity (NGRI) to a charge of murder. The hypothesis in this study is that these seriously violent individuals have localised brain damage in a variety of regions: the prefrontal cortex, angular gyrus, amygdala, hippocampus, thalamus and corpus callosum.

Raine *et al.* used **PET scans** (see Figure 19.1) to discover whether there are brain abnormalities in murderers who plead NGRI. If significant differences could be found between the patterns of glucose metabolism in the brains of such individuals compared with those of non-murderers, the correlation might indicate that murderers (pleading NGRI) are more prone to violence than non-murderers. Until this study, no previous brain imaging had been conducted to either support or refute this notion.

the **amygdala** is an almond-shaped set of neurones located deep in the brain's medial temporal lobe. It has been shown to play a key role in the processing of emotions. The amygdala forms part of the limbic system.

Figure 19.1 A PET scanner

a **PET (Positron Emission Tomography) scan** detects the metabolism level of injected substances (such as glucose) made mildly radioactive to show which parts of the brain are most active (using up energy) over a period of minutes.

In a preliminary report on a pilot sample of 22 NGRI offenders compared with 22 'normals', Raine *et al.* (1994) showed support for the idea of prefrontal dysfunction in NGRIs.

The aim of this study was therefore to build on previous research. Two hypotheses were tested:
1 Seriously violent individuals pleading NGRI have relatively localised brain dysfunction in the prefrontal cortex, angular gyrus, amygdala, hippocampus, thalamus and corpus callosum (areas of the brain previously linked empirically or conceptually to violence).
2 Seriously violent individuals pleading NGRI show no dysfunction in other brain areas, i.e. caudate, putamen, globus pallidus, midbrain, cerebellum, which have been implicated in other psychiatric conditions but have not been related to violence.

Research method

This was a natural (quasi) experiment because the IV – whether the participant was a murderer pleading NGRI or 'normal', non-murderer (taking no medication and with no history of psychiatric illness or current significant medical illness, with the exception of six schizophrenics who were selected as matches for six schizophrenic murderers) – was naturally occurring and so could not be manipulated or controlled by the researchers. The DV was whether the participant showed evidence of brain dysfunction in their prefrontal cortex and other areas such as the angular gyrus, amygdala, hippocampus, thalamus and corpus callosum which had previously been linked to violent behaviour.

The study used a matched participants design. Participants were matched on age and gender and the six schizophrenics in the experimental group were matched with six schizophrenic controls ('normal', non-murderers) who had not committed murder.

Outline of the procedure/study

The experimental group consisted of 41 participants (39 men and 2 women) tried in the state of California with a mean age of 34.3 years. They had been charged with either murder or manslaughter (referred to from here on as 'murderers') and had been sent to the University of California, Irvine (UCI) imaging centre for one of three reasons:
1 To obtain evidence as to whether they were NGRI.
2 To find out whether they were competent to understand the judicial process.
3 To see whether there was any evidence of diminished mental capacity which might affect the nature of the sentence they received.

They were referred for the following reasons:
● Six had schizophrenia.
● Twenty-three had head injuries or organic brain damage.
● Three had a history of psychoactive drug abuse.
● Two had affective disorders.
● Two had epilepsy.
● Three had a history of hyperactivity and learning disability.
● Two had personality disorders (passive-aggressive or paranoid personality disorder).

In seven of the above cases there were also unusual circumstances surrounding the crime that additionally led to the suspicion of some mental impairment.

Now test yourself

2 Describe how a PET scan works.

TESTED

Now test yourself

3 Identify three features by which the two groups of participants were matched.

TESTED

The control group of 41 participants (39 men, 2 women), none of whom had committed murder, were matched by age and gender and had a mean age of 31.7 years, which was considered not significantly different to the experimental group. The six schizophrenics in the experimental group were matched with six schizophrenic controls who had not committed murder. The rest of the control group were thoroughly screened and showed no history of psychiatric illness.

Subjects participated under protocols and consent forms approved by the Human Subjects Committee of UCI were completed.

Materials

- Thermoplastic head holder, individually modelled/moulded, to hold the participant's head still while being scanned.
- PET machine to image brain functioning.
- Fluorodeoxyglucose (FDG) tracer injected to trace brain metabolism.
- A degraded stimulus version of a continuous performance task (CPT) which required participants to detect target signals for 32 minutes, a task which had been shown to make the frontal lobes work especially hard, together with the right temporal and parietal lobes, so investigators could see how the different areas functioned.

Procedure

- All offenders were in custody and were kept medication free for the two weeks before brain scanning. No one in the control group was taking medication.
- Ten minutes before receiving the FDG injection, participants were given practice trials on the CPT.
- Thirty seconds before the FDG injection, participants started the actual CPT so that the initial novelty would not be FDG labelled and to get their brains 'working'.
- Thirty-two minutes after the FDG injection, the participant was transferred to an adjacent PET scanner room.
- The plastic head holder was used to hold the head still during the scan so that 10 slices (pictures) at 10 mm intervals could be obtained in relation to differences in brain metabolism in both six main cortical areas (the outside of the brain) and eight sub-cortical areas (inside the brain). This detail was precise so that the study could be replicated.

Key findings

Brain differences are shown in Table 19.1.

Table 19.1 Brain differences in murderers

	Brain structure	Murderers' metabolic activity level	Interpretation
Cortex	Prefrontal cortex	Lower activity than controls	Linked to loss of self-control and altered emotion
	Parietal cortex	Lower activity than controls, especially in the left angular gyrus ($p \leq .06$) and both left ($p \leq .02$) and right ($p \leq .05$) superior parietal gyri	Lower left angular gyrus activity linked to lower verbal ability, educational failure and thus crime
	Temporal cortex	No significant difference compared with controls ($p \geq .86$)	No difference was expected
	Occipital cortex	Higher activity than controls ($p \leq .02$) (unexpected)	May compensate on CPT for lower frontal activity

Answers at www.hoddereducation.co.uk/myrevisionnotes

	Brain structure	Murderers' metabolic activity level	Interpretation
Sub-cortex	Corpus callosum	Lower activity than controls	May stop left brain inhibiting the right's violence
	Amygdala	Lower activity in left than right side of the brain in murderers than in controls ($p \leq .02$)	These structures form part of the limbic system (thought to control emotional expression). Problems with these structures may cause a lack of inhibition for violent behaviour, fearlessness and a failure to learn the negative effects of violence
	Medial (inner) temporal, including hippocampus	Lower activity in left than right side of the brain in murderers than in controls ($p \leq .006$)	
	Thalamus	Murderers had lower left than right thalamic activity compared with controls ($p \leq .05$)	
	Cingulate, caudate, putamen, globus pallidus, midbrain and cerebellum	No significant differences were found in these structures between murderers and controls	No differences were expected in these structures (which are involved in other disorders), supporting the specificity of brain areas involved in violence

Table 19.2 shows overall findings.

Table 19.2 Overall findings

Reduced activity	Areas previously linked to violence: prefrontal cortex, left angular gyrus, corpus callosum	Left side: amygdala, thalamus, hippocampus (previously linked to violence)
Increased activity	Area not previously linked to violence: cerebellum	Right side: amygdala, thalamus, hippocampus

Fourteen of the murderers were non-white but when they were compared with the white control participants on PET measures there was no significant difference between them. Twenty-three of the murderers had a history of head injury, but again they showed no significant difference between non-head injured murderers except in the functioning of their corpus callosum ($p \leq .08$), and the authors accepted that this may have contributed towards a reduction in the murderers' brain activity.

No significant differences were found for performance on the CPT or handedness (except left-handed murderers had significantly less abnormal amygdala asymmetry than right-handed murderers).

Conclusions

Murderers pleading NGRI have significant differences in the metabolism of glucose in a number of brain areas compared with non-murderers.

The study identifies some specific physiological processes which may predispose some criminals to violent behaviour. Reduced activity in the prefrontal, parietal and callosal regions of the brain, together with asymmetries of activity in the amygdala, thalamus and medial temporal lobe, including the hippocampus, may be one of many predispositions towards violence in murderers pleading NGRI. This reduced activity in the prefrontal areas may explain impulsive behaviour, a loss of self-control, evidence of immaturity, altered emotionality and the inability to modify behaviour. All of these may make it easier to carry out different kinds of aggressive acts because the normal constraints on behaviour may be reduced.

Exam tip

Know the key findings and be able to draw conclusions from the findings.

Now test yourself

5 Identify two regions of the sub-cortex where NGRIs showed lower brain activity than controls (non-murderers).
6 Identify two regions of the brain linked to violence.
7 Outline two key findings from this study.

TESTED

The results do not show that violent behaviour is determined by biology alone. There are a number of other factors which must be taken into account. Social experiences, situational factors, psychological predispositions and learned responses will all have their part to play and perhaps the physiological elements may only produce predispositions to extreme forms of violent behaviour rather than being a cause in themselves. One should therefore be cautious about attributing the reason why individuals commit murder simply to the fact that they are found to have mental disorders.

Results do not show that brain dysfunction causes violence. It may even be that brain dysfunction is an effect of violence.

Results do not show that all violent offenders have such brain dysfunctions; the study can only draw conclusions about this kind of violent offender, i.e. murderers pleading NGRI.

Application

At least one biological strategy for preventing criminal behaviour: for example, plastic surgery for prisoners to improve their appearance, making them look less 'criminal'; participation by pregnant women in health and nutrition programmes to reduce antisocial behaviour in their offspring; the use of drugs to reduce violent tendencies.

The collection and processing of forensic evidence (Biological)

REVISED

Motivating factors and bias in the collection and processing of forensic evidence: for example, emotional factors, the need to get a result/make a conviction, fingerprints, ballistics, blood samples, boot/shoe prints, tyre marks, hair/fibre samples, DNA.

Key research: Hall and Player (2008): Will the introduction of an emotional context affect fingerprint analysis and decision-making?

Theory/theories on which the study is based

The analysis and comparison of fingerprints relies on the ability of an individual to recognise the differences or similarities between the ridge details of a fingermark obtained from a crime scene and one taken from a suspect. The process is open to the questioning of an expert's ability to accurately analyse and interpret friction ridges. It has been suggested that the interpretation and analysis of fingermarks becomes more subjective as clarity decreases and as a consequence the expert is more vulnerable to external stimuli. See Figure 19.2.

Now test yourself

8 Suggest one conclusion that can be drawn from the findings of this study.

TESTED

forensic evidence is the information gathered and analysed by forensic scientists. Forensic science is the application of science to criminal and civil laws. Forensic scientists collect, preserve and analyse scientific evidence during the course of an investigation.

Now test yourself

9 Describe the term 'forensic evidence'.

TESTED

Experimental research suggests that emotional effects based on external stimuli impact on decision-making processes during the examination of fingerprints (Dror *et al.*, 2005).

Background to the study

In the United Kingdom the training of a fingerprint expert involves a structured programme of formal courses, which teaches and assesses a series of competencies, including the scientific theories of foetal fingerprint development and the factors that give rise to their observed individuality; methods for the recovery of latent fingermarks; applied examination techniques, utilising analysis, comparison, evaluation and verification (ACE-V) methodology. The practitioner then utilises these competencies through practical work experience. During their progression to 'expert' status the practitioner's work is constantly peer reviewed and assessed. The training process requires the achievement and demonstration of competence before a practitioner is deemed proficient to give fingerprint evidence in a court of law.

In many cases the marks available from a crime scene are far from ideal – they may be incomplete, smudged, distorted, rotated or obscured by the substrate. In order to secure quality, it is standard operating procedure for the identification process to be conducted independently by at least two fingerprint experts.

It has been suggested that the circumstances surrounding a crime case and the pressure experts are put under to produce results may influence the reported outcome (Risinger *et al.*, 2002).

Dror *et al.* (2005) gave university research students either good quality or incomplete, poor quality fingerprints to study. They were also given emotional stimuli deemed low level (case details pertaining to a theft) or high level (case details pertaining to a murder). The results showed that the volunteers were affected by the emotional context and this interfered with their decisions, making them more likely to make matches or identifications when analysing poor quality or ambiguous pairs of fingerprints. This research raised the following questions:
a) Would the same results be found with trained fingerprint experts?
b) Are mis-identifications due to emotional bias?

Hall and Player thought it was important to ascertain whether the normal working practices employed by the Metropolitan Police Fingerprint Bureau introduce an emotional bias. They therefore designed an experiment to test the effect of context on fingerprint identification by fingerprint experts. The research set out to answer the following questions:
a) Does the written report of a crime, as routinely supplied with the fingerprint evidence, affect a fingerprint expert's interpretation of a poor quality mark?
b) Are the fingerprint experts emotionally affected by the circumstances of the case?

The latter was addressed by a specially devised feedback questionnaire and the former by the analysis of an artificially obscured fingermark.

Research method

This was a laboratory experiment. Although designed to be as naturalistic as possible, with participants being asked to participate in work time,

Figure 19.2 Fingerprints were analysed by fingerprint experts

> **Exam tip**
>
> Be able to describe several factors that may influence the collection and processing of forensic evidence.

> ## Now test yourself
>
> 10 What is the fingerprint examiner working for the Metropolitan Police Service provided with?
> 11 Outline the two questions this study aimed to answer.
>
> TESTED ☐

in a typical fingerprint examination room within the New Scotland Yard Fingerprint Bureau, the task itself was artificially generated and participants were randomly allocated to one of two conditions. Furthermore, some control over the experimental conditions was preferred as in a naturalistic setting there would be no capacity to prevent the experts from asking each other's opinions.

The IV was whether the participant was allocated to the low-context or the high-context group and the DVs were (a) whether the participant read the crime scene examination report prior to examining the fingerprint, (b) whether the participant considered the fingermark was (i) identification – a match, (ii) not an identification – not a match, (iii) insufficient – not enough detail to undertake a comparison, (iv) insufficient detail to establish identity, some detail in agreement but not enough to individualise, and (c) whether the participant would be confident to present the fingerprint as evidence in court.

The experiment used an independent measures design.

Outline of the procedure/study

The participants were all respondents to a request for volunteers to take part in an experiment. The request did not go into the details of the experiment.

Seventy fingerprint experts working for the Metropolitan Police Fingerprint Bureau took part. Their length of experience as experts ranged from less than three months to over 30 years. The mean length of experience was 11 years.

Materials

- In order to validate the experts' decisions, a finger impression from a known source was used. A volunteer's right forefinger was inked and introduced to a piece of paper. This good quality, clear mark was then scanned on to a computer and superimposed on a scanned image of a £50 note. The fingermark was positioned so the background of the note obscured the majority of the ridge detail. The mark was then manipulated to control the contrast and further obscure the discernible detail within the fingermark. Fourteen copies of this mark were then printed for use in the experiment. The images used were of actual size and the colour, size and detail of the image contained on the card were representative of the quality and clarity received on a regular basis.
- All 14 copies of the mark were compared against each other to ensure consistency.
- The fingermark and the corresponding set of fingerprint impressions (all 10 printed fingers, donated by the same source as the mark) were then given to participants, who were asked to give their expert opinions as to whether there was a match using the procedure outlined below.
- Each participant was allowed access to a fingerprint magnifying glass and a Russell comparator (an optical magnifying unit for comparing two images).

Procedure

- The volunteers were randomly assigned in groups of eight and were asked to treat the experiment as they would a typical day. They could come and go as they pleased, and talk among themselves as long as they did not discuss the fingermarks that they were analysing in the experiment, or the experiment itself. No time limit was placed on the participants and they were told to consider the experiment material as an ordinary case.

- The participants were assigned into one of two groups, low-emotional context or high-emotional context, on the day of the experiment. The low-context group (35 participants) were given an examination report referring to an allegation of forgery. This was chosen as it is considered a victimless crime and carries a relatively minor sentence. The high-context group (35 participants) were given an examination report referring to an allegation of murder. This was chosen because there is, inevitably, a victim and it carries the most severe sentence.
- The participants were given an envelope containing one of the test marks, the relevant 10-print fingerprint form, the relevant crime scene examiner's report and a sheet of paper advising participants of the contents, which also stated that the mark was made by the right forefinger.
- The experts were then asked to consider whether the mark was:
  - identification (a match)
  - not an identification (not a match)
  - insufficient – not enough detail to undertake a comparison, or
  - insufficient detail to establish identity, some detail in agreement but not enough to individualise.

  They were also asked to elaborate on their findings by providing observations and opinions.
- Finally, when they had finished the experiment, they were given a feedback sheet which asked whether or not they had referred to the crime scene examination report prior to their assessment of the marks and to indicate what information they had read, i.e. the allegation, modus operandi, date, venue, victim and details of examination. If they had referred to the crime scene examination report they were also asked whether, in their judgement, they felt that the information contained on the examination report had affected their analysis and if so, how.

Key findings

A total of 57 of the 70 participants (81.4 per cent) indicated that they had read the crime scene examination report prior to examining the prints – 30 of the 57 were in the high-context scenario group. Therefore 13 experts (18.6 per cent) stated on their feedback forms that they did not read the crime scene examiner's report presented with the fingermarks (so were unaware of the crime-type context when making their judgements).

Of the experts who had read the high-context scenario 50 per cent felt that they were affected by the information given on the examination report, which was significantly greater than the six per cent who had read and reported that they were affected by the low-context scenario. This indicates that there is a relationship between the type of context and the perceived effect on the experts.

To establish whether this perceived effect altered the expert's final decision, the difference between the decisions made between the two groups was compared. These findings are displayed in Table 19.3.

Table 19.3 **The experts' final opinions of the fingermark comparison for the low and high contexts**

	Identification	Insufficient/not suitable for comparison	Some detail in agreement but not sufficient to identify	No identification
High context	6	15	13	1
Low context	7	12	16	0

Now test yourself

14 Describe one way in which confidentiality was maintained.
15 Describe the high (emotional) context condition.
16 Identify the four options the fingerprint expert had chosen from when examining the mark.

TESTED

Table 19.3 shows the final decisions made by the experts to be very similar regardless of the emotional context. Chi-square analysis of the table was carried out and no significant difference was found.

The only variation between the two groups occurred in whether they thought the mark had insufficient detail to undertake a comparison or some detail in agreement but not enough to establish identity. Within the low-context scenario, 46 per cent of experts stated that they had some points in agreement but not enough to individualise as opposed to 37 per cent of the experts given a high context.

The experts were also asked whether they would be prepared to present the mark in court. These findings are displayed in the graph below.

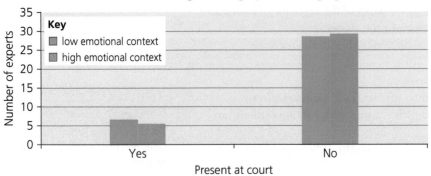

Figure 19.3 The effect of context on the decision to present evidence at court

The graph shows that 17 per cent of those given the high-context and 20 per cent of those given the low-context scenario were sufficiently confident to present the mark as a positive identification to the court. A Pearson Chi-square test showed there was no relationship between an emotional context and presenting the mark as evidence for judicial proceedings.

Overall, the results showed that the manipulated fingermarks lay at the boundary of making a conclusive match. This confirmed the mark to be ambiguous, i.e. of poor quality and open to different interpretations.

Conclusions

Both emotional context and severity of a case affect a fingerprint expert's analysis but this does not have any actual effect on their final decisions.

Details of an individual crime provided with fingermarks may be considered surplus to requirements.

There may be motivating factors and bias in the collection and processing of forensic evidence.

Application

At least one strategy for reducing bias in the collection and processing of forensic evidence: for example, educating detectives, judges, juries, etc. about the strengths and weaknesses of forensic science; conducting an independent analysis of a latent fingerprint and the comparison print; training forensic examiners to acknowledge and minimise bias, e.g. using the 'filler-control' method to combat circular reasoning and bias, working in isolation from other evidence and conclusions to combat context effects, employing 'sequential unmasking', using a 'blind testing' protocol, etc.

Now test yourself

17 Outline the findings in relation to the number of participants who read the crime scene report.
18 Outline the overall findings in relation to the two emotional contexts.
19 Draw one conclusion from the findings of this study.
20 Describe one strategy for reducing bias in the collection and processing of forensic evidence.

TESTED

Collection of evidence (Cognitive)

REVISED

Collection and use of evidence from witnesses and suspects: for example, identity parades, identikits (photo-fits, FACES, E-fits, SketchCop), the difference between an interview and an interrogation, the Reid technique's nine steps of interrogation, PEACE, interviews (the standard interview, the cognitive interview – CI, the structured interview – SI, the enhanced cognitive interview – ECI).

Retrieval techniques used in a cognitive interview: (i) context reinstatement, (ii) in-depth reporting, (iii) narrative re-ordering, (iv) reporting from different perspectives.

The nine phases of an enhanced cognitive interview are: (i) greet and personalise the interview and establish rapport, (ii) explain the aims of the interview, (iii) initiate a free rapport, (iv) compatible questioning, (v) varied and extensive retrieval, (vi) investigatively important questions, (vii) summary, (viii) closure, (ix) evaluation.

Key research: Memon and Higham (1999): A review of the cognitive interview

Theory/theories on which the study is based

Interviewing techniques should incorporate basic psychological findings about memory. Research in cue-dependent forgetting has shown that memory traces contain many different types of information: some internal factors such as mood and psychological state and some external cues such as smell and colour of surroundings. According to the encoding specificity principle, the retrieval of a memory trace is more likely if the information in a cue overlaps with the information in a memory trace. Retrieval can be improved by using as many cues as possible. The implication for police procedure is that a witness interview should use cues to stimulate memory while at the same time avoiding leading questions (cited in Putwain and Sammons, 2002).

Questioning produces much better recall if it follows the chronological order of events rather than asking questions in any order.

Background to the study

The traditional technique used by the police for witness interviews is known as the standard interview. This involves a period of free recall followed by specific questions asked by the police officer. According to Gudjonsson (1992), the standard interview has four stages:
1 Orientation.
2 Listening.
3 Questions and answers.
4 Advice.

Geiselman *et al.* (1985) developed the cognitive interview, an alternative to the standard interview. It takes into account psychological findings about cue-dependent forgetting and has four stages designed to stimulate as many cues as possible in order to maximise different retrieval routes:
Stage 1: Reinstate the context.
Stage 2: Recall events in reverse order.
Stage 3: Report everything they can remember.
Stage 4: Describe events from someone else's point of view.

Now test yourself

21 Identify the four memory-retrieval techniques used in a cognitive interview.
22 Identify the nine phases of an enhanced cognitive interview.

TESTED

Exam tip

Be able to describe several ways evidence can be collected from witnesses and suspects.

19 Section B: Option 2 – Criminal psychology

Geiselman *et al.* (1986) compared a cognitive interview, with a standard police interview and a hypnotic interview. Although this was laboratory-based research, it did suggest that the cognitive interview can produce more correct details without increasing witness error (cited in Putwain and Sammons, 2002).

In a real-life test, Fisher *et al.* (1990) trained detectives from the Miami Police Department to use the cognitive interview. Compared to the standard procedure used, the cognitive interview produced 46 per cent increase in recall and 90 per cent accuracy. The findings suggested that the cognitive interview is more effective than the standard interview, producing higher recall and reducing errors (cited in Putwain and Sammons, 2002).

Research method

This study is a review article which critiques (reviews) the cognitive interview. Discussion is organised around four themes:
1 The effectiveness of various components of the CI.
2 The relationship between the CI and other interviewing methods such as the guided memory interview (GMI), the standard interview and the structured interview, i.e. comparison interviews.
3 Different measures of memory performance.
4 The effect of training quality on interviewer performance.

Comments are made on some of the theoretical and methodological issues to be considered in CI research and the practical considerations relating to the use of the CI in the field.

Outline of the article

Section 1: The effectiveness of various components of the cognitive interview

One of the most frequently used components of the CI is for the witness to mentally reconstruct the physical (external) and personal (internal) contexts which existed at the time of the crime: mental context reinstatement. The interviewer can help witnesses recreate context by asking them to form an image or impression of the environmental aspects of the original scene (such as the location of objects in a room), to comment on their emotional reactions and feelings (surprise, anger, etc.) at the time, and to describe any sounds, smells and physical conditions (hot, humid, smoky, etc.) that were present. Increasing the overlap between test context and the context of acquisition (i.e. contextual reinstatement) will ensure the operation of effective retrieval cues and maximise memory retrieval. There is some evidence to suggest that context reinstatement is a technique that witnesses spontaneously use to remember events (Memon *et al.*, 1997c; Milne, 1997) and Milne (1997) showed that context reinstatement yields as much information as the full CI procedure.

A second technique is to ask the witness to report everything. Witnesses are encouraged to report in full without screening out anything they consider irrelevant or for which they have only partial recall. In addition to facilitating the recall of additional information, this technique may yield information that may be valuable in putting together details from different witnesses to the same crime (see Memon and Bull, 1991).

The third component is to ask for recall from a variety of perspectives. This technique tries to encourage the witnesses to place themselves in the

Now test yourself

23 Identify the four stages of a standard interview.

TESTED

Exam tip

Know the research method used in the study.

victim's shoes (if the witness is not a victim) or of another witness and to report what they saw or would have seen. The theoretical assumption is that a change in perspective forces a change in retrieval description, thus allowing additional information to be recalled from the new perspective. Again the aim is to use multiple pathways to increase both retrieval and the amount of detail elicited. There is some recent evidence that when compared to the other CI techniques, the perspective instruction can produce as accurate information as the other CI techniques, although it does not appear to increase the amount of information recalled any more than the other techniques (Milne, 1997).

The fourth component of the CI is the instruction to make retrieval attempts from different starting points. Witnesses usually feel they have to start at the beginning and are usually asked to do so. However, the CI encourages extra focused and extensive retrieval by encouraging witnesses to recall in a variety of orders from the end, or from the middle or from the most memorable event. This technique, like the change perspective instruction, is assumed to change the retrieval description, resulting in the recall of additional details. So far there is no evidence that this technique yields any more information than a second retrieval attempt when used in a cognitive interview (Memon et al., 1997a), although Milne (1997) has found the instruction to be of some benefit when applied with specific prompts.

Section 2: (a) Isolating the effective components of the CI

One way of pinpointing how a procedure like the CI works is to experimentally isolate and test the effectiveness of each of the components, yet there have been only a couple of attempts to do this (see Milne, 1997 for a recent review).

In a study using five- and eight-year-old children as witnesses, Memon et al. (1996a, Experiment 1) interviewed the children about a staged event using one of the three cognitive techniques described in the previous section, i.e. context reinstatement (CR), change perspective (CP) and change order (CO). As a control, a fourth group were merely instructed to 'try harder'. The control group was included in order to test the hypothesis that the increase in recall with the CI may be a result of the additional retrieval attempts when each new instruction is applied. The hypothesis was supported and there were no significant differences in recall performance across CP, CR, CO and control groups. However, it was noted that younger children had difficulty using the cognitive techniques.

Milne (1997) extended the studies conducted by Memon et al. (1996a) by comparing the full CI procedure with each of the cognitive techniques, including the 'report everything' (RE) instruction. She also included a control group who were merely asked to make a second retrieval attempt. Overall she found no differences in number of correct or incorrect details across the four cognitive conditions (CP, CO, CR and RE) and the control condition, thus supporting Memon et al.'s findings. She did find, however, that the full CI condition elicited more recall than the other single-technique conditions except the CR condition. As indicated earlier, this leads one to conclude that context reinstatement is the most effective component of the CI.

(b) The enhanced CI

The enhanced version of the CI combines the four cognitive techniques with some strategies for improving interviewer–witness communication and flow of information in the interview. Several techniques are used

Now test yourself

24 Identify the four main cognitive techniques used in the CI.

TESTED

to facilitate the communication, including the 'transfer of control' of the interview from the interviewer to the witness. This is put into place during the rapport-building phase in several ways, for example through the use of open questions which request an elaborated response from the witness.

During the course of training student and police interviewers on the CI techniques, Memon noted that the various elements of the CI work interactively. For example, building rapport with the witness: if this is done appropriately, the witness will be more relaxed and open to using the various cognitive techniques – by not interrupting a witness and pausing after questions, the interviewer can facilitate contextual reinstatement. It is possible therefore to suggest that the effectiveness of the CI is due to improved communication, improved access/retrieval of information as well as the interaction of these factors.

Further refinements of the CI include additional cognitive techniques for activating and probing a witness's mental image of the various parts of an event, such as a suspect's face, clothing, objects, etc. A distinction is drawn between conceptual image codes (an image stored as a concept or dictionary definition) and pictorial codes (the mental representation of an image). The instructions to form an image are used in conjunction with the context reinstatement technique during the questioning phase of the interview. When contextual reinstatement is accompanied by instructions to imagine the parts of the events and the witness's images are probed with questions, further details (correct and incorrect) are elicited.

The effects of imagery on the retrieval of information depend on a number of factors, such as reality monitoring, task demands and the ease with which an image may come to mind. However, research by Marcia Johnson *et al.* (1993) suggests that imaging could potentially be problematic to accurate memory performance. Therefore, it has been suggested that imagery instructions should be used with some caution until there is better understanding of how they influence source monitoring and corresponding decision processes.

To summarise: contextual reinstatement, possibly accompanied by the cautious use of imagery that (a) limits the possibility of source monitoring confusions and (b) is non-suggestive, seems to be the only effective cognitive technique employed with the CI. Instructions to change perspective or to recall in reverse order have not proven to be effective by themselves and may even introduce some problems. Research on these issues is sparse, however.

(c) Comparison interviews

In attempts to evaluate the efficacy of the CI, it has been compared with other interview procedures such as the typical police interview (standard interview), the guided memory interview, the structured interview and hypnosis. This article does not focus on hypnosis because of the lack of clear evidence that it can facilitate recall, the controversy surrounding the use of hypnosis and the ambiguity about exactly what techniques are used in an hypnosis interview. Instead, recent reviews by Fisher (1995) and Das Gupta *et al.* (1995), which compare the cognitive interview with hypnosis, are considered.

The standard interview

In early studies, results from using the CI were compared to results using the standard police interview. This was a sensible research strategy given

Now test yourself

25 Identify the only cognitive technique used in a CI that Memon and Higham consider to be effective.

TESTED

that few other interview techniques were widely used when the CI was first introduced.

From the practical point of view, the CI offers a clear advantage over the standard interview as undesirable elements are absent. However, for the purposes of memory research, the disadvantage of the standard interview is that it differs from the CI in many ways and so does not provide a tight experimental control against which to measure the effectiveness of the cognitive techniques employed specifically with the CI – for example, there is no control over the effects of training and interviewer motivation. Memon and Higham recommend against using the standard interview as a comparison group to evaluate the efficacy of the CI, especially when the research is focused on determining the specific effects that CI techniques might have on memory.

The guided memory interview (GMI), the cognitive interview and the enhanced cognitive interview

The GMI draws upon principles of contextual reinstatement, as does the CI, and by encouraging the witness to mentally reinstate contexts, guides their memory.

Techniques employed in the GMI resemble the context reinstatement and imagery components of the most recent version of the CI. Therefore, because the CI is made up of a number of different techniques (such as changed perspective, change order, report everything) as well as context reinstatement, the GMI may be a reasonable comparison group for determining whether the CI effects can be attributed to context reinstatement alone or whether a combination of cognitive techniques is responsible for the effects. However, there is more to the CI than the cognitive techniques; the ECI relies on the ability of the interviewer to communicate effectively in an interview. Perhaps a more appropriate control would be a procedure that achieves good rapport with the witness without the use of any special mnemonic techniques.

The structured interview and the cognitive interview

Koehnken and colleagues (for example, Koehnken et al., 1994) first used the SI as a comparison interview in CI research.

SI interviewers are persuaded to build rapport with the witness, to allow the witness the opportunity to give narrative descriptions and to provide ample time for interviewees to respond. Additionally, the SI is non-interruptive, expansive, confidence building and fosters the use of good questioning techniques, such as active listening, use of open questions, appropriate non-verbal behaviour. Many of these positive aspects of the SI are also present in the enhanced CI. However, the SI and the CI are different in that the cognitive techniques, such as contextual reinstatement, are employed only with the CI. Therefore, the amount of information elicited in a CI exceeds that which is elicited by interviewers trained in the SI, even though both procedures produce comparable accuracy rates.

Section 3: Measures of memory

Although one of the strong points of the CI is its employment of well-established laboratory principles, researchers of CI effectiveness have not typically been as concerned with measures of performance as have their laboratory counterparts. In practically all studies, performance is measured in terms of the percentage of correct interview statements or the absolute

Now test yourself

26 Outline why Memon and Higham recommend that a standard interview should not be compared with a cognitive interview.

TESTED

Exam tip

Know the key suggestions made by the researchers.

Now test yourself

27 Outline why Memon and Higham suggest the GMI interview would provide a good comparison with the CI.

TESTED

Now test yourself

28 Outline one difference between a CI and an SI.

TESTED

number of correct and incorrect statements. One potential problem of limiting research to these measures is that it ignores the amount and the nature of unreported information, which is as important to determining the efficacy of any interview procedure as is the reported information.

Without this unreported information, it is impossible to determine hit and false alarm rates which are necessary to calculate measures of sensitivity and bias. However, there is a clear need for the incorporation of analogous ideas into measures of interview performance. One reason for this need is that the CI may affect an interviewee's report criterion – for example, the instruction to 'report everything' may cause people to lower their response criterion and report more information than they might normally.

In a series of articles Koriat and Goldsmith (1994) presented a formal model that outlines the effect of retrieval, memory monitoring and output control on memory performance. According to the model, a person retrieves candidate answers from long-term memory in response to an input question (retrieval). The probability that the best candidate answer is correct is then assessed (monitoring) and this probability is then compared to a response criterion probability set by situational demands and payoff (control). If the assessed probability that the best candidate answer is correct is greater than the response criterion, then the candidate answer is reported. If not, it is withheld (performance). This model makes the important distinction between retrieval and meta-memory issues such as memory monitoring. It also makes some clear predictions about the effect of shifts in response criterion on interview accuracy measures. In general, it predicts that as the response criterion becomes more conservative, accuracy should improve.

If accuracy is compared between the SI and the CI, output is generally greater for the CI but there is no associated loss in accuracy. This finding runs counter to Koriat and Goldsmith's model, which predicts poorer accuracy with increased output (all other factors held constant). One possible reason for this is that the cognitive techniques employed with the CI improve retrieval, monitoring or both, relative to the SI, and so the loss of accuracy due to the criterion shift is compensated for.

Section Four: Quality of training

A criticism of early studies of the CI was that the amount and quality of training that interviewers were given was not specified. Based on the description of the interview protocol, it seems that interviewers were merely provided with a set of instructions to follow and were not 'trained' in any depth.

In some studies, interviewers were required to read the CI instructions to the interviewees verbatim, thus possibly obviating the need to have properly trained interviewers. The original CI procedure was perhaps easier to communicate to witnesses than the enhanced version. It appears to be the case that the enhanced version places far greater demands on the interviewer. Post-interview discussion with the student interviewers in the various Memon studies yielded the following observation: the cognitive interviewers reported that they found the procedure more demanding and exhausting as compared with the structured interviewers.

It is likely that differences in the attitudes, motivation and experience of the interviewers play a big role in determining the kinds of results obtained with the CI.

> ## Now test yourself
>
> 29 Explain why Memon and Higham suggest Koriat and Goldsmith's model of how retrieval, memory monitoring and output control affect memory performance may be useful.
>
> TESTED ☐

Geiselman and Fisher (1997), in a review of ten years of research on cognitive interviewing, also stress the importance of providing feedback on interviewers' performance.

Memon and Higham therefore make the following suggestions for training:
a) Interviewers should be given adequate training in CI techniques – a two-day training programme is recommended.
b) A possible strategy would be to direct training to a select group of officers.

Conclusions

Research into the effectiveness of the CI remains inconclusive. There is a need for further research investigating the particular effects the CI has on memory, as well as how the various elements of the CI work.

It is not yet clear how the CI relates to other interviewing procedures and what would make a suitable control group.

Interviewers differ in their ability and motivation to conduct a good interview. If research is limited to comparisons between interviews with established protocols, such as the CI and the SI, the problem of interviewer variability is not alleviated.

Further research is needed to improve understanding of the conditions under which the CI procedure may be most useful as a forensic tool.

> **Exam tips**
>
> Know how the study relates to the component 'Criminal psychology'.
>
> Know how the study relates to the topic 'Collection of evidence (Cognitive)'.
>
> Know how the study relates to the collection and use of evidence from witnesses and suspects.

Application

At least one strategy for police interviews: for example, the PEACE model of interviewing, forensic hypnosis.

Psychology and the courtroom (Cognitive)

How juries can be persuaded by the characteristics of witnesses and defendants: for example, attractiveness, race, language, accent, confidence, dress, the use of mock juries to research such factors.

Key research: Dixon *et al.* (2002): The role of accent and context in perceptions of guilt

Theory/theories on which the study is based

Accents may affect listeners' impressions of speakers (Giles *et al.*, 1987; Giles and Powesland, 1975). Standard accents are rated more positively than non-standard accents, especially on traits associated with competence or status. Therefore, accent use may systematically (dis)advantage speakers in such institutional contexts as job interviews, medical consultations and classrooms (Kalin, 1982).

> **Now test yourself**
>
> 30 Outline Memon and Higham's suggestions in relation to witness interviewers.
>
> TESTED ☐

> **Exam tip**
>
> Be able to draw conclusions from the article.

> **Exam tips**
>
> The question is likely to be worded generically so focus on the specific strategy selected for police interviews.
>
> Be able to apply at least one strategy for police interviews to a novel situation.

> **Now test yourself**
>
> 31 Describe one strategy for police interviews.
>
> TESTED ☐

REVISED ☐

> **Now test yourself**
>
> 32 Outline how any one witness or defendant characteristic might influence jury decision making.
>
> TESTED ☐

> **Exam tip**
>
> Be able to describe several ways in which juries can be influenced by the characteristics of witnesses and defendants.

'Third-class' urban accents are evaluated more negatively than either rural regional or British received pronunciation (RP) accents (Giles, 1970; Giles, Baker and Fielding, 1975).

A foreign accent undermines a person's credibility. Because an accent makes a person harder to understand, listeners are less likely to find what the person says as truthful (Lev-Ari and Keysar, 2010).

Background to the study

The effects of accent on attributions of guilt would appear to be an issue of particular concern, yet until this study had received comparatively little research.

Seggie (1983) investigated the effects of three local accents – **British Received Pronunciation** (RP), broad Australian and Asian – on Australian raters' attributions of guilt. Seggie found that the suspect's accent significantly influenced raters' responses but that the nature of this influence varied as a function of crime type (**blue collar** vs. **white collar**).

In a South African study, Dixon *et al.* (1994) found that a 'coloured' suspect who switched from English into Cape Afrikaans speech was rated as more guilty by white English-speaking listeners than a suspect who did not exhibit speech divergence.

The Birmingham or 'Brummie' accent has featured in accent evaluation research since the early 1970s and has generally been evaluated more negatively than either rural regional or RP accents (for example, Giles, 1970; Giles, Baker and Fielding, 1975).

This study aimed to further document the evaluative consequences of accent in a legal context by investigating the influence of an English regional accent, the Brummie accent, on listeners' attributions of guilt towards a criminal suspect. The main hypothesis tested was therefore: 'A Brummie-accented suspect will elicit stronger attributions of guilt than a standard-accented suspect.'

This research also examined the effects of two contextual variables on the attribution of guilt: the suspect's race and the type of crime committed.

Research method

This was a laboratory experiment. The IV was which of the conditions the participant was assigned to – accent type: Brummie/standard, race of suspect: black/white, crime type: blue collar/white collar. The main DV was participants' attributions of guilt. The study therefore used a 2 × 2 × 2 factorial design. The experiment used an independent measures design.

Outline of the procedure/study

The study took place in the Department of Psychology at the University College, Worcester. The sample consisted of 119 white undergraduate psychology students (24 men and 95 women, with a mean age of 25.2 years), who participated as part of their course requirements.

As the focus was on the reactions of individuals who did not speak with a Brummie accent, participants who grew up in Birmingham were excluded from the sample.

Participants were randomly allocated to one of the conditions. They were then asked to listen to a two-minute recorded conversation based

British Received Pronunciation is the accent of Standard English in the United Kingdom. This is based on the standard accent of English as spoken in the south of England.

blue-collar crime is any crime committed by an individual from a lower social class as opposed to white-collar crime which is associated with crime committed by someone of a higher-level social class. Today, blue collar crimes are typically those crimes that are considered to be fuelled by passion, rage or other emotions, as compared with those that are carefully calculated and executed. Crimes that cause injury to people or property, such as burglary or other property crimes, theft crimes, sex crimes, assault and drug crimes are all considered to be blue-collar crimes.

white-collar crimes are those crimes which are generally committed in a business setting and are considered to be non-violent. Some people refer to white-collar crimes as 'paper crimes'. Examples include wire fraud, forgery and embezzlement.

Now test yourself

33 State the hypothesis for this study.

TESTED

Exam tip

Know the research method and sample.

on a transcript of an interview that occurred in a British police station in 1995. The conversation featured a middle-aged male police inspector interrogating a young male suspect who pleaded his innocence to a crime of which he had been accused. Actors hired for the purposes of the study played both speakers: a standard-accented student in his mid-forties played the role of inspector while the role of the suspect was played by a student in his early twenties who spoke with a standard accent. He was a natural code-switcher who grew up near Birmingham and had lived in various parts of England.

To manipulate accent types, two matched guises of the police interview were created: a guise in which the suspect spoke with a standard accent and a guise in which he spoke with a Brummie accent. Moreover, confirming the success of the matching process, the guises did not differ significantly in terms of loudness, though the Brummie guise was rated as higher than the RP guise in terms of speech rate because in authentic speech contexts urban accents tend to be faster than both rural regional and RP accents (Wells, 1982), this difference was not eradicated.

The two contextual variables were manipulated by varying the information given to respondents as shown in the excerpt below from the transcript of the taped exchange between suspect (S) and police officer (PO):

PO: Okay, would you like to just briefly tell me what your understanding is of the arrest?

S: Well, eh, I was told last night that I was arrested on suspicion of armed robbery/cheque fraud?

PO: Okay. Are you involved in that robbery/fraud?

S: No, I'm not.

PO: In any way, are you involved in that robbery/fraud?

S: Not in any way whatsoever. It's absolutely not true, not true at all. I speak only for myself and I am not involved in any armed robbery/ fraud, in any way whatsoever.

PO: Well the person that carried out this crime is described as male, white/black, put at 5'9" tall.

Note: the type of crime and race of the suspect variables were manipulated by varying the transcript as indicated.

Crime type was manipulated by having the suspect accused of different criminal acts, either armed robbery (blue-collar condition) or cheque fraud (white-collar condition).

The race of the suspect was manipulated by varying the racial cues provided to respondents. At one point in the taped interview, the police inspector provided a physical description of the person who committed the crime and this description was systematically altered across experimental conditions.

Having listened to their version of the tape-recorded exchange, participants completed two sets of rating scales. First, they rated the suspect's guilt on a seven-point scale ranging from innocent to guilty. Second, they rated the suspect more generally by completing the **Speech Evaluation Instrument** (SEI), an 'omnibus' measure of language attitudes (Zahn and Hopper, 1985).

Now test yourself

34 Identify the conditions that made up the 2 × 2 × 2 factorial design of this study.
35 Explain how excluding people who grew up in Birmingham acted as a control in this study.

TESTED

Exam tip

Know the procedure and all six experimental conditions.

the **Speech Evaluation Instrument** is a method used to evaluate linguistic diversity and attitudes to language.

Now test yourself

36 Outline the two rating scales used to gather data in this study.

TESTED

Key findings

The Brummie suspect was rated as more guilty than the RP suspect, which is an effect of moderate strength.

There was a significant three-way interaction: the Brummie accent/black suspect/blue-collar crime had significantly higher guilt ratings than the other five conditions.

Analysis treating guilt as a criterion and the SEI dimensions as predictors showed that the suspect's Superiority and Attractiveness significantly predicted guilt but that Dynamism did not.

Conclusions

Attributions of guilt may be affected by accent in a British context.

Non-standard (English) speakers are perceived as guiltier than standard speakers. Suspects speaking with a Brummie accent are more likely to be perceived as guilty of an offence than RP suspects.

Suspects accused of a blue-collar crime who are black and speak with a Brummie accent are likely to be perceived as guilty.

A suspect's perceived Superiority and Attractiveness may predict whether they are guilty or not guilty.

Juries may be influenced and persuaded by the characteristics of witnesses and defendants.

> **Exam tips**
>
> Know how the study relates to the component 'Criminal psychology'.
>
> Know how the study relates to the topic 'Psychology and the courtroom (Cognitive)'.
>
> Know how the study relates to how juries can be persuaded by the characteristics of witnesses and defendants.

Application

At least one strategy to influence jury decision making: for example, the influence of inadmissible evidence; the CSI effect; the impact of fMRI scans as evidence; using order presentation of evidence (story order and witness order); using expert witnesses; the Yale model of persuasion; use of rhetorical strategies.

Crime prevention (Social)

How the features of neighbourhoods can influence crime: for example, defining territory, marking territory, protecting territory, defensible space, architecture, type of accommodation, town planning, factors important in explaining differences in crime rate: zone of territorial influence, opportunities for surveillance, image, milieu, research by Oscar Newman, Wilson and Kelling's broken windows theory.

How a zero tolerance policy can influence crime: for example, the work by William Bratton in New York, the work by Ray Mallon in Hartlepool, Japan's zero tolerance policy for alcohol and driving, zero tolerance policies in schools and other educational establishments in relation to drugs and weapons, the 1996 zero tolerance initiative of the London Metropolitan Police together with the London Transport Police, City of London Police and other local borough councils to deal with homeless beggars, drug dealers, prostitutes and pimps who were congregating at St Pancras Railway Station.

Key research: Wilson and Kelling (1982): The police and neighbourhood safety: broken windows

Theory/theories on which the study is based

It has been proposed that public opinion in relation to the value of foot patrolling by police reflects a desire for a style of policing. What the public finds attractive about foot patrols is that they are non-threatening and they do not engage the public exclusively in confrontational situations (Wakefield, 2006; www.police-foundation.org.uk/uploads/catalogerfiles/the-value-of-foot-patrol/foot_patrol.pdf).

The public's expectations of foot patrol suggest that it is commonly associated with a range of expected outcomes (most frequently, crime prevention and reassurance) and a set of specific policing interventions or activities that the police 'should do more of' (such as gathering local intelligence, dealing with disturbances, providing advice on crime prevention or more proactive targeting of criminals) (Wakefield, 2006).

Background to the study

Previous research has shown how features of a community can influence crime rates. Newman (1972) compared the rate of crime in two New York housing projects. Brownsville was designed in small blocks around a courtyard and housed five or six families, while Van Dyke consisted of high-rise buildings set a distance apart with parkland between. Although the same number of residents lived in both housing complexes, the crime rate was 50 per cent higher in Van Dyke. Newman suggested that four factors were important in explaining the different crime rate: zone of territorial influence, opportunities for surveillance, image and milieu.

Five thousand civilian police community support officers (PCSOs) have been employed across the police forces of England and Wales, carrying out their foot patrol duties alongside a growing number of police officers and civilian support staff. The Home Office announced plans to provide every area of the country with multi-agency 'neighbourhood policing teams' by 2008, designed to be 'citizen-focused' and promote local 'reassurance' (Wakefield 2006).

In 1973, the New Jersey state legislature in the USA passed the Safe and Clean Neighborhoods Act. This legislation sought to create safe, clean neighbourhoods and foot patrol was specifically mandated as part of an effort to expand the presence and visibility of police protection.

Research method

This was an article published in *The Atlantic Online* in March 1982. It describes features of neighbourhoods that can be linked to high incidences of crime, and developments in policing strategies and changes in the concept of policing initiated in an attempt to reduce crime rates, focusing initially on the usefulness of foot patrols. The article also considers a variety of explanations for the fear of crime and victimisation, and how communities can help maintain order and make their neighbourhoods safe.

Now test yourself

40 Explain the term 'zero tolerance policy' in relation to crime.

TESTED ☐

Now test yourself

41 Outline the aim of this article.

TESTED ☐

Exam tip

Know the research method used in the study.

The article can be seen to be composed of three main sections: safe neighbourhoods, the changing role of the police and maintaining order.

Outline of the article

Part 1: Safe neighbourhoods

Finding the answer to the question 'how can a neighbourhood be 'safer' when the crime rate has not gone down – in fact, may have gone up?' requires an understanding of what often frightens people in public places. Many individuals are primarily frightened by crime, especially crime involving a sudden, violent attack by a stranger. This risk is very real, in Newark as in many large cities. However, there is another source of fear – that of being bothered by disorderly people who are not violent or, necessarily, criminals, but disreputable or unpredictable people, for example drunks, addicts, rowdy teenagers, prostitutes, loiterers. What foot-patrol officers did in the 'Safe and Clean Neighborhoods Program' was to elevate the level of public order in the neighbourhoods of Newark they patrolled. Though the neighbourhoods were predominantly black and the foot patrol men were mostly white, this 'order-maintenance' function of the police was performed to the general satisfaction of both parties.

Kelling himself spent many hours walking with Newark foot-patrol officers to see how they defined 'order' and what they did to maintain it. The population of one typical beat area included both 'regulars' and 'strangers'. The officer on that beat knew who the regulars were and they knew him. As he saw his job, he was to keep an eye on strangers and make certain that the disreputable regulars observed some informal but widely understood rules – for example, people could drink on side streets but not at the main intersection; bottles had to be in paper bags; talking to, bothering or begging from people waiting at the bus stop was forbidden. Individuals who broke the informal rules were arrested for vagrancy. Noisy teenagers were told to keep quiet.

At the community level, disorder and crime are usually inextricably linked. Social psychologists and police officers tend to agree that if a window in a building is broken and left unrepaired, all the rest of the windows will soon be broken – the broken window theory. This is true in both nice and rundown neighbourhoods. Window breaking does not necessarily occur on a large scale because some areas are inhabited by determined window breakers whereas others are populated by window lovers; rather, one unrepaired broken window is a signal that no one cares and so breaking more windows costs nothing.

'Untended' behaviour also leads to the breakdown of community controls. A stable, law-abiding community can easily change to an inhospitable and frightening jungle. If a property is abandoned, it will become derelict and windows get smashed. The behaviour of some of the inhabitants deteriorates, so 'nice' families move out and unattached adults move in. Teenagers start to gather in front of the corner store, the shopkeeper asks them to move, they refuse, fights occur, litter accumulates and the community continues its downward spiral. Such areas then become increasingly vulnerable to criminal invasion – drugs will change hands, prostitutes will solicit, cars will be stripped and muggings will occur.

In response to fear, people avoid each other, weakening controls. Sometimes they call the police. Patrol cars arrive, an occasional arrest occurs, but crime continues and disorder is not abated. Citizens complain to the police chief, but he explains that his department is low on personnel and that the courts do not punish petty or first-time offenders. To the residents, the police who arrive in squad cars are either ineffective or uncaring; to the police, the residents are animals who deserve each other. The citizens may soon stop calling the police because 'they can't do anything'.

The process we call urban decay has occurred for centuries in every city. However, what is happening today is different in at least two important respects: (i) mobility has become easy for all but the very poor or those who are blocked from moving because of racial prejudice; (ii) the police no longer help to reassert law and order by acting on behalf of the community. This is probably because the role of the police has slowly changed from maintaining order to fighting crimes and making arrests.

Part 2: The changing role of the police

Over the past two decades, the shift of police from order maintenance to law enforcement has brought them increasingly under the influence of legal restrictions, provoked by media complaints and enforced by court decisions and departmental orders. As a consequence, the order maintenance functions of the police are now governed by rules developed to control police relations with suspected criminals.

Wilson and Kelling think it is a mistake to 'decriminalise' disreputable behaviour that 'harms no one' as it removes the ultimate sanction the police can employ to maintain neighbourhood order. Although arresting a single drunk or vagrant who has harmed no identifiable person seems unjust, failing to arrest a group of drunks or a group of vagrants may destroy an entire community.

It may be their greater sensitivity to communal as opposed to individual needs that helps explain why the residents of small communities are more satisfied with their police than are the residents of similar neighbourhoods in big cities.

This raises the problem of how a police chief should deploy his meagre forces. Wilson and Kelling offer the following possibilities:
- Try further variations of the Newark experiment.
- Have minimal police involvement and use informal methods of social control such as community rules and agreements.
- Employ citizen patrols, for example the Guardian Angels who patrol the New York City streets.

Part 3: Maintaining order: the way forward

Though citizens can do a great deal, the police are plainly the key to order maintenance. However, they cannot do this job by themselves, they need the public's support.

Psychologists have carried out many studies on why people fail to go to the aid of people being attacked or seeking help and they have learned that the cause is not 'apathy' or 'selfishness' but the absence of some plausible grounds for feeling that one must personally accept responsibility.

Now test yourself

44 Outline the broken windows theory.
45 Explain why the link between order maintenance and crime prevention became forgotten over time.

TESTED

Figure 19.4 Broken windows can be linked to high incidences of crime

Now test yourself

46 Explain why Wilson and Kelling think that disreputable behaviour that harms no one should not be decriminalised.

TESTED

Police forces in the USA are losing not gaining members, with some cities suffering substantial cuts in the number of officers available for duty. The key objective must therefore be to identify neighbourhoods at the tipping point – where public order is deteriorating but not unreclaimable, where the streets are used frequently but by apprehensive people, where a window is likely to be broken at any time and must quickly be fixed if all are not to be shattered.

Unfortunately, few police departments have ways of systematically identifying such areas and assigning officers to them. To allocate patrols wisely, the department must look at the neighbourhoods and decide, from first-hand evidence, where an additional officer will make the greatest difference in promoting a sense of safety.

Wilson and Kelling suggest the following strategies could help communities instil a sense of security and maintain order:
- Employ private watchmen/security guards.
- Tenant organisations can hire off-duty police officers for patrol work in their buildings.
- Encourage patrol officers to go to and from duty stations on public transportation and while on the bus or subway car, enforce rules about smoking, drinking, disorderly conduct and the like.

It is time to return to the long-abandoned view that the police should protect communities as well as individuals. The police ought to recognise the importance of maintaining, intact, communities without broken windows.

Conclusions

Features of neighbourhoods influence crime rates.

The role of the police has changed over recent years and policing strategies are continually changing.

Foot patrols enhance community feelings of safety.

Application

At least one strategy for crime prevention: for example, target hardening, creating defensible space, access control, increasing risk of detection (surveillance), facilitating compliance.

Effect of imprisonment (Social)

Punishment and reform as responses to criminal behaviour: for example, imprisonment, fines, probation, reparation (for example, community service) and restitution.

Key research: Haney *et al.* (1973): Study of prisoners and guards in a simulated prison

Theory/theories on which the study is based

Attempts to provide an explanation of the deplorable condition of the American penal system and its dehumanising effects upon prisoners and guards often focus on what is known as the **dispositional hypothesis**. In relation to this study this would mean that the state of the social institution of prison is due to the 'nature' of the people who administer it, or the 'nature' of the people who populate it, or both. This hypothesis

---

Exam tip

Know the key observations and suggestions made by the authors.

Now test yourself

47 Identify the two criteria used to assign police offers to areas.
48 Outline two strategies that Wilson and Kelling feel could help communities instil a sense of security and maintain order.

TESTED ☐

Exam tips

The question is likely to be worded generically so focus on the specific strategy selected for crime prevention.

Be able to apply at least one strategy for crime prevention to a novel situation.

Now test yourself

49 Describe one strategy for crime prevention.

TESTED ☐

REVISED ☐

Now test yourself

50 Outline the purpose of imprisonment.

TESTED ☐

Exam tip

Be able to describe several ways punishment and reform are used to motivate criminals not to reoffend.

would propose that both prisoners and guards have personalities or dispositions that make conflict inevitable. Prisoners are, by definition, lacking in respect for law and order. As guards have to be domineering and use physical force to control aggressive inmates, they are likely to be attracted to the job because of a desire for power (an aspect of their personality). If this is so, it is obvious why conflict occurs. Both prisoners and guards are inevitably 'evil'.

Background to the study

Although the physical conditions within prisons have improved over the years, the social institution of prison has continued to fail. On purely pragmatic grounds, there is substantial evidence that prisons really neither 'rehabilitate' nor act as a deterrent to future crime – in the USA at the time this study was conducted, recidivism rates were upwards of 75 per cent (Haney, Banks & Zimbardo, 1973).

Prisons have also been found to fail on humanitarian grounds. The mass media are increasingly filled with accounts of atrocities committed daily, man against man, in reaction to the penal system or in the name of it (Haney, Banks and Zimbardo, 1973).

The customary explanation for the dreadful conditions of the American penal system and its dehumanising effects on both prisoners and guards is based on the dispositional hypothesis. However, Haney, Banks and Zimbardo claimed that this proposition could not be critically evaluated through direct observation in existing prison settings 'because such naturalistic observation necessarily confounds the acute effects of the environment with the chronic characteristics of the inmate and guard populations' (Haney, Banks and Zimbardo, 1973).

Therefore, to separate the effects of the prison environment itself from the natural dispositions of its inhabitants they created a 'new/simulated' prison. This was comparable in its fundamental socio-psychological milieu to existing prison systems but was entirely populated by individuals who were undifferentiated in all essential dimensions from the rest of society. If the guards and prisoners in a mock prison behaved in a non-aggressive manner, this would support the dispositional hypothesis. If these 'ordinary' people came to behave in the same way that we see in real prisons, then one can conclude that the environment plays a major role in influencing behaviour.

In this study, therefore, the situational hypothesis, as favoured by Haney, Banks and Zimbardo, proposed that the social structure and conditions of a prison cause the behaviour of prisoners and guards alike.

The aim of the study was therefore to investigate the effects of an environment on a group of students, and to see whether the roles they were randomly assigned to play would significantly influence their behaviour.

This study shows some possible effects of imprisonment and offers possibilities for prison reform.

Research method

This was a laboratory experiment, designed to be as naturalistic as possible.

the **dispositional hypothesis** in relation to crime infers that it is not the prison environment that makes people act in the ways that they do but rather the dispositions (character traits) of those who live and work there.

Now test yourself

51 Explain the difference between a dispositional explanation and a situational explanation for behaviour.

TESTED ☐

Figure 19.5 The independent variable (IV) was: guard or prisoner

The IV was the condition the participant was randomly allocated to, i.e. the role of prisoner or guard (see Figure 19.5 on page 193). The DV was the resulting behaviour.

The study used an independent measures design.

Outline of the procedure/study

Twenty-four males were selected from an original pool of 75 who answered a newspaper advertisement asking for male volunteers to take part in a psychological study of 'prison life' in return for a payment of $15 a day for up to two weeks. The volunteers completed a questionnaire concerning their family background, physical and mental health history, experience and attitudinal propensities with respect to sources of psychopathology (including their involvements in crime). Each respondent was interviewed by one of two experimenters. The 24 individuals who were deemed to be the most stable (physically and mentally), most mature and least involved in antisocial behaviours were selected. On a random basis, half of the participants were assigned to the role of 'guard' and half to the role of 'prisoner'.

All participants were normal, healthy male college students who were in the Stanford area during the summer. They were largely of middle-class socio-economic status and Caucasians (with the exception of one Oriental participant). They did not know each other as existing friendships might have affected the study or led to the breakup of the friendship. Two standby prisoners were not called and one guard dropped out before the start of the study, which left 10 prisoners and 11 guards.

This final sample was administered a battery of psychological tests on the day prior to the simulation, but to avoid any selective bias on the part of the experimenter-observers, scores were not tabulated until the study was completed.

Physical aspects of the prison

The prison was built in a 35 ft section of a basement corridor in the Psychology building at Stanford University. It was partitioned by two fabricated walls; one was fitted with the only entrance door to the cell block and the other contained a small observation screen. Three small cells (six by nine foot) were made from converted laboratory rooms by replacing the usual doors with steel barred, black painted ones and removing all furniture.

A cot (with mattress, sheet and pillow) for each prisoner was the only furniture in the cells. A small closet across from the cells served as a solitary confinement facility; its dimensions were extremely small (two by two by seven foot) and it was unlit.

In addition, several rooms in an adjacent wing of the building were used as guards' quarters (to change in and out of uniform or for rest and relaxation), a bedroom for the 'warden' and 'superintendent', and an interview-testing room. Behind the observation screen at one end of the 'yard' (small enclosed room representing the fenced prison grounds) was video-recording equipment and sufficient space for several observers.

Operational details

The prisoners remained in the mock prison 24 hours per day for the duration of the study. Three were arbitrarily assigned to each of the three

Now test yourself

52 Outline the aim of this study.
53 Describe how the independent variable was operationalised in this study.

TESTED ☐

Exam tip

Know the research method and sample.

Now test yourself

54 Identify the sampling technique used in this study.
55 Describe why it was important that all participants were unknown to each other.

TESTED ☐

Answers at **www.hoddereducation.co.uk/myrevisionnotes**

cells; the others were on stand-by call at their homes. The guards worked on three-man, eight-hour shifts, remaining in the prison environment only during their working shift and going about their usual lives at other times.

Role instructions

All participants were told they would be randomly assigned to the guard or prisoner role and all had voluntarily agreed to play either role for $15 per day for up to two weeks. They signed a contract guaranteeing a minimally adequate diet, clothing, housing and medical care as well as the financial remuneration in return for playing their assigned role for the duration of the study. The contract made it clear that those assigned the role of prisoner should expect to be under surveillance (have little or no privacy) and that some of their human rights would be suspended. They were given no further information but were informed by phone to be available at their place of residence on a given Sunday when the experiment would start.

Those assigned the role of guard attended an orientation meeting on the day prior to the induction of the prisoners. At this time, they were introduced to the principal investigators, the 'superintendent' of the prison (the author, Zimbardo) and an undergraduate research assistant who assumed the administrative role of 'warden'. They were told that the aim was to simulate a prison environment and, although given no specific instructions as to how to behave, that their assigned task was to 'maintain a reasonable degree of order within the prison necessary for its effective functioning' without the use of any physical punishment or physical aggression. The 'warden' instructed the guards in administration details. including the work shifts, the mandatory completion of shift reports concerning the activity of guards and prisoners, the completion of 'critical incident' reports which detailed unusual occurrences, and the administration of meals, work and recreation programmes for the prisoners. To help the guards get into their roles they assisted in the final phases of completing the prison complex by putting the cots in the cells, putting signs on the walls, setting up the guards' quarters, moving furniture, water coolers, refrigerators, etc.

Uniforms

In order to promote feelings of anonymity, participants in each group were issued with identical uniforms. Prisoners wore loose-fitting muslin smocks with identification numbers on front and back, a cap made from a nylon stocking, no underwear, rubber sandals and a light lock and chain around one ankle. They were issued with washing gear (toothbrush, soap, soap dish, towel) and bed linen but were not allowed personal possessions.

Guards wore plain khaki shirts and trousers and reflective sunglasses (to make eye contact impossible) and carried a wooden baton and whistle. The khaki uniforms were intended to convey a military attitude, while the whistle and baton were carried as symbols of power.

The prisoners' uniforms were designed not only to deindividuate the prisoners but also to be humiliating and serve as symbols of their dependence and subservience.

Induction procedure

With the co-operation of the Palo Alto City Police Department, prisoners were unexpectedly arrested from their homes the day before the study was due to start. A police officer charged them with suspicion of burglary

> **Now test yourself**
>
> 56 What instructions were given to the guards at the orientation meeting?
>
> TESTED ☐

or armed robbery, advised them of their legal rights, handcuffed them, thoroughly searched them (often as curious neighbours looked on) and took them off to the police station in the back of a police car. At the station they went through the standard procedure of being fingerprinted, having an identification file prepared and then being placed in a detention cell. Each prisoner was then blindfolded and driven by one of the experimenters and a guard participant to the mock prison.

Upon arrival at the mock prison each prisoner was stripped, deloused (with a harmless deodorant!) and made to stand alone, naked, for a while in the cell yard. He was then given a prisoner's uniform, had an ID photograph taken, put in his cell and ordered to remain silent.

Administrative routine

When all the cells were occupied the warden greeted the prisoners and read them the prison rules (developed by the guards and the warden). They were to memorise and follow these rules. From that moment onwards they were referred to by number only.

Prisoners were to be served three bland meals a day, allowed three supervised toilet visits and given two hours daily for reading or letter writing. Work assignments were issued for which prisoners were to receive an hourly wage to constitute their $15 daily payment. Two visiting periods per week were scheduled, as were movie rights and exercise periods. Three times a day prisoners were lined up for a 'count' (one on each guard shift) – this was to ascertain that all prisoners were present and to test them on their knowledge of the rules and their ID numbers. The first 'count' lasted about ten minutes, but as the study progressed counts spontaneously increased in duration until some lasted several hours.

Subsequent behaviour by both guards and prisoners was observed by the researchers in the observation room and recorded on video tape.

Key findings

The experiment had to be stopped after six days, principally because of the pathological reactions of the participants. The results were recorded by observation but were backed up by video and audio tape, dialogue, self-report questionnaires and interviews.

In general, guards and prisoners showed a marked tendency towards increased negativity, with the nature of their interactions becoming increasingly hostile, affrontive and dehumanising. From the beginning the prisoners adopted a generally passive response mode while the guards assumed a very active initiative role in all interactions.

Although physical violence was prohibited, varieties of less direct aggressive behaviour were frequently observed, especially by the guards, with verbal affronts being used as one of the most frequent forms of interpersonal contact between guards and prisoners.

The most dramatic impact of the situation was seen in the extreme reactions of five prisoners who had to be released because of emotional depression, crying, rage and acute anxiety. When the experiment was terminated prematurely, all the remaining prisoners were delighted with their unexpected good fortune whereas most of the guards seemed to be distressed by the decision to stop the experiment as it appeared they had become absorbed in their roles and enjoyed the extreme control and power which they exercised and were reluctant to give up.

Now test yourself
57 Describe how the guards were dressed.
58 Describe the prisoners' induction procedure.
TESTED

Exam tip
Know the procedure in relation to both the guards and the prisoners.

None of the guards ever failed to come to work on time for their shift and on several occasions they remained on duty voluntarily for extra hours – without additional pay. Some guards were tough but fair, some went far beyond their roles to engage in creative cruelty and harassment, while a few were passive and rarely instigated any coercive control over the prisoners.

When prisoners' private conversations were monitored, it was found that 90 per cent of what they talked about was directly related to immediate prison conditions, i.e. food, privileges, punishment, guard harassment, etc., with only 10 per cent of their conversations being concerned with their lives outside the prison. Likewise, during their relaxation breaks, the guards either talked about 'problem prisoners' or other prison topics, or did not talk at all.

When questioned after the study about their persistent affrontive and harassing behaviour in the face of prisoner emotional trauma, most guards replied that they were 'just playing the role' of a tough guard, although none ever doubted the validity of the prisoners' emotional response.

When introduced to a Catholic priest, many of the prisoners referred to themselves by their prison number rather than their Christian names.

During a parole board hearing, when each of five prisoners eligible for parole was asked whether he would be willing to forfeit all the money earned as a prisoner if he were to be paroled, three of the five said 'Yes'. When told the possibility of parole would have to be discussed with the members of staff before a decision could be made, each prisoner got up quietly and was escorted by a guard back to his cell to await the decision.

The prisoners developed the 'pathological prisoner syndrome' and became extremely negative, which manifested itself as depression or as excessive obedience. This situation was thought to be brought about due to the loss of personal identity, the arbitrary control shown by the guards, dependency and emasculation (reinforced by their uniforms which resembled frocks or dresses, lack of underwear, etc.).

The guards became absorbed in what has been described as the 'pathology of power' where they enjoyed and misused the power they felt they had been given. This was demonstrated in terms of the increasingly extreme sanctions, punishment and demands made on the prisoners – for example, after the first day, practically all prisoner rights were redefined by the guards as 'privileges' which were to be earned through obedient behaviour. 'Reward' then became granting approval for prisoners to eat, sleep, go to the toilet, talk, smoke, wear glasses.

Conclusions

Being confined within a prison environment can have negative effects on the interpersonal processes that take place between prisoners and guards.

Incarceration can lead to prisoners developing a pathological prisoner syndrome.

Prison guards can develop a pathology of power.

There are individual differences in the way people cope in novel experiences.

The behaviour of the participants is best explained by situational, not dispositional, factors.

Exam tip

Know the key findings and be able to draw conclusions from the findings.

Now test yourself

59 Describe how 'pathological prisoner syndrome' was shown in this study.
60 Describe how 'pathology of power' was shown in this study.
61 Suggest one conclusion that can be drawn from the findings of this study.

TESTED

Application

At least one strategy for reducing reoffending: for example, the use of token economies, anger management programmes, restorative justice programmes, social skills training, cognitive behaviour therapy.

Practice questions

Criminal psychology

1 Describe how research by Raine *et al.* (1997) offers a biological explanation for criminal behaviour. [10]
2 Discuss the nature/nurture debate in relation to Raine *et al.*'s study. [15]
3 Gary has been in prison for eight years, having been found guilty of committing three 'breaking and entering' offences. Several times during his first few months in prison Gary got involved in fights with other prisoners. Those incidences have left him with a scarred face and misshapen nose. He is due to be released in three months' time; however, his self-esteem is very low and he is worried that his physical appearance will make life difficult for him once he is released. He feels he will not be able to get a job or make any friends and will therefore be drawn back into crime. Suggest a biological strategy to reduce the chances of Gary reoffending. [10]

ONLINE

Summary

By the end of this chapter you should:
- know and understand a physiological and non-physiological explanation of criminal behaviour, Raine *et al.*'s study, at least one biological strategy for preventing criminal behaviour
- be able to describe motivating factors and biases in the collection and processing of forensic evidence, Hall and Player's study, at least one strategy for reducing bias in the collection and processing of forensic evidence
- be able to describe how evidence can be collected and used from witnesses and suspects, Memon and Higham's study, at least one strategy for police interviews

- be able to describe how the characteristics of witnesses and defendants can influence jury decision making, Dixon *et al.*'s study, at least one strategy used to influence jury decision making
- be able to describe how the features of neighbourhoods and a zero tolerance policy can influence crime, Wilson and Kelling's study, at least one strategy for crime prevention
- be able to describe how punishment and reform are used as responses to criminal behaviour, Haney *et al.*'s study, at least one strategy for reducing reoffending.

20 Section B: Option 3 – Environmental psychology

Stressors in the environment (Biological)

REVISED

Environmental stressors: for example, heat, noise, architecture, pollution, crowding, environmental catastrophes.

The impact of environmental stressors on biological responses: for example, the role of the central nervous system, the peripheral nervous system, the autonomic nervous system, the adrenal glands and hormones; the fight or flight response; Selye's General Adaptation Syndrome.

Key research: Black and Black (2007): Aircraft noise exposure and residents' stress and hypertension

Theory/theories on which the study is based

Exposure to aircraft noise suggests there are several kinds of reflex responses (Spreng, 2000, 2004) that cause a stress reaction (emotional stress).

Stress means that the individual is experiencing a physical reaction to something that is perceived as threatening or dangerous to their survival. Hypertension is the medical term for elevated blood pressure. Sound can impact on blood pressure.

Noise-sensitive people have a low capability to cope with a noise stimulus, leading them to get more stressed than normal.

Background to the study

Health effects have been ignored when formulating environmental management plans at airports.

Previous research – for example, Brozaft *et al.* (1998), Meister and Donatelle (2000), Miyakita *et al.* (2002), Franssen *et al.* (2004) – has shown that exposure to high levels of aircraft noise had a significant negative relationship with general health status.

The World Health Organization definition that health includes physical, psychological and social well-being (Berglund and Lindvall, 1995) was taken as a starting point for this research. The research presented in this paper aimed to develop a better understanding of the impacts of aircraft noise on community health and well-being by seeking to answer two core questions:
1 Is health-related quality of life worse in a community chronically exposed to aircraft noise than in a community not exposed?
2 Is long-term aircraft noise exposure associated with elevated blood pressure in adults via noise stress as a mediating factor?

The research also considered implications for future public policy.

Suggestions were made in relation to stress management techniques as methods that could be employed to help individuals who suffer from health-related issues relating to long-term exposure to aircraft noise – for example, cognitive behavioural therapy.

Now test yourself

1 Outline Selye's General Adaptation Syndrome (GAS).

TESTED

Exam tips

Be able to describe a variety of environmental stressors.

Be able to describe some biological responses to environmental stressors.

> **stress** is the feeling of being under too much mental or emotional pressure. Pressure turns into stress when an individual feels unable to cope.

Now test yourself

2 Give a definition of stress.

TESTED

Now test yourself

3 Identify the two questions this research aimed to answer.

TESTED

Research method

This is a literary review of research undertaken by a multi-disciplinary team. A pilot study of a small suburb south of Sydney Airport, Australia is described. Subsequently, a wider-ranging study is reported that involved the selection of a highly exposed, noise-affected area and a control study area, not exposed to aircraft noise, with similar demographic and socio-economic characteristics.

It is a cross-sectional study with a matched control group with data gathered through the use of a questionnaire (a form of self-report).

Outline of the procedure/study

Pilot study

A small residential suburb at Kurnell, located to the south of Sydney Airport, acted as a case study for the pilot test with sample size of 100. The analysis of the findings showed that several values of the noise stress scale and the noise sensitivity scale duplicated the results of other items so the exclusion of some noise stress items and noise sensitivity items was recommended for the final study.

The questionnaire

Subjective health outcomes were measured by a questionnaire that measured seven major characteristics of each participant: (1) health related quality of life (HRQoL); (2) hypertension condition; (3) noise stress; (4) noise sensitivity; (5) noise annoyance; (6) demographic characteristics; and (7) confounding factors. For each health measure, a summary score in the range of 0 to 100 was obtained, with a higher score implying a more positive health status.

A set of closed questions was used to assess hypertension, for example, 'Have you ever been told by a doctor or nurse that you have high blood pressure sometimes called hypertension?' (1) Yes, (2) Yes, but only temporarily, (3) No. And then 'If Yes, do you currently have high blood pressure?' (1) Yes, (2) No. Questions were also included to prevent distortion effects from the variables of hypertension history in participants' parents and cholesterol levels.

The annoyance measurement included in the questionnaire consisted of two sections, each of which had two questions assessing annoyance from traffic noise and aircraft noise:

1 The first section measured participants' annoyance from daily activity disturbances (during the past 12 months) when at home.
2 The second section asked participants to consider all items from the first section and rate their overall annoyance from each noise source by using an opinion scale (0 to 10) where zero meant not at all annoyed and 10 meant extremely annoyed.

The study area

For the aircraft noise exposure area, highly exposed areas around Sydney (Kingsford Smith) Airport were selected and were matched on the socio-economic status of the exposure areas with a control group area, a suburb (South Penrith), located in the western suburbs of Sydney (approximately 55 km from Sydney Airport, a location not exposed to aircraft noise, i.e. outside flight paths).

The procedure

When contacting potential respondents, the cover letter explained that the study was one of environmental noise – not mentioning aircraft noise in an attempt to neutralise the likelihood of an increased response rate of those residents who are especially annoyed by aircraft noise.

Field measurements of environmental noise were undertaken according to Australian standards (Australian Standard, 1997) to determine noise at the points of receptors in the control and noise-exposed study areas. Noise data was collected at 26 stations located around Sydney Airport and three stations in the control area from 7 a.m. to 6 p.m. on various days from October 2003 to November 2004.

Key findings

Response rate

The questionnaire was completely filled in by 704 respondents. The number of responses from participants in the control group area was a little lower than from the noise exposure area.

Overall, the total response rate was slightly lower than the expected rate of 50 per cent.

Demographic and socio-economic states of the samples (data gathered from the questionnaires)

In the total sample, ages ranged from 15 to 87 – considered normal. The mean age in the control group was approximately four years higher than the noise exposure group. In the control group, 66.1 per cent of the sample was female – 10.1 per cent higher than in the noise exposure group.

In terms of socio-economic status, participants in the noise exposure group seemed to have a higher education and better employment status than the control group. Both groups were similar in terms of household income.

Participants' consumption of alcohol and salty food in both groups was not significantly different, though participants in the noise exposure group were more likely to be smokers than those in the control group.

In the control group, participants took proportionately less exercise than in the noise exposure group. Therefore the percentage of obesity in the control group was considerably higher.

The marital status between both groups was significantly different, with a higher proportion being married in the control group.

Only 3 per cent of the participants in the control group had insulated their house from noise compared with around 37 per cent of the participants in the noise exposure group.

Health and related measures

Table 20.1 summarises some of the descriptive statistics of health and related measures of both study groups.

Table 20.1 Health and related measures

Variable	Noise exposure group	Control group
Mean physical functioning score	79.09	79.23
Mean general health score	64.49	66.08
Mean mental health score	68.02	73.53
Mean noise stress score	6.44	4.25
Mean aircraft noise annoyance	6.27	1.03

Now test yourself

5 List the seven participant characteristics measured by the questionnaire.
6 Outline the areas to which questionnaires were sent.
7 Describe the procedure followed in this study.

TESTED

Exam tip

Know the key findings and be able to draw conclusions from the findings.

Relationships between health quality of life (QoL) factors and aircraft noise

The study rejected the null hypotheses and concluded that the mean scores of physical functioning, general health, vitality and mental health of the aircraft noise exposure group was significantly lower than for the matched control group.

Prevalence of hypertension and aircraft noise

The analyses of association between prevalence of hypertension and aircraft noise exposure were divided into two sub-sections:

a) Aircraft noise exposure – chronic noise stress: analysis of results showed that there was a significant positive association/relationship between noise exposure and chronic noise stress with those exposed to high aircraft noise level having the odds of 2.61 (95 per cent) on having chronic noise stress.

b) Chronic noise stress – prevalence of hypertension, based on an assumption that 'aircraft noise has indirect impacts to hypertension. It disturbs daily activities and creates chronic noise stress which becomes a mediating factor for hypertension in the future': analysis of results showed there was a significant positive relationship between chronic noise stress and the prevalence of hypertension with individuals who suffer chronic noise stress having the odds of 2.74 (95 per cent) on having hypertension compared with those without chronic noise stress.

Conclusions

Individuals who are exposed long term to high levels of aircraft noise are more likely to report stress and hypertension compared with those not exposed to aircraft noise.

There is a statistically significant relationship between long-term exposure to aircraft noise and well-being.

HRQoL – health-related quality of life – (in terms of physical functioning, general health, vitality and mental health) of individuals from aircraft noise exposure groups is worse than that of individuals who live in areas not affected by aircraft noise.

Application

At least one strategy for managing environmental stress: for example, problem-focused strategies (directed at changing the situation that is causing the problem) such as architectural improvements like double glazing, soundproofing, limiting how close to airports residential housing can be built, building more runways; emotion-focused strategies (directed at managing an individual's distress rather than changing the situation), for example rational emotive therapy, mindfulness, cognitive behavioural therapy, imaginal exposure therapy.

> **Now test yourself**
>
> 8 Outline two findings from this study.
>
> TESTED

> **Exam tips**
>
> Know how the study relates to the component 'Environmental psychology'.
>
> Know how the study relates to the topic 'Stressors in the environment (Biological)'.
>
> Know how the study relates to the impact of environmental stressors on biological responses.

> **Now test yourself**
>
> 9 Outline one strategy for managing environmental stress.
>
> TESTED

> **Exam tips**
>
> The question is likely to be worded generically so focus on the specific biological strategy selected for managing environmental stress.
>
> Be able to apply at least one strategy for managing environmental stress to a novel situation.

Biological rhythms (Biological)

Biological rhythms: for example, temporal (time) conditions and their impact on behaviour, **circadian rhythms**, circadian rhythms – are they **endogenous** or are they **exogenous**, ultradian rhythms, infradian rhythms.

The impact of the disruption of biological rhythms on behaviour: for example, the role of the **suprachiasmatic nucleus (SCN)** and the **pineal gland** in controlling circadian rhythms, how the disruption of circadian rhythms impacts on behaviour, the influence of **zeitgeber** changes on behaviour, the effects of sleep deprivation on behaviour, why jetlag occurs, the effects of jetlag and shift work on behaviour – phase advanced, phase delayed.

> **Exam tip**
>
> Be able to describe how the disruption of biological rhythms can have a negative impact on behaviour.

Key research: Czeisler *et al.* (1982): Rotating shift work schedules that disrupt sleep are improved by applying circadian principles

Theory/theories on which the study is based

Circadian rhythms occur once every 24 hours. The human sleep/wake cycle is a good example of a circadian rhythm. The normal circadian clock is set by the light/dark cycle over 24 hours. Circadian rhythm disorders can be caused by many factors, including shift work, pregnancy, time zone changes, medication, mental health problems, changes in routine for example, staying up late or sleeping in.

There are numerous medical and psychosocial problems associated with rotating shift work schedules – see research by Reinberg (1979), for example. Field studies indicate that there are sleep and digestive disorders among workers on rotating shifts (Rutenfranz *et al.*, 1977).

Background to the study

Within the past 50 years, the need for round-the-clock operations in many industrial plants and emergency services has led to major changes in the day–night schedules to which 26.8 per cent of the US workforce is exposed, many of whom work shifts which rotate between night, evening and daytime duties.

Previous research has shown that rotating shift workers are often dissatisfied with the features of their schedules that violate circadian principles.

Prior to this study, three major strategies had been used to address the problems of adaptation to shift work:
1 To schedule workers on straight shifts without rotation.
2 To rotate from one shift to the next rapidly in order to escape the consequences of partial temporal adaptation.
3 To take advantage of differences between individuals in measurable properties of the circadian timing system, to select individuals with the greatest tolerance for working or sleeping on abnormal schedules.

Now test yourself

10 What is a circadian rhythm?

TESTED

---

a **circadian rhythm** is a roughly 24-hour cycle which shows a repeating pattern of physical changes. Examples of circadian rhythms include the sleep/wake cycle, hormone secretion and blood pressure.

endogenous is a general term referring to anything whose origins are from within the individual whereas **exogenous** is a general term referring to anything whose origins are from outside the individual.

the **suprachiasmatic nucleus (SCN)** is a small group of brain cells located in the hypothalamus that controls the circadian cycles and influences many physiological and behavioural rhythms occurring over a 24-hour period, including the sleep/wake cycle.

the **pineal gland** is a small endocrine gland in the vertebrate brain. It produces melatonin, a serotonin derived hormone, which affects the modulation of sleep patterns in both seasonal and circadian rhythms.

a **zeitgeber** is any external or environmental cue that synchronises an organism's biological rhythms to the Earth's 24-hour light/dark cycle and 12-month cycle.

Because previous research has indicated that most rotating work schedules are outside the range of adjustment of the pacemaker timing the human circadian sleep–wake cycle, Czeisler *et al.* proposed that a practical and effective intervention would be to resolve this aspect of the shift work problem. Their aim was to show that when schedules are introduced which take into account the properties of the human circadian system, subjective estimates of work schedule satisfaction and health improve, personnel turnover decreases and worker productivity increases.

The researchers proposed that work schedules that rotate should do so by successive phase delays and that the interval between phase shifts should be as great as was practical.

Research method

This study used the self-report method through questionnaires to gather data in relation to measures of worker satisfaction, worker health, personnel turnover, and productivity before and after the introduction of new shift work schedules.

Outline of the procedure/study

Participants were 85 male rotating shift workers, aged 19 to 68 (mean age: 31.4 years), with a control group of 68 male non–rotating day and swing shift workers with comparable jobs, aged 19 to 56 (mean age: 27.3 years), at the Great Salt Lake Minerals and Chemicals Corporation plant in Ogden, Utah. The response rate was 84 per cent.

Each worker (participant) was given Smith, Kendall and Hulin's (1969) job description and health indices, and sleep/wake and schedule preferences questionnaires to complete before new shift work schedules were introduced. A rotating work schedule was designed and introduced that would take into account the properties of the circadian timing system, which focused on two key issues: the direction of rotation and the interval between phase shifts.

Shift workers (the participants) on phase advancing work schedules were divided into two groups and placed on phase delay schedules: 33 workers continued to change shifts each week and 52 others rotated shifts by phase delay once every 21 days. The 21-day phase delay schedule was originally designed so that work hours were shifted gradually by one to two hours per day for five days until the new shift time was attained. This procedure was eliminated after a month when it proved inconvenient for the workers' family life and car-pooling arrangements; thereafter an eight-hour phase delay was undertaken on every twenty-first day.

Before implementation of the schedule, all workers and managers attended an audiovisual presentation on the basic properties of the circadian sleep/wake cycle that offered suggestions for adjusting their sleep time to their schedule, and each received an educational booklet designed for the workers at this facility.

The workers' preferences were evaluated from other questionnaires distributed three months after the introduction of the new schedules, and personnel turnover and plant productivity were analysed nine months after the introduction of the new schedules.

Now test yourself

11 State what the researchers proposed in relation to optimal work schedules.

TESTED ☐

Now test yourself

12 Describe how the self-report method was used in this study.

TESTED ☐

Exam tips

Know the research method and sample (in relation to both the experimental and control groups).

Know the procedure and how data was gathered.

Now test yourself

13 Describe the sample used in this study.

TESTED ☐

Answers at www.hoddereducation.co.uk/myrevisionnotes

Key findings

Prior to the introduction of the new shift schedules:

- the rotators reported significantly more problems with insomnia than did non-rotators
- 29 per cent of the rotators reported that they had fallen asleep at work at least once during the previous three months
- a major complaint was that the schedule changed too often
- 81 per cent reported that it took two to four days or more for their sleep schedule to adjust after each phase advance; this included 26 per cent who said they were never able to adjust before being rotated again.

After the introduction of the new shift schedules:

- the workers clearly preferred the phase delay direction of rotation
- complaints that the schedule changed too often dropped from 90 per cent to 20 per cent among the workers on the 21-day phase delay rotation schedule
- there was a substantial increase on the schedule satisfaction index, improvements in the health index and a reduction in personnel turnover.

Measures taken after nine months of the new rotation schedules showed:

- staff turnover on the new phase delay schedules had reduced to the same range as the control group of non-rotating shift workers
- the rate of potash harvesting by men operating front-end loaders in the evaporation ponds and the rate of processed potash production in the plant increased after the introduction of the new schedule.

Conclusions

Work schedules that rotate by phase delay with an extended interval between each rotation are most compatible with the properties of the human circadian timing system.

The application of circadian principles to the design of schedules improves shift workers' job satisfaction and health indices.

The application of circadian principles to the design of schedules decreases personnel turnover and increases productivity.

Application

At least one strategy for reducing effects of jetlag or shift work: for example, induce biological changes such as taking melatonin supplements to control sleeping patterns, make schedule changes, initiate behavioural changes, control exposure to light and dark (using a light box).

> **Exam tips**
>
> The question is likely to be worded generically so focus on the specific strategy selected for reducing the effects of jetlag or shift work.
>
> Be able to apply at least one strategy for reducing the effects of jetlag or shift work to a novel situation.

> **Exam tip**
>
> Know the key findings and be able to draw conclusions from the findings.

> ## Now test yourself
>
> 14 Outline one finding from data gathered prior to the introduction of the new shift schedules.
> 15 Outline one finding from data gathered after the introduction of the new work shift schedules.
> 16 Suggest two conclusions that could be drawn from the findings of this study.
>
> TESTED ☐

> **Exam tips**
>
> Know how the study relates to the component 'Environmental psychology'.
>
> Know how the study relates to the topic 'Biological rhythms (Biological)'.
>
> Know how the study relates to the impact of the disruption of biological rhythms on behaviour.

20 Section B: Option 3 – Environmental psychology

Recycling and other conservation behaviours (Cognitive)

Conservation behaviours: for example, conservation behaviour is all behaviours that minimise damage to the environment/ are environmentally friendly, recycling, water conservation, heat conservation, fuel conservation, wildlife conservation, litter control, air quality control, emotions control.

Factors which influence the tendency to conserve or recycle: for example, situational factors, individual factors, cognitive factors, social value orientations, biospheric values, social norms.

Key research: Lord (1994): Motivating recycling behaviour: a quasi-experimental investigation of message and source strategies

Theory/theories on which the study is based

Recycling is an essential element of any long-term solution to the increasing problem of refuse disposal. Therefore, how to motivate full participation in recycling programmes is a critical concern of policy makers.

Inducing individuals to make a public commitment to environmentally responsible behaviours – for example, reduced energy consumption, increased use of public transport, newspaper recycling – results in greater compliance (for example, Wang and Katzev, 1990).

Self-monitoring which requires individuals to keep a record of their behaviour (Pallak *et al.*, 1980) and providing financial incentives (Bachman and Katzev, 1982) can also have a positive effect on environmentally responsible behaviours. Fear appeals may also be effective.

Individuals apply a cost–benefit strategy when deciding whether or not to adopt environmentally responsible behaviours.

Background to the study

Refuse disposal problems have plagued America's largest cities in recent years. These problems are now being felt in smaller communities and across national borders. In 1990, Americans threw out 196 million tons of refuse, more than twice as much as in 1960.

This study examines the relative efficacy of:
- two different message approaches – positively and negatively framed appeals (positively framed messages emphasise the 'relative benefits associated with compliance'; negatively framed messages draw attention to the 'detriments associated with rejection')
- three source strategies to encourage beliefs about, attitude towards and behavioural compliance with community recycling programmes – message sources examined are (a) advertising appeals, (b) publicity-generated news items, (c) personal influence appeals.

Now test yourself

17 Identify three things that have to be conserved in order to minimise damage to the environment.

TESTED

Exam tips

Be able to define the term 'conservation behaviour'.

Know a variety of ways through which conservation behaviours can be demonstrated.

Know some factors that may influence the likelihood of an individual showing conservation behaviours.

Now test yourself

18 Identify one strategy that individuals use when deciding whether or not to be environmentally responsible.

TESTED

This study aimed to show that exposure to each of the above message and source strategies yields more favourable attitudes towards recycling and a higher level of participation in recycling programmes than no message exposure. The researchers anticipated that a positively framed message would have a better opportunity of affecting beliefs than a negative appeal because individuals will respond to the feelings of satisfaction and other benefits gained from recycling.

The study therefore had the following hypotheses:

- Attitude towards recycling is improved for households receiving an **advocacy message**, relative to unexposed (control) households (H1).
- Delivery of an advocacy message yields an increase in observed recycling, with households receiving no message (control) showing no significant change in kerbside (pavement) collection amounts (H2).
- Consumer beliefs about positively valenced benefits of recycling are more readily formed upon exposure to an advocacy message than are beliefs about negatively framed consequences of failure to recycle (H3).
- Positively framed messages result in a more favourable attitude towards recycling than negatively framed messages (H4).
- Consumer belief in negatively framed arguments about the consequences of failure to recycle is greatest when those arguments are conveyed in the form of a publicity-generated news story and least when they appear as part of an advertising message (H5).
- Among consumers exposed to negatively framed messages, attitude towards recycling is greatest when the message is conveyed in the form of a publicity-generated news story (H6).
- Messages conveyed via social influence (i.e. from a personal acquaintance) result in a more favourable attitude towards recycling in a positively framed than in a negatively framed condition (H7).
- An advocacy message from a personal acquaintance elicits a greater increase in recycling behaviour than a comparable message from an advertising or news (publicity) source, with strongest behavioural change arising in the personal influence–negatively framed message condition (H8).

> an **advocacy message** is a message that aims to encourage an individual's support.

Research method

This is best viewed as an experimental field study/field experiment. Observations and self-reports were used to gather data.

The design was a full-factional three (message source: advertisement, newspaper article, personal letter from acquaintance) × two (message framing: positive, negative) between-subjects/participants design, plus a control condition.

Outline of the procedure/study

Data was obtained from 140 households in a north-eastern metropolitan community in the USA served by a kerbside (pavement) recycling programme such as that shown in Figure 20.1 on page 208.

- Twenty households received the advertisement with a positive message.
- Twenty households received the advertisement with a negative message.
- Twenty households received a newspaper article with a positive message.

Now test yourself

19 Outline two of the hypotheses tested in this study.
20 Outline why this study is best considered a field experiment.

TESTED ☐

- Twenty households received a newspaper article with a negative message.
- Twenty households received a personal letter from acquaintance with a positive message.
- Twenty households received a personal letter from acquaintance with a negative message.
- Twenty households received no message at all.

Figure 20.1 **Kerbside recycling**

Quota sampling was employed to try to ensure that the households selected for the study matched as closely as possible the community's demographic diversity.

The sample was somewhat upwardly skewed demographically, relative to the average socio-economic status from which it was drawn (presumably as a consequence of a slight bias towards the inclusion of suburban neighbourhoods in the quota sample – an attempt to avoid, for safety reasons, sending student assistants into certain inner-city neighbourhoods to collect data).

Of the questionnaire respondents:
- 57 per cent were female
- ages ranged from 19 to 65 years, with a mean of 34.9 years
- educational attainments ranged from some high school to graduate degrees (median – some college)
- household income ranged from $10,000 to 130,000 (mean $40,920)
- demographic profiles did not differ significantly between conditions.

The stimuli

Negatively framed messages described the risks (physical, environmental and social) of failing to recycle and some of the possible measures failure could necessitate. Positive appeals focused on environmental benefits, savings to the community and personal and social satisfactions arising from full participation in the recycling programme. Both messages reminded recipients of the items that were recyclable and the mode of pickup.

In the advertisement condition, the message had the appearance of an advert and was attributed to a fictitious company claiming to be a distributor of environmentally friendly products in the region. In the publicity (news article) condition, it was described as having recently appeared in a local news publication. In the personal influence condition, it appeared in the form of a letter, signed by a student assistant and addressed to a personal acquaintance.

> **Exam tips**
>
> Know the research method and sample.
>
> Know the procedure and how data was gathered.

Data collection proceeded in the following stages:

a) On kerbside collection day of the first week, student assistants discreetly observed and recorded on an observation form the contents of the test household's recycling bin.

b) On the following day, they left the stimulus message (the version appropriate to the condition to which the household had been assigned) at the front door of the test household, avoiding face-to-face contact (this step was omitted for the 20 households in the control condition).

c) On kerbside collection day of the following week, the observation of recycling bin contents was repeated (to assess behavioural impact of the test message).

d) On the day after the second observation, the student assistants contacted and delivered a questionnaire to the adult member of the household most involved with sorting and taking out the refuse (this comprised the first face-to-face contact between the student assistants and sample household members). The respondent was assured of anonymity and was asked to return the questionnaire in a sealed envelope, which would be submitted unopened and without household identifiers to the individual responsible for data entry.

Measures

The observation form assessed the quantity of items placed in recycling bins by the sample households in each of the categories accepted by the community's recycling programme (newspapers/magazines, corrugated cardboard, glass bottles/jars, etc.).

The follow-up questionnaire:

- Assessed beliefs in the arguments raised by the messages by asking participants to evaluate the truthfulness of each of several statements.
- Four seven-point semantic-differential items measured attitude towards recycling (good–bad, wise–foolish, harmful–beneficial, favourable–unfavourable).
- Demographic information was collected from the test households.
- Attitude towards the message (obviously, omitted in the control condition) was measured using eight seven-point semantic-differential items (good–bad, wise–foolish, harmful–beneficial, favourable–unfavourable, persuasive–unpersuasive, uninformative–informative, weak–strong and believable–unbelievable).

Key findings

H1: at an aggregate level this hypothesis was supported. Participants in the experimental groups demonstrated a more favourable attitude towards recycling than did respondents from control households. Attitude was significantly more favourable in the personal-positive, advertising-positive and publicity-negative conditions and marginally so in the advertising-negative and publicity-positive conditions. In the personal-negative condition, attitude towards recycling was not significantly different from that observed in the control condition.

H2: the combined treatment (experimental) groups showed a significant increase in both the number of recycling categories and the total number of items set out for recycling. The control group showed no significant change.

H3: those exposed to the positively framed message manifested a significantly higher level of belief in statements that constituted that

Now test yourself

21 Outline how the observation method was used to gather data in this study.
22 Outline how the self-report method was used to gather data in this study.
23 Outline what the follow-up questionnaire aimed to measure.

TESTED ☐

message's rationale for participation in the community recycling programme than did individuals in the control group and those exposed to the negatively framed message. Participants in the negative-appeal condition did not differ significantly in their perception of truthfulness of that message's arguments from their control group counterparts who were not exposed to the message.

H4: there was a significant effect of message framing, showing that the positively framed message led to a more favourable attitude towards recycling than did the negative appeal.

H5: findings did not support this hypothesis as no significant difference between sources was found.

H6: the source-framing interaction was significant and directionally consistent with the hypothesis. However, although attitude towards recycling as observed in the negative-appeal publicity condition was significantly greater than that obtained for the same message conveyed by a personal acquaintance, it did not differ significantly from that generated by the advertising source so H6 was only partially supported.

H7: attitude towards recycling was significantly higher among households receiving the positively framed message than among those in the negative-appeal condition.

H8: the personal negative condition showed the greatest increase in recycling behaviour.

Overall, the pooled data from the experimental groups revealed an increase in recycling behaviour that was not observed within the control group.

Conclusions

Consumers prefer positively framed messages over those that expose them to the unpleasantness of the adverse consequences of failure to recycle.

Individuals are more likely to believe arguments raised in positive appeals than those raised in negative appeals in relation to recycling behaviours.

Positively framed messages have a more favourable impact on attitude towards recycling than negative appeals.

Conveying a negatively framed message via a message from a personal acquaintance exacerbates its negative attitudinal consequences.

The most effective way to increase recycling behaviour is to convey a negatively framed message via a personal acquaintance.

Application

At least one technique used to increase recycling or other conservation behaviour: for example, information campaigns, reinforcing social norms, changing attitudes, prompts, positive reinforcement, punishment, feedback.

Exam tips

The question is likely to be worded generically so focus on the specific technique selected to increase recycling or other conservation behaviours.

Be able to apply at least one technique for increasing recycling or other conservation behaviours to a novel situation.

Exam tip

Know the key findings and be able to draw conclusions from the findings.

Now test yourself

24 Summarise the findings of this study.

TESTED

Exam tips

Know how the study relates to the component 'Environmental psychology'.

Know how the study relates to the topic 'Recycling and other conservation behaviours (Cognitive)'.

Know how the study relates to factors which influence the tendency to recycle.

Now test yourself

25 Suggest one conclusion that can be drawn from the findings of this study.
26 Outline one technique that could be used to increase recycling or other conservation behaviours.

TESTED

Ergonomics – human factors (Cognitive)

Cognitive overload: for example, Atkinson and Shiffrin's model, Baddeley and Hitch's working memory model, Bell *et al.*'s concept of environmental overload, secondary task performance ability, the use of self-reports to assess cognitive overload.

The impact of observation in the workplace environment: for example, social facilitation; audience effects; co-action effects.

> ## Exam tips
>
> Be able to describe the term 'cognitive overload'.
>
> Be able to explain how cognitive overload comes about.
>
> Know how observation in the workplace environment can have a negative effect on behaviour.

> ## Now test yourself
>
> 27 Outline one way in which observation may impact in the workplace environment.
>
> TESTED

Key research: Drews and Doig (2014): Evaluation of a configural vital signs display for intensive care unit nurses

Theory/theories on which the study is based

The intensive care unit (ICU) is a specialised hospital environment where critically ill and injured patients receive continuous physiologic monitoring (Drews, 2013). Standard vital signs acquired continuously and displayed on patient monitors include blood pressure, oxygen saturation, and heart and respiratory rates. Traditionally, these are displayed numerically.

ICU nurses typically care for two patients in different rooms, intermittently monitoring their patients at the bedside and from remote monitoring displays. One of their primary cognitive tasks is to determine whether a patient is stable.

Processing information from multiple data sources requires considerable cognitive effort as each variable is examined and integrated to form an assessment (Vicente, Christoffersen and Pereklita, 1995).

Background to the study

ICU nurses using a graphical display had less diagnostic accuracy than when using a traditional display. In contrast, anaesthesiologists who used the graphical display were more accurate (Agutter *et al.*, 2003; Albert *et al.*, 2007).

Current display technology in the ICU is not optimised for fast recognition and identification of physiological changes in patients.

The aim of this study was therefore to (a) develop and (b) evaluate a CVS display designed to support rapid detection and identification of physiological deterioration by graphically presenting patient vital signs data.

> ## Now test yourself
>
> 28 Outline the aim of this study.
>
> TESTED

Research method

This was a laboratory experiment for which a CVS display was developed based on findings from studies of the cognitive work of ICU nurses during patient monitoring. An independent measures design was used.

The IV was whether the nurse was asked to interpret data presented in a traditional numerical format or using the CVS display. The DV was the response time and accuracy in clinical data interpretation (assessed across four scenarios).

The study was approved by the institutional review board (University of Utah). The simulation took place in the Applied and Basic Cognition Laboratory of the Department of Psychology at the University of Utah.

> **Exam tip**
>
> Know the research method and design.

Now test yourself

29 Explain why this study is said to have used an independent measures design.

TESTED

Outline of the procedure/study

A total of 42 registered nurses with critical care training and a minimum of one year's ICU experience interpreted data. Their mean age was 44.59 years (range 25 to 64 years), their mean amount of ICU experience was 8.48 years (range 2 to 30 years) and 69 per cent of the sample was female.

● Twenty-one nurses interpreted data in a traditional, numerical form (the control group).
● Twenty-one nurses interpreted data on the CVS display (the experimental group).

The development of a CVS display suitable for nurses in an ICU

Based on nurse interviews, a literature review and interviews with data visualisation experts, the design requirements for the graphical display were identified. Three experienced ICU nurses then iteratively reviewed display design prototypes, resulting in the final version of the CVS display, shown in Figure 20.2.

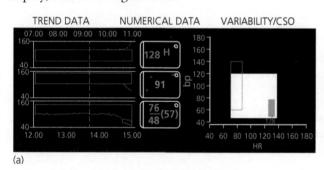
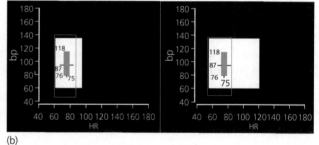

(a)

(b)

Figure 20.2 Configural vital signs (CVS) display

The centre panel (numerical data) is identical to the control display.
● CSO = current state object.
● **Trend data:** this shows trend data in relation to heart rate, blood oxygen saturation, systolic (SBP), diastolic (DBP) and mean arterial (MAP) blood pressures.
● **Variability/CSO:** the solid white rectangle shows a continuously updated representation of high and low values (range) for patient physiology over the past hour.

> **Exam tips**
>
> Know the sample (in relation to both the experimental and the control groups).
>
> Know the procedure.

Three clinical scenarios examined whether the CVS display supported nurses' decision making better than the traditional display – one relating to early sepsis, one to septic shock and one to pulmonary embolism. In all three scenarios, the information required to make a correct assessment was available on both displays.

A fourth scenario represented a stable patient and was included to determine whether the CVS display facilitates more rapid recognition of a 'normal' patient, that is, one without acute physiological changes or deterioration.

Procedure

Each participant in one display condition received a random order of scenarios that matched the scenario order received by another participant in the second display condition.

Participants were randomly assigned to either one or the other of the two display conditions until one condition had its full complement of participants.

All participants received a standardised 20-minute training that included procedural instructions and explained elements and functionality of the CVS and the control display. Each study lasted a total of approximately 90 minutes.

Prior to beginning the experiment, participants were instructed that they were to verbally evaluate the patient's physiologic status, interpret the data and recommend appropriate interventions as quickly and accurately as possible. Next, participants received scenario-specific patient information containing medical diagnoses, medical history, and previous and current administered medications.

Participants were given 300 seconds (five minutes) to complete each scenario. The last two steps were repeated until completion of all four scenarios.

For each scenario, a paper patient record was provided for clinical context. The vital signs displays were presented on a 15 inch desktop computer screen. Upon completion of all scenarios, all participants performed the NASA-TLX to assess workload (Hart and Staveland, 1988) and answered on a seven-point Likert-type scale (1 = lowest to 7 = highest) questions concerning the clinical desirability of the CVS display and the realism of the study scenarios.

Response time was measured from the start of the scenario to the time when the nurse verbalised their assessment. If the nurse did not verbalise an assessment within 300 seconds, 300 seconds was coded as that response time. Accuracy was determined by whether or not the nurse correctly identified the patient state.

For the control display condition, the frequency with which trend information was accessed was measured to assess the impact of information access costs on seeking out trending information.

Key findings

Response time

Overall, there was a significant difference in response time between the two display conditions, with participants in the CVS display condition identifying the patient's state more rapidly than in the control display condition.

The interaction between display and scenario was significant, indicating that in some of the scenarios the nurses using the CVS display correctly identified the patient state more rapidly than in others, compared with the nurses using the control display.

None of the covariates reached significance.

The scenario-specific analyses indicated that nurses in the CVS display condition were significantly faster in the septic shock and pulmonary embolism scenarios.

In the stable scenario the CVS display also yielded faster responses of participants compared with the control display.

Now test yourself

30 Explain the purpose of the fourth scenario.

TESTED

Now test yourself

31 Describe what participants had to do prior to the experiment.
32 Describe what participants had to do upon conclusion of all scenarios.
33 Outline how response time and accuracy were measured.

TESTED

Accuracy of data interpretation

Nurses using the CVS display correctly identified the patient's condition more frequently than nurses in the control condition.

Statistically significant differences were found for the septic shock scenario and the pulmonary embolism scenario, but not quite for the stable scenario. No difference between display conditions was found in the early sepsis scenario.

Workload and questionnaire data

There was a significant difference on the mental demand scale, with lower mental demand reported by nurses in the CVS display condition than by those in the control display condition.

Conclusions

Providing patient information in a configural display with readily visible trends and data variability can improve the speed and accuracy of data interpretation by ICU nurses.

The provision of integrated vital signs, variability information as spatial patient state and trend information can improve nurses' performance.

Application

At least one workplace design based on ergonomic research: for example, designing equipment that fits with how people think, using Feng Shui by designing the environmental space and organising furniture so people feel comfortable, considering colour schemes, noise levels, temperature, overcrowding to reduce cognitive stress.

> **Exam tips**
>
> The question is likely to be worded generically so focus on the specific workplace design based on ergonomic research selected.
>
> Be able to apply at least one workplace design based on ergonomic research to a novel situation.

Psychological effects of built environment (Social)

REVISED

The impact of the built environment on well-being: for example, environmental stressors such as overcrowding, commuting and noise in relation to both physical and mental well-being, the health-giving properties of nature, restorative environments.

The impact of urban renewal on well-being: for example, defensible space schemes, the development of green spaces, the ability to maintain privacy, encouraging heterogeneous communities.

> **Exam tips**
>
> Know how the built environment can have either a positive or a negative effect on health and well-being.
>
> Know how urban renewal can have a positive effect on health and well-being.

> **Exam tip**
>
> Know the key findings and be able to draw conclusions from the findings.

Now test yourself

34 Give one finding in relation to response time.
35 Give one finding in relation to accuracy.
36 Suggest one conclusion that could be drawn from the findings of this study.

TESTED

> **Exam tips**
>
> Know how the study relates to the component 'Environmental psychology'.
>
> Know how the study relates to the topic 'Ergonomics – human factors (Cognitive)'.
>
> Know how the study relates to cognitive overload in the workplace environment.

Now test yourself

37 Outline one workplace design based on ergonomic research.

TESTED

Now test yourself

38 Outline one way in which the built environment can impact on well-being.

TESTED

Key research: Ulrich (1984): View through a window may influence recovery from surgery

Theory/theories on which the study is based

Views of vegetation and especially water appear to sustain interest and attention more effectively than urban views with the same level of visual complexity (Ulrich, 1981). Most natural views apparently elicit positive feelings, reduce fear in stressed individuals, hold interest and may block or reduce stressful thoughts; they might also foster restoration from anxiety or stress (Altman and Wohlwill, 1983).

Surgical patients often experience considerable anxiety (for example, Chapman and Cox, 1977) and hospital confinements limit their access to outdoor environments almost entirely to views through windows. It is therefore possible that a hospital window view could influence a patient's emotional state and might accordingly affect recovery (Ulrich, 1984).

Background to the study

Investigations have shown a strong tendency for American and European groups to prefer natural scenes over urban views that lack natural elements (for example, Zube *et al.*, 1975; Weidemann and Anderson, 1978).

For this study, the restorative effect of natural views on surgical patients was examined in a suburban Pennsylvania hospital. Records of patients assigned to rooms on the second and third floors of a three-storey wing of the hospital between 1972 and 1981 were examined to determine whether assignment to a room with a window view of a natural setting might have restorative influences.

Research method

This is a review article that examined recovery data from hospital records of patients who had undergone cholecystectomy (a common type of gall bladder operation).

Outline of the procedure/study

Participants were 46 patients who had undergone cholecystectomy in a suburban Pennsylvania hospital between 1 May and 20 October 1972 and 1981. (May to October were selected because the trees have foliage on them during those months.) Patients younger than 20 years or older than 69, patients who developed serious complications and those with a history of psychological disturbances were excluded.

Participants were:
- twenty-three (15 female, 8 male) patients who had been assigned to rooms with windows looking out over a natural scene
- twenty-three (15 female, 8 male) patients matched on sex, age (within five years), being a smoker/non-smoker, obese/within normal weight limits, general nature of previous hospitalisation, year of surgery (within six years) and floor level who had been assigned to similar rooms with windows facing a brick building wall.

Patients on the second floor were also matched by the colour of their rooms (rooms on that floor alternated between blue and green).

> **Now test yourself**
>
> 39 Suggest why a hospital window view could influence a patient's emotional state and might accordingly affect recovery.
>
> TESTED ☐

> **Exam tips**
>
> Know the research method and sample.
>
> Know how and what data was gathered.

Records of patients assigned to rooms on the second and third floors of a three-storey wing of the hospital between 1972 and 1981 were obtained. The same nurses had been assigned to the rooms on a given floor.

The rooms were all for double occupancy and were nearly identical in terms of dimensions, window size, arrangement of beds, furniture and other major physical characteristics. Each room had a single window 1.83 m high and 1.22 m wide with the lower edge 74 cm above the floor. The size and placement of the window allowed an unobstructed view out for a patient lying in bed on either side of the room. The only real difference in the rooms was therefore what could be seen through the windows.

Recovery data was extracted from patients' records by a nurse with extensive surgical floor experience. The nurse did not know which scene was visible from a patient's window.

Five types of information were taken from each record:
a) Length of hospitalisation.
b) Number and strength of analgesics each day.
c) Number and strength of doses for anxiety each day.
d) Minor complications.
e) All nurses' notes relating to a patient's condition or course of recovery.

Key findings

Records showed that patients with window views of trees spent less time in the hospital than those with views of the brick wall: 7.69 days compared with 8.70 days per patient. More negative notes were made on patients with the brick well view: 3.96 per patient compared with 1.13 per patient with the tree view.

For the primary period of interest (days 2 to 5) there were statistically significant variation between the tree-view and wall-view patients in the mean number of **analgesic** doses. Patients with the tree view took fewer moderate and strong pain doses than did the wall-view group but more doses in the weak category.

With respect to doses of anti-anxiety drugs, there was no significant variation between the groups.

A weighted score of minor post-surgical complications was computed for each patient. Although tree-view patients had lower scores, the difference was not statistically significant.

Conclusions

A natural scene has positive therapeutic influences (for patients recovering from cholecystectomy). Patients (recovering from cholecystectomy) who can see a natural view from their hospital window have shorter post-operative hospital stays and display more positive behaviours than those who have only featureless views such as brick walls.

Patients (recovering from cholecystectomy) who can see a natural view from their hospital window take fewer moderate and strong analgesic doses than patients who have only featureless views. They tend to experience fewer minor post-operative complications than patients who have only featureless views.

Answers at **www.hoddereducation.co.uk/myrevisionnotes**

Now test yourself

40 Describe the sample used in this study and the conditions to which they were assigned.
41 Identify the types of information taken from each patient's records.
TESTED

analgesic intake refers to the quantity and frequency of pain-relieving drugs taken by an individual.

Exam tip

Know the key findings and be able to draw conclusions from the findings.

Now test yourself

42 Outline two findings from this study.
43 Suggest one conclusion that could be drawn from the findings of this study.
TESTED

REVISED

Exam tip

Know how the study relates to the component 'Environmental psychology'.

Know how the study relates to the topic 'Psychological effects of built environment (Social)'.

Know how the study relates to the impact of the built environment on well-being.

Application

At least one example of environmental design used to improve health/well-being: for example, painting rooms in light colours, designing residential developments with limited connectivity and through-movement to reduce crime opportunities, constructing low-level rather than high-level buildings, developing nature parks in and around urban areas, reducing overcrowding by enlarging defensible spaces around both working and domestic buildings.

Exam tips

The question is likely to be worded generically so focus on the specific environmental design selected to improve health/well-being.

Be able to apply at least one example of environmental design used to improve health/well-being to a novel situation.

Territory and personal space (Social)

Territory in the workplace: for example, what is **personal space** (for example, Sommer's definition), how can personal space be invaded, Hall's four personal space distances, what is **territory** (for example, Sommer's definition), types of territory (for example, Altman's three types of territory), research into territory and personal space (for example, Felipe and Sommer (1966), Fisher and Byrne (1975), Middlemist (1976), Haber (1980), Smith (1981)).

Personal space in the workplace: for example, open-plan or closed-plan office designs, type and design of work spaces – desks or cubicles, allocated or first-come-first-occupied work spaces policies, personalisation of the office/working area.

personal space is often described as an emotionally charged bubble of space which surrounds each individual and which accompanies them wherever they go.

territory generally refers to a physical area which is generally immovable and is considered to belong to or be connected with a particular country or person.

Exam tips

Be able to describe the term 'territory' in relation to the workspace.

Be able to describe at least one piece of research into personal space and territory.

Be able to describe the term 'personal space' in relation to the workplace.

Know at least one way that personal space in the workplace can be identified.

Now test yourself

44 Define the term 'personal space'
45 Define the term 'territory'.
46 Outline one way in which personal space can be maintained in the workplace.

TESTED

Key research: Wells (2000): Office clutter or meaningful personal displays: the role of office personalisation in employee and organisational well-being

Theory/theories on which the study is based

Socio-cultural trends impact the way in which Americans conduct business (Wells, 2000). Communications technology has created major changes in today's offices (Wells, 2000) and socio-cultural changes have a significant impact on office designs (Wells, 2000).

With the changing nature of offices (from permanent offices to temporary workspaces), employee **personalisation** of office environments takes on special significance.

Personalisation is said to have three different classifications (Heidmets, 1994):

a) Personalisation may be done by (a) individuals to their own spaces – for example, their bedrooms or workspaces, (b) groups to their collective spaces – for example, their school or office building.

b) Personalisation can be done to places (for example, bedrooms, offices, hospital rooms) or objects (for example, computers, work instruments, clothing).

c) Personalisation may be done to a place or an object that belongs to the user either permanently (for example, their house or their computer) or temporarily (for example, their seat on a bus or their library books).

Personalisation is generally considered a form of territorial behaviour by which people use their belongings to mark and defend their territories and to regulate their social interactions (Altman, 1975; Brown, 1987). It is also thought that personalisation may guard against the negative physiological and psychological consequences of inadequate privacy regulation (for example, illness, stress and anxiety, Altman, 1975; Scheiberg, 1990).

Men and women employ different personalisation practices.

Organisational well-being may be defined as the overall health of an organisation which is comprised of many constructs, including organisational climate, social climate, employee productivity, performance, turnover and absenteeism. Organisational consultants have suggested that allowing employees to personalise their workspaces is very important to organisational climate (Becker, 1990).

Background to the study

Increased female employment over the past couple of decades (Quinn *et al.*, 1995) has resulted in many companies adopting more family-friendly policies such as flexitime, which allows employees to choose their own working hours (Lueder, 1986; Werts, 1996).

A design technique that is becoming increasingly common among large companies that frequently have a large percentage of their employees working at home or in the field rather than in the office is 'hot-desking', a type of officing in which employees are not given permanent offices (Brill and Keable, 1998). Instead, on the days they are in the office, employees are assigned one of several temporary workspaces.

Personalisation of a space may lead to feelings of personal control (Edney and Buda, 1976) which has been found to increase satisfaction, reduce stress, enhance work performance and enhance well-being and mental health (for example, Averill, 1973; Halper, 1995).

Despite the findings of previous research, some facilities managers adopt policies that restrict workspace personalisation. However, studies have indicated that even when companies have clear policies restricting personalisation, employees do it anyway (Clearwater, 1980; Becker, 1981; Brill *et al.*, 1984).

Research has shown that women tend to personalise their homes in a more intimate manner than men. Vinsel *et al.* (1980) found that female students

> **personalisation** is the deliberate decoration or modification of an environment by its occupants to reflect their identities.

Now test yourself

47 Define the term 'personalisation'.

48 Suggest one purpose of personalisation.

TESTED

tended to personalise with symbols of personal relationships such as photos, whereas male students tended to personalise with such things as sports themes and entertainment equipment.

The focus of this paper is on individuals' personalisation of their permanent places, specifically employees' personalisation of their workspaces. The paper poses four research questions and hypotheses:

1 Q: Do men and women personalise their workspaces differently?
   H: Men and women will personalise their offices differently.

2 Q: Is personalisation associated with enhanced employee well-being?
   H: Personalisation will be positively associated with satisfaction with the physical work environment, which will be positively associated with job satisfaction, which will be positively associated with employee well-being.

3 Q: Is personalisation more important to women's well-being than to that of men?
   H: Workspace personalisation will be more integral to the well-being of women than men.

4 Q: Is a company's personalisation policy associated with organisational well-being?

   H: Companies that have more lenient personalisation policies will report higher levels of organisational well-being (i.e. lower turnover, lower absenteeism, higher employee morale, and higher productivity) than companies having stricter personalisation policies.

This study used the model of office personalisation and employee well-being shown in Figure 20.3 to examine the questions and test the hypotheses.

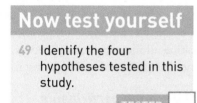

Now test yourself

49 Identify the four hypotheses tested in this study.

TESTED ☐

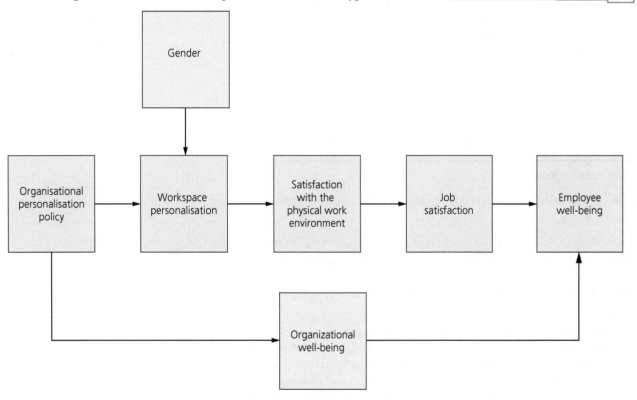

Figure 20.3 Model of office personalisation and employee well-being

Research method

This study used the self-report method to gather data in relation to the four research questions and hypotheses to determine whether office personalisation is associated with employee well-being and to determine the effect of gender on this relationship.

The self-reports included:
● an employee survey
● a co-ordinator survey.

The researcher also observed and photographed workspaces and interviewed some employees at five of the companies which agreed to participate as case studies.

Now test yourself

50 Outline what the self-report method was used for in this study.

TESTED

> **Exam tip**
>
> Know the research method and sample (in relation to both the employee surveys and the case studies).

Outline of the procedure/study

The participating companies

The participants were 20 companies and their employees who were recruited from 2,000 companies participating in the Small Business Workplace Wellness Project (SBWWP). 763 companies that employed at least 30 employees were selected to be approached for this project. The SBWWP contact person at each of the 763 companies was then sent a letter explaining that this was a study of office environments and employee well-being and asking all interested companies with at least 15 office employees to fill out the enclosed participant interest form and fax it back to the researcher.

The human participants

661 surveys were given out to office workers and 338 surveys were returned – 187 (55 per cent) were from males and 138 (41 per cent) were from females; 13 people (4 per cent) did not report their gender. Most of the participants (62 per cent) were between the ages of 25 and 44.

The sample was 69 per cent Caucasian/white, 13 per cent Hispanic, 10 per cent Asian-American, 3 per cent African-American, 1 per cent Native American and 4 per cent 'other'.

Most of the respondents (55 per cent) were married, whereas 24 per cent were single, 14 per cent divorced, 6 per cent living with a partner and 1 per cent widowed.

The average number of years the respondents had spent at their companies was 5.6 years.

Twenty-three employees (15 women, 8 men) agreed to be interviewed as part of the case studies. Employees were asked to complete a survey. This had several sections:
a) The first assessed workspace personalisation (for example, the number of personal items displayed).
b) The second assessed satisfaction with the physical work environment (using a nine-item, five-point scale with items such as 'I like my workplace').
c) The third assessed job satisfaction using a job-satisfaction scale (a five-item, five-point scale with items such as 'In general I like my job').
d) The fourth assessed well-being using measures of global well-being, physical health and psychological well-being (all used rating scales).
e) The fifth assessed employee perceptions of organisational well-being, including social climate, organisational climate, employee morale, productivity, performance and absenteeism (again using rating scales).
f) The sixth assessed personality traits predicted to be associated with office personalisation for example, need for affiliation, need for privacy, and creativity (all again assessed using rating scales).

Answers at **www.hoddereducation.co.uk/myrevisionnotes**

g) The final section consisted of personal demographic information including gender, age, ethnicity, marital status, parental status, education, salary, job title, full/part-time employment, length of time with the company and length of time at the present workplace. Other questions assessed the employee's type of workspace (enclosed or open) and the quality of their workspace.

Co-ordinators at each company completed the employee survey with the addition of several questions regarding the company's personalisation policy and organisational well-being (assessed using rating scales).

Case studies: to add depth and richness to the survey data, five of the 20 companies agreed to participate as case studies. After completing the surveys, these companies allowed the researcher to interview some employees and observe and photograph their workspaces.

The interview: participating employees were interviewed at their workspaces for 10 to 15 minutes. The interviews were structured interviews with open-ended questions and were tape-recorded.

The observation checklist: once the interview was complete, the researcher examined the workspace using an observation checklist which consisted of (a) a list of personalisation categories so that the number of items pertaining to each category could be counted, (b) space to list unusual items and themes, (c) a scale measuring aesthetic quality of the workspace, (d) the gender of the workspace occupant. Upon completion of the checklist, the workspace was photographed.

Key findings

Hypothesis 1

Over half (56 per cent) of respondents indicated that they personalised their workspace to express their identity and individuality, 30 per cent to improve the feel of the workplace, 16 per cent to express their emotions, 15 per cent to show that the workspace belonged to them, 6 per cent to show their status within the organisation, 5 per cent to control their interactions with co-workers, 3 per cent because everyone else did.

Men and women tended to personalise for different reasons. More women than men reported personalising to express their identities and their individuality, to express their emotions and to improve feel of the workplace. However, more men than women reported personalising their workspace to show their status within the company.

Gender differences also appeared in the extent of personalisation, with women personalising their workspaces significantly more than men. The average number of items displayed by men was 7.68, whereas for women this was 11.2. The women interviewed displayed an average of 18.5 personal items compared with an average of 8.3 by men.

The types of items displayed also varied by gender. Results indicate that most people (68 per cent) display symbols of personal relationships. Results showed that women's displays contained significantly more symbols of personal relationships, such as friends and pets, than men's. Women's displays also included more plants and trinkets than men's but men's displays contained more sports-related items than women's. These gender differences were also supported by the observational data – for example, women tended to display figurines, posters, greetings cards whereas men tended to display diplomas, trophies, training programme certificates.

Exam tip

Know the procedure and the focus of the surveys and case studies.

Now test yourself

51 Describe the sample used in the interview part of this study.
52 Describe what participants were asked about in the interview part of this study.

TESTED

Therefore both the survey and observational data supported the first hypothesis.

Hypothesis 2

Results showed that, as predicted, personalisation is significantly associated with satisfaction within the physical work environment:
a) The association between satisfaction with the physical environment and job satisfaction was found to have a positive correlation.
b) Job satisfaction was found to be positively associated with employee well-being in relation to global well-being, physical health and psychological well-being.
c) Personalisation was not directly associated with employee well-being when satisfaction with physical work environment and job satisfaction were controlled for.

Hypothesis 3

Survey results showed that personalisation was no more important to the well-being of women than to that of men, thus not supporting the hypothesis. However, the hypothesis was supported by the interview data.

When asked how they would feel if their company strictly prohibited workspace personalisation, women consistently replied that they would feel restricted, controlled and that management did not care about them. Men, however, were divided on the issue.

Hypothesis 4

Results indicated that companies that allow more personalisation have a more positive organisational climate, a more positive social climate, greater levels of employee morale and reduced turnover.

Secondary analyses

The extent to which employees personalise their workspace was positively correlated with the amount of personalisation allowed by the company. Organisational well-being was positively correlated with employee well-being.

There was a good fit between the proposed model of the relationships between office personalisation, gender, employee well-being and organisational well-being and the data gathered.

People who personalised the most tended to be managers as opposed to supervisors or lower-level staff members. They also tended to be older and married.

Correlational analysis showed that people personalised more in companies having employee-friendly policies, for example telecommuting, flexitime.

The company owner's ethnicity was significantly associated with the amount of personalisation allowed, with companies owned by Asian-Americans allowing less personalisation than companies owned by Caucasian/white Americans.

Conclusions

Men and women personalise their workspaces differently. Women personalise their workspaces more than men and place more importance on personalisation (of their workspace).

Exam tip

Know the key findings and be able to draw conclusions from the findings.

Now test yourself

53 Outline one finding in relation to the hypothesis: men and women will personalise their offices differently.
54 Outline one finding in relation to the hypothesis: companies that have more lenient personalisation policies will report higher levels of organisational well-being.

TESTED

Answers at www.hoddereducation.co.uk/myrevisionnotes

Employee well-being is enhanced if individuals are allowed to personalise their workspace.

The workplace organisational climate and social climate have significant implications for employee well-being.

Companies with lenient personalisation policies have greater levels of organisational well-being.

Companies with lenient personalisation policies have greater levels of employee morale and lower staff turnover than companies with strict personalisation policies.

Application

At least one office design strategy based on research into territory or personal space: for example, open-plan offices/hot-desking/working at a treadmill desk with lenient company policies with regard to personalisation.

Now test yourself

55 Suggest one conclusion that could be drawn from the findings of this study.
56 Outline one office design strategy based on research into territory and personal space.

TESTED

Practice questions

Environmental psychology

1 Describe what Ulrich's (1984) study into the impact of the built environment tells us about health and well-being. [10]
2 Discuss the usefulness of research into the effects of the built environment in relation to health and well-being. [15]
3 Alex is an environmental psychologist who has been asked to make recommendations to town and country planners. Describe at least one suggestion that Alex could make to promote health and well-being in the design of a proposed housing estate. [10]

ONLINE

Summary

By the end of this chapter you should:
- know some environmental stressors and how they may impact on biological responses, Black and Black's study, at least one strategy for managing environmental stress
- be able to describe how the disruption of biological rhythms can impact on behaviour, Czeisler *et al.*'s study, at least one strategy for reducing the effects of jetlag or shift work
- be able to describe factors which influence the tendency to conserve or recycle, Lord's study, at least one technique used to increase recycling or other conservation behaviour
- be able to describe the term 'cognitive overload' and the impact of observation in the workplace environment, Drews and Doig's study, at least one workplace design based on ergonomic research
- be able to describe how the built environment and urban renewal can impact on our well-being, Ulrich's study, at least one example of environmental design used to improve health/well-being
- be able to describe the terms 'territory' and 'personal space' in relation to the workplace, Wells' study, at least one office design strategy based on research into territory or personal space.

Arousal and anxiety (Biological)

Optimising arousal (in sport): for example, definitions of '**arousal**' and '**anxiety**', arousal and performance (for example, drive theory and the Yerkes–Dodson's inverted–U hypothesis and Oxendine's revision of the hypothesis).

Controlling anxiety (in sport): for example, the effects of the anxiety/stress spiral, trait anxiety, state anxiety – somatic and cognitive, techniques for controlling anxiety and arousal (for example, breathing techniques, relaxation techniques).

Measuring anxiety in sport: for example, physiological measures (for example, monitoring heart rate, breathing rate, measuring muscle response, measuring sweating, measuring hormone and steroid levels in the blood or urine), the use of observation in relation to the individual's behaviour and aspects of their performance, self-report questionnaires (for example, SCAT (Sport Competition Anxiety Test), CSAI-2 (Competitive State Anxiety Inventory)).

> **arousal** refers to a state of alertness and anticipation that prepares the body for action: it involves physiological activity (such as increased heart rate) and cognitive activity (such as an increase in attention).
>
> **anxiety** refers to feelings of fear and apprehension caused because a situation is seen as threatening.

Exam tips

Be able to define 'arousal' and 'anxiety' in relation to sports performance.

Be able to explain the relationship between arousal and sports performance.

Know at least one way that anxiety can be controlled in a sports situation.

Know at least one way that sports anxiety can be measured.

Now test yourself

1 Define the term 'arousal'.
2 Define the term 'anxiety'.
3 Outline drive theory.
4 Outline one way in which anxiety in sport can be measured.

TESTED

Key research: Fazey and Hardy (1988): The inverted-U hypothesis: a catastrophe for sport psychology

Theory/theories on which the study is based

The inverted–U hypothesis (Figure 21.1) describes how performance initially increases with the increase in intensity of a stimulus, but then performance tails off if the intensity or frequency of the stimulus continues to increase.

The inverted–U hypothesis does not account for individual differences in performance or the fact that different types of skill require different levels of arousal to achieve optimum performance. The hypothesis was therefore extended by Oxendine (1970) to describe the relationship between 'arousal' and motor performance in a range of different conditions. Oxendine suggested that the inverted–U hypothesis should be extended to include the following generalisations: (a) a high level of arousal is necessary for optimal performance in gross motor activities involving strength, endurance and speed, (b) a high level of arousal interferes with performance involving complex skills, fine muscle movements, co-ordination and concentration, (c) for all motor tasks, a slightly above average level of arousal is preferable to a normal or below average level of arousal.

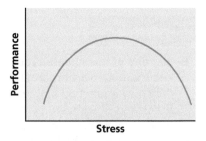

Figure 21.1 A traditional representation of the inverted-U hypothesis

Catastrophe theory was first developed by René Thom (1975) as a means of modelling certain naturally occurring discontinuities in functions which were normally continuous. His original theory showed that any catastrophe which might naturally occur in real time and space can be classified as being of the 'same type' as one of seven elementary catastrophes (fold catastrophe, cusp catastrophe, swallowtail catastrophe, butterfly catastrophe, hyperbolic catastrophe, elliptic catastrophe and parabolic catastrophe).

Background to the study

The inverted-U hypothesis originated from a study of habit-strength formation in mice under different conditions of punishment stimulus frequency (Yerkes and Dodson, 1908).

Fazey and Hardy claim there are at least three issues which present serious problems for the inverted-U hypothesis as it stands:
a) Difficulties with the basic ideas involved in the hypothesis.
b) Lack of convincing evidence for the validity of the predicted relationship between stress and performance.
c) Difficulties with applying the model, suggesting there are problems with the construct validity of the hypothesis.

This study considers these three issues and then proposes two catastrophe models of motor performance under anxiety which attempt to describe the relative contributions to performance of cognitive anxiety, 'on the day' physiological arousal, task difficulty and self-confidence.

Research method

This is a monograph (a specialist work of writing on a single subject or an aspect of a subject, usually by a single author) which identifies and considers three different areas of difficulty associated with the inverted-U hypothesis – difficulties with the basic constructs (ideas), difficulties with the corroborative evidence and difficulties in applying the model.

Outline of the identified difficulties with the inverted-U hypothesis

Difficulties with the basic constructs (ideas)

Many psychologists were using the terms 'arousal', 'stress' and 'anxiety' interchangeably when, in fact, they are different. While the inverted-U hypothesis described the relationship between arousal and performance, it did not adequately explain the more important relationship between anxiety and performance.

Difficulties with the corroborative evidence

There is still little convincing, sound experimental evidence for the inverted-U hypothesis as a model of the relationship between stress and performance.

Difficulties in applying the model

Fazey and Hardy's experiences when working with athletes performing in potentially highly stressful situations did not engender any real confidence that the traditional inverted-U concept was applicable. Instead, it appeared that when an athlete went 'over the top' two things occurred:

Now test yourself

5 Outline the inverted-U hypothesis.

TESTED

Now test yourself

6 Identify the three difficulties Fazey and Hardy found with the inverted-U hypothesis.

TESTED

Exam tip

Know the research method and sample and know how data was gathered.

a) The drop-off in performance was very large and dramatic (not a process of getting gradually worse).

b) Once the athlete started to experience a performance disaster in competition it was very difficult to get performance back to even a mediocre level, suggesting that small reductions in the stress being experienced by the athlete made no real difference to performance once this stage had been reached.

Fazey and Hardy therefore proposed a model that showed that as stress increased, so too did performance until a critical point was reached where it suddenly and dramatically fell to a very low level. In addition, their model proposed that once a performer was on the lower curve, it required a considerable reduction in stress for them to be able to jump back onto the upper performance curve (see Figure 21.2).

To summarise, Fazey and Hardy present three major criticisms of the inverted-U hypothesis:

1 The failure to recognise the multi-dimensionality of the anxiety and arousal systems.

2 The general lack of sound experimental support for the detailed predictions of the hypothesis.

3 The apparent lack of predictive validity in practical situations.

Outline of the proposed catastrophe model of anxiety and performance

Fazey and Hardy therefore proposed a catastrophe model to explain the relationship between anxiety and performance when athletes are performing under stress. The model's main assumption is that an athlete's level of **cognitive anxiety** determines whether the effect of physiological arousal is 'smooth and small, large and catastrophic, or somewhere between these two extremes'.

Fazey and Hardy's catastrophe model of anxiety and performance is shown in Figure 21.3. It proposes that where physiological demand is high and cognitive demands are low, cognitive anxiety will be associated with good performance. However, where physiological demand is low but cognitive demands are high, cognitive anxiety will be associated with poor performance.

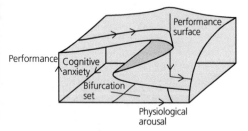

Figure 21.3 **A cusp catastrophe model of the effects of anxiety upon performance**

Fazey and Hardy's proposed catastrophe model makes the following testable predictions:

a) Physiological arousal (and any associated **somatic anxiety**) is not necessarily detrimental to performance. However, it will be associated with catastrophic effects when cognitive anxiety is high.

b) Under conditions of high cognitive anxiety, hysterics will occur. Under conditions of low cognitive anxiety, hysterics will not occur.

c) Intermediate levels of performance are most unlikely in conditions of high cognitive anxiety.

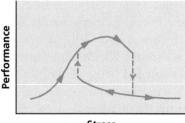

Figure 21.2 **Hardy's (1985) model of the relationship between stress and performance**

---

cognitive anxiety refers to the mental manifestations of anxiety, or the specific thought processes that occur during anxiety, such as concern or worry.

somatic anxiety is the physical symptoms of anxiety, such as butterflies in the stomach.

Now test yourself

7 Describe two of Fazey and Hardy's criticisms of the inverted-U hypothesis.

TESTED

Exam tip

Know the key findings and be able to draw conclusions from the findings.

Now test yourself

8 Outline the main assumption of Fazey and Hardy's catastrophe model.

9 Outline two of the testable predictions proposed by Fazey and Hardy.

TESTED

Conclusions

The inverted-U hypothesis is flawed.

Catastrophe models of motor performance under anxiety can be applied to describe the relative contributions to performance of cognitive anxiety, 'on the day' physiological arousal, task difficulty and self-confidence.

> **Exam tips**
>
> Know how the study relates to the component 'Sport and exercise psychology'.
>
> Know how the study relates to the topic 'Arousal and anxiety (Biological)'.
>
> Know how the study relates to the impact of optimising arousal and controlling anxiety in sport.

Application

At least one technique for managing arousal and anxiety in sport: for example, the use of biofeedback, the supplication of cognitive behavioural therapy, energising strategies to increase arousal (for example, energising self-talk, rituals), strategies to reduce arousal and anxiety (for example, relaxation training programmes).

> **Exam tips**
>
> The question is likely to be worded generically so focus on the specific technique selected to manage arousal and anxiety in sport.
>
> Be able to apply at least one technique for managing arousal and anxiety in sport to a novel situation.

Exercise and mental health (Biological)

REVISED

Benefits of exercise to mental health: for example, definitions of 'exercise' and 'mental health', exercise and mood, biological explanations of mental health, psychological explanations of how exercise might be beneficial to mental health, measuring the benefits of exercise on mental health and psychological well-being.

> **Exam tips**
>
> Be able to define the terms 'exercise' and 'mental health'.
>
> Be able to suggest several benefits of exercise to mental health and well-being.

Key research: Lewis *et al.* (2014): Mood changes following social dance sessions in people with Parkinson's

Theory/theories on which the study is based

Parkinson's (PD), a neurodegenerative disease, typically developing in people above the age of 50 years, is associated with the motor signs of tremor, bradykinesia (slow movement), muscle rigidity and postural instability.

Now test yourself

10 Suggest one conclusion that can be drawn from this study.

TESTED

Now test yourself

11 Outline one technique that could be used to manage anxiety in sport.

TESTED

Now test yourself

12 Define the term 'exercise'.
13 Define the term 'mental health'.
14 Outline one way the benefits of exercise on mental health and psychological well-being can be measured.

TESTED

Although PD is predominantly identified by these motor symptoms, non-motor features are also shown to be associated with the condition, including sleep disturbances, deficits in tasks of executive functioning and altered mood.

Dance can help the motor symptoms of PD (Hackney and Earhart, 2009; Hackney *et al.*, 2007). Dance may have particular psychological benefits due to the mental challenges that dance steps and timing can provide, such as memory, learning and spatial awareness (Lima and Vieira, 2007). Also, dance is a sociable form of exercise. Lack of sociability is linked to depression in elderly (Anderson, 2001), thus potentially explaining positive benefits of mood from dance.

Background to the study

Research has consistently shown that there is a high prevalence of depression in people with PD, such that up to 60 per cent of scores in relation to quality of life can be explained by depression (Global Parkinson's Disease Survey (GPDS) Steering Committee, 2002) and perhaps even more than the severity of the motor symptoms of the disease (Suzukamo *et al.*, 2006).

Research has shown that dance can help to regulate mood such that positive mood is increased and negative mood is decreased following dance exercise interventions over short-term, progressive periods of up to 50 minutes (Hansen *et al.*, 2001; Kennedy and Newton, 1997) and over a longer period of seven weeks (Steinberg *et al.*, 1998).

In a qualitative study by Paulson (2011), who interviewed elderly dancers, the main themes to emerge were feelings of psychological well-being and a sense of belonging. Lima and Vieira (2007) followed dance classes with the elderly over the period of one year. Participants reported 'being transported to a world of happiness' and being able to 'forget their problems'.

The objective of this study was, therefore, to examine the moderating effect of dance on mood in the elderly and more specifically in a group of people with PD across a long cycle of 12 weeks and a short cycle of one hour.

Research method

This study formed part of a larger study investigating dance as an intervention for PD. The research method was an experiment.

A mixed design (matched participants and repeated measures) was used with two independent variables:
- The first (IV1) was the naturally occurring variable of group – whether participants were sufferers of PD or whether participants did not suffer with PD (the control group). This part of the experiment used a matched participants design.
- The second (IV2) which was manipulated by the researchers was the time cycle: long cycle time (week 1 vs. week 12) or short cycle time (before class vs. after class). This part of the experiment used a repeated measures design.

The DVs were participants' mood scores.

Outline of the procedure/study

A total of 37 participants, aged between 50 and 80 years (M = 65.5 years), took part in the study. Of these, 22 participants (12 males, 10 females) had been diagnosed with PD and were all rated as having mild to moderate

Now test yourself

15 Identify two mood states for which exercise is proposed to be particularly beneficial.
16 Identify two ways in which dance is thought to be beneficial.

TESTED

Now test yourself

17 Outline the aims of this study.
18 Describe the two independent variables.

TESTED

symptoms by trained physiotherapists. The remaining 15 participants (7 males, 8 females) acted as age-matched controls.

Participants were recruited though local advertisements and through contact with local PD support groups (therefore a self-selecting sample). Eight of the controls were partners of those in the PD group. Many participants in the control group were carers for the people taking part with PD.

This study was ethically approved at an institution in the United Kingdom. All participants gave informed consent.

Materials

To measure the long cycle time: the POMS. The POMS is a 64-item mood scale and is scored on six sub-categories: Tension–Anxiety, Vigour–Activity, Depression–Dejection, Fatigue–Inertia, Anger–Hostility and Confusion–Bewilderment. The POMS also produces a total mood disturbance (TMD) score, calculated by adding all responses and subtracting Vigour from the rest of the sub-scales. Responses to mood are indicated on a five-point Likert scale (0 = Not at all to 4 = Extremely). Lower scores indicate a more positive mood state in all sub-scales other than Vigour, where a higher score suggests higher energy and elevated mood.

To measure the short cycle time: the BRUMS (Brunel University Mood Scale) was used. This is based on the POMS but has only 24 items, though it still measures the same mood states as the full POMS.

Procedure

Participants were asked to fill out a demographics questionnaire and the POMS according to how they had felt in the past month. They were also administered the Mini Mental State Examination (MMSE) at baseline, in a meeting prior to the first dance class (week 1). Participants then attended a weekly dance class, run by a qualified dance instructor, for a period of ten weeks (weeks 2 to 11).

Dance classes lasted for 50 minutes and consisted of a ten-minute warm-up, 30 minutes of dancing and a five-minute cool-down. A five-minute break was given midway. Each class was based on rhythmic dancing to a strong beat, designed to be appropriate for the age, mobility and constraints of people with mild to moderate PD. They completed the classes standing, with the option to sit down if desired. The style of dancing changed every two weeks and consisted of Bollywood, Tango, Cheerleading, Old Time Music Hall and Party dancing based on the Charleston and Saturday Night Fever.

Participants were taught in two separate, yet identical, dance classes.

In the ninth week, participants were asked to complete the BRUMS, according to how they felt 'right now', before and after the dance class (short cycle).

Following completion of the dance classes, participants were asked to complete the POMS for a second time a few days later in week 12 (long cycle).

Key findings

Comparisons between mean scores of the PD and control groups revealed no significant differences between the two groups for age, MMSE scores or baseline mood scores. Differences were found in the PD POMS baseline figures for tension, confusion, anger, vigour and TMD from the

Exam tip

Know the research method and sample and know how data was gathered.

Now test yourself

19 Outline how the self-selecting sampling technique was used in this study.
20 Identify the measurement tools used in the long cycle time and the short cycle time.

TESTED

Now test yourself

21 Describe when these BRUMS and POMS were administered.
22 Describe how the dance programme was organised.

TESTED

POMS geriatric norms. Participants in the control group did not differ from the POMS geriatric norms.

PD participants showed higher TMD scores throughout the study than participants in the control group.

Long cycle time:
● Results showed a significant reduction in mood disturbance over the long cycle time in all participants. Anger declined most significantly, with Anxiety–Tension also declining significantly. Vigour increased slightly but did not reach significance.

Short cycle time:
● Tests on BRUMS short cycle scores showed TMD scores improved significantly from baseline.
● BRUMS sub-scales of Tension–Anxiety and Vigour were significantly improved, though other improvements – for example, depression – did not reach significance.

Conclusions

Dance interventions have physical benefits for the elderly, especially those with Parkinson's.

Dance can provide positive benefits over both a long and a short cycle time for the elderly, including those with PD. It can help improve mood states and reduce anger in elderly people, especially those suffering with Parkinson's.

Exercise, including dance aerobics, can improve levels of vigour, TMD and fatigue.

> **Exam tips**
>
> Know how the study relates to the component 'Sport and exercise psychology'.
>
> Know how the study relates to the topic 'Exercise and mental health (Biological)'.
>
> Know how the study relates to the benefits of exercise to mental health.

Application

At least one exercise strategy to improve mental health: for example, weekly classes in dance/yoga/pilates/keep fit/aqua aerobics, etc., cardio-vascular exercise, green exercise, meditation.

Motivation (Cognitive)

REVISED

Self-efficacy and sports confidence: for example, definitions of 'motivation', 'self-efficacy' and 'sports self-confidence'; intrinsic motivation and extrinsic motivation.

Imagery and sports orientation: for example, imagery, its use and purpose in a sporting context; factors involved in sports orientation for example, competitiveness, win orientation, goal orientation, measuring sports-orientation (for example, the Sports Orientation Questionnaire, SOQ).

> **Exam tip**
>
> Know the key findings and be able to draw conclusions from the findings.

> **Now test yourself**
>
> 23 Outline two findings from this study.
>
> TESTED

> **Now test yourself**
>
> 24 Suggest one conclusion that can be drawn from the findings of this study.
>
> TESTED

> **Exam tips**
>
> The question is likely to be worded generically so focus on the specific exercise strategy selected to improve mental health.
>
> Be able to apply at least one exercise strategy to improve mental health to a novel situation.

> **self-efficacy** can be defined as one's belief in one's ability to succeed in specific situations or accomplish a task.
>
> **motivation** can be described as the desire to fulfil a need.

Key research: Munroe-Chandler *et al.* (2008): Playing with confidence: the relationship between imagery use and self-confidence and self-efficacy in youth soccer players

Theory/theories on which the study is based

Imagery is one way to enhance self-confidence and self-efficacy (Bandura, 1997). It is defined as an 'experience that mimics real experiences' (White and Hardy, 1998).

Athletes can benefit from using imagery in sport to enhance performance (Morris, Spittle and Watt, 2005).

Imagery in sport has both cognitive and motivational functions that operate on either a specific or a general level, as shown in Table 21.1.

Table 21.1 Imagery in sport: cognitive and motivational functions

Function	Imaging
Cognitive general (CG) function	Imaging strategies, game plans or routines (for example, a two on one in soccer)
Cognitive specific (CS) function	Imaging specific sport skills (for example, taking a free kick)
Motivational general (MG) function	Imaging physiological arousal levels and emotions (for example, getting psyched up before a game)
Motivational specific (MS) function	Imaging individual goals (for example, standing on the podium)

In sport, self-confidence is a general term which is most often measured as trait sports confidence. It refers to an athlete's certainty about their ability to be successful in sport (Vealey, 1986). Self-efficacy refers to a person's belief that they can be successful in specific tasks, skills or under specific conditions (Bandura, 1986).

Confidence is one of the most consistent factors in distinguishing successful from non-successful athletes (Gould, Weiss and Weinberg, 1981).

Background to the study

Recent qualitative research conducted by Munroe-Chandler, Hall, Fishburne and Strachan (2007) and Munroe-Chandler, Hall, Fishburne and Hall (2007) demonstrated that all ages of child athletes from the range 7 to 14 years used imagery for both cognitive and motivational purposes. However, younger athletes used imagery related to individual goals, whereas older athletes used imagery related to team goals. Additionally, the 11 to 14-year-old athletes reported using imagery more than their younger counterparts (7 to 10 years).

Research specifically examining MG-M imagery supports Bandura's (1997) proposal that imagery is one way to enhance self-confidence and self-efficacy. For example, Callow, Hardy and Hall (2001) examined the effects of MG-M imagery on the confidence of elite adult badminton players. The results showed that a 20-week imagery intervention improved the sport confidence for two of the players and stabilised the sport confidence of the third player.

Hall (2001) and Gregg and Hall (2006) found that higher-skilled athletes employ more imagery than lower-skilled athletes.

Although there seems to be considerable evidence that the use of MG-M imagery is associated with increased self-confidence and self-efficacy, the research has been conducted with relatively elite athletes who are adolescents or adults, so the question remains: does this relationship hold for recreational athletes and younger athletes?

The purpose of the present study was to examine the relationship between imagery use and confidence (self-confidence and self-efficacy) in soccer (football) players aged 11 to 14 years competing at both the recreational and competitive levels.

The researchers had two hypotheses:
1 MG-M imagery will be a significant predictor of both self-confidence and self-efficacy in young athletes (a non-directional hypothesis).
2 The relationship between MG-M imagery use and self-confidence and self-efficacy will be stronger in competitive athletes than recreational athletes (because self-confidence and self-efficacy are important to success in competitive sport) (a directional hypothesis).

Research method

This study used the self-report research method to gather data in relation to young soccer players' use of imagery (using the SIQ-C), their general self-confidence (using the CTAI-2C) and their self-efficacy in soccer (using the SEQ-S).

Data was collected mid soccer season over the course of a two-week period. Correlation was used to analyse the data gathered (so cause and effect could not be determined).

Outline of the procedure/study

NB. The sport of soccer was targeted because it has two clearly defined levels, house league (i.e. non-elite) and travel (i.e. elite), and is equally represented by both males and females (Canadian Soccer Association). Soccer is the largest youth participation sport in Canada, with over 702,000 youths (under 18 years old) registered in 2004 (Canadian Soccer Association).

A sample of young athletes was recruited from house and travel soccer leagues from south-western Ontario. The sample consisted of 125 participants (56 male, 69 female), all of whom were soccer athletes aged 11 to 14 years. The total sample of athletes reported a mean of 6.11 years of soccer playing experience.

The participants competed at both house/recreation ($n = 72$) and travel/competitive ($n = 50$) levels. Three participants did not report their level and as such were removed from any further analysis, resulting in a total sample of 122 athletes.

Measures

Imagery use was measured using the Sport Imagery Questionnaire for Children (SIQ-C). The SIQ-C is a 21-item questionnaire with statements measuring the frequency of children's imagery use. Statements were

Now test yourself

30 Outline one piece of research linked to the use of imagery that showed positive effects on sports performance.
31 State the non-directional hypothesis tested in this study.
32 Outline how the self-report method was used in this study.

TESTED

Exam tip

Know the research method and sample and know how data was gathered.

Now test yourself

33 Outline the final sample used in this study.

TESTED

scored from 1 (not at all) to 5 (very often) and participants were asked to circle the number that most applied to that particular statement. Each of the five functions of imagery was assessed throughout the 21 items, for example:

- 'I can usually control how a skill looks in my head' addressed the CS function of imagery.
- 'I make up new game plans, or routines in my head' addressed CG imagery.
- 'I see myself being mentally strong' addressed MG-M imagery.
- 'In my head, I imagine how calm I feel before I compete' addressed the MG-A imagery function.
- 'I see myself doing my very best' addressed MS imagery.

Confidence was measured using the Competitive State Anxiety Inventory – 2 for Children (CSAI-2C) – moderated for this study to the Competitive Trait Anxiety Inventory – 2 for Children (CTAI-2C) as the study was concerned with the athletes' trait measures of confidence. It is a 15-item questionnaire that measures somatic and cognitive anxiety as well as confidence. As this study was only interested in the confidence sub-scale, the anxiety sub-scales were not employed. The confidence sub-scale consists of five items that are rated on a four-point Likert scale from 1 (not at all) to 4 (very much so).

Self-efficacy was measured using the Self-efficacy Questionnaire for Soccer (SEQ-S). It is a five-item questionnaire which asks participants to record the strength of their belief in their mental abilities (for example, focused, in control, mentally tough) based on a 100-point scale, ranging in 10-unit intervals from 0 (no confidence) to 100 (complete confidence). The five items were:

1 'I am confident I can work through difficult situations.'
2 'I am confident I can remain focused during a challenging situation.'
3 'I am confident I can be mentally tough throughout a competition.'
4 'I am confident I can remain in control in challenging situations.'
5 'I am confident I can appear confident in front of others.'

Procedure

After receiving clearance from the university's research ethics board (University of Windsor, Windsor, Ontario, Canada), the soccer teams were contacted by the researchers through email and mailed letters to the coach. Parental consent and player assent were also obtained.

The players first were asked to complete a general demographics questionnaire including their age, gender, level and number of years playing soccer. Next, the participants completed the three questionnaires in the following order: the SIQ-C to assess their frequency of imagery use, the CTAI-2C to measure their generalised confidence, and finally the SEQ-S to assess their self-efficacy in soccer.

Completion of the questionnaires took approximately 15 minutes. They were completed prior to the athletes' practice at their respective practice fields.

Data was collected mid soccer season over the course of a two-week period.

Key findings

No significant differences were found between level of play (competitive and recreational) and gender (male and females) with respect to any of the dependent variables (five imagery functions, self-confidence, or self-efficacy) or the number of years playing.

Now test yourself

34 Describe how confidence was measured in this study.

TESTED

Now test yourself

35 Describe two ways in which ethical concerns were managed in this study.

TESTED

Pearson correlations found:
- a strong positive correlation between the use of MG-M imagery and self-confidence
- a strong positive correlation between the use of MG-M imagery and self-efficacy
- all types of imagery were positively correlated with self-confidence and self-efficacy but to a lesser extent than with MG-M imagery
- the relationship between MG-M imagery and self-confidence and self-efficacy was stronger in the recreational group than the competitive group but did not reach a significant level.

Conclusions

MG-M imagery is a significant predictor of self-confidence and self-efficacy in young soccer players. If a youth athlete, regardless of competitive level, wants to increase their self-confidence or self-efficacy through the use of imagery, the MG-M function should be emphasised.

MG-A and MS (motivational specific) imagery contribute to the prediction of self-confidence in recreational athletes.

The relationship between MG-M imagery and self-confidence and self-efficacy does not differ greatly between recreational and competitive soccer players. Competitive level has no influence on the relationship between MG-M imagery and self-confidence and self-efficacy.

Application

At least one strategy for motivating athletes: for example, working with intrinsic and extrinsic motivation, training athletes in the use of imagery techniques, developing greater self-efficacy through the use of goal setting/using positive language, positive feedback and encouragement/using positive role models.

> **Exam tips**
>
> The question is likely to be worded generically so focus on the specific strategy selected for motivating athletes.
>
> Be able to apply at least one strategy for motivating athletes to a novel situation.

Personality (cognitive)

Measuring personality: for example, definitions of personality, theories of personality (for example, trait theories – Eysenck, Cattell), Freud's psychodynamic theory, measuring personality (for example, the Rorschach Test, Eysenck's EPI, EPQ and EPQ-R, Cattell's 16PF questionnaire).

The relationship between personality and sport: for example, personality and sporting participation, personality and sporting success, personality and choice of sport.

Key research: Kroll and Crenshaw (1970): Multivariate personality profile analysis of four athletic groups

Theory/theories on which the study is based

Personality is an important factor in successful sports performance. Certain personality characteristics are (a) prerequisites for success and (b) necessarily different for different athletic activities.

Answers at **www.hoddereducation.co.uk/myrevisionnotes**

> **Now test yourself**
>
> 36 Outline two findings from this study.
>
> TESTED ☐

> **Exam tip**
>
> Know the key findings and be able to draw conclusions from them.

> **Now test yourself**
>
> 37 Suggest one conclusion that can be drawn from the findings of this study.
> 38 Outline one strategy for motivating athletes.
>
> TESTED ☐

> **Exam tips**
>
> Know how the study relates to the component 'Sport and exercise psychology'.
>
> Know how the study relates to the topic 'Motivation (Cognitive)'.
>
> Know how the study relates to self-efficacy and sports confidence, including imagery and sports orientation.

REVISED ☐

> **personality** is the combination of characteristics or qualities that forms an individual's distinctive character.

> **Now test yourself**
>
> 39 Define personality.
> 40 Outline one way in which personality can be measured.
>
> TESTED ☐

Certain personality characteristics can be linked for entering, continuing with or dropping out of participation in sport. Certain personality characteristics can be affected by participation and associated experiences dependent upon features found in both the participant and in the specific sport.

Background to the study

Since 1950, steady progress has been made in the clarification of major personality theories, in particular in relation to the development of instruments for personality assessment.

One problem with studies relating to personality and sport has been the lack of suitably defined criterion samples which are truly representative of the sports being investigated. Information concerning the quality of sport participants being investigated is quite scarce.

Researchers (Kroll, 1967; Kroll and Carlson, 1967; Kroll and Peterson, 1965) have analysed personality profiles of participants with known quality levels of athletic achievement from samples which represented more than a particular local situation. This in-sport analysis provided pertinent and essential information in relation to within-sport personality composition.

The purpose of this study was to build on the previous research into within-sport personality composition by making a between-sport comparison of personalities using the Cattell Sixteen Personality Factor Questionnaire (16PF Test).

The aim of this study was to investigate what differences, if any, there would be in the personality profiles of participants with a high level of skill in the four sports of football, gymnastics, wrestling and karate.

Research method

This study used the self-report research method to gather data in relation to athletes' personality characteristics

The self-report method used was the 16PF Test. To control for falsification and ensure validity of responses, participants also completed the 15-item lie test from the Minnesota Multiphasic Personality Inventory (MMPI) – data was discarded for any participant who scored seven or higher on this scale.

Outline of the procedure/study

A total of 387 athletes were included in the analysis:
- 81 American football players
- 141 gymnasts
- 94 wrestlers
- 71 amateur karate participants.

They were all of regional or national level.

Key findings

Significant differences between groups on personality profiles were shown to exist.

Significant differences in personality profiles were found between sporting pairs, except football and wrestling where no differences were observed. Results are shown in Table 21.2 on page 236.

Now test yourself

41 Suggest why there may be a relationship between personality and choice of sport.

TESTED ☐

Exam tips

Be able to define the term 'personality'.

Be able to describe at least one personality theory.

Be able to describe at least one general way for measuring personality and one sport-specific way of measuring personality.

Be able to describe the relationship between personality and sport.

Now test yourself

42 Outline the aim of this study.
43 Outline how falsification was controlled for in this study.
44 Identify the four sports used in this study.
45 Outline the sample used in this study.

TESTED ☐

Table 21.2 Major contributors to differences in the sporting profiles in pairs of sports

Comparison teams	Components on the 16PF where the major differences were observed
Football–Wrestling	No differences
Football–Gymnastics	Shy vs. venturesome; affected by feelings vs. emotionally stable; trusting vs. suspicious; group-dependent vs. self-sufficient
Football–Karate	Group-dependent vs. self-sufficient; shy vs. venturesome; trusting vs. suspicious; non-conforming vs. conforming
Wrestling–Gymnastics	Shy vs. venturesome; less intelligent vs. more intelligent; group-dependent vs. self-sufficient; traditional vs. open-to-change
Wrestling–Karate	Group-dependent vs. self-sufficient; patient vs. over-wrought; forthright vs. private; non-conforming vs. conforming
Gymnastics–Karate	Relaxed vs. tense; expedient vs. conscientious; sober vs. happy-go-lucky; less intelligent vs. more intelligent

Gymnasts scored lowest of all four groups on the relaxed vs. tense factors while karate participants scored the highest. Gymnasts scored lowest and karate participants highest on the non-conforming vs. conforming factor.

Gymnasts scored the lowest on the sober vs. happy-go-lucky factor, denoting a silent, introspective demeanour, but highest on the intelligence factor.

The biggest overall difference between groups was between footballers and gymnasts.

Conclusions

Sportspeople exhibit different personality characteristics.

Football players and wrestlers exhibit 16PF profiles that are homogeneous.

Football players and wrestlers exhibit 16PF profiles that differ from those exhibited by gymnasts and karate participants.

Gymnasts and karate participants exhibit different personality profiles.

The sports of football and wrestling (in the USA) share many similar personality characteristics.

Exam tips

Know how the study relates to the component 'Sport and exercise psychology'.

Know how the study relates to the topic 'Personality (Cognitive)'.

Know how the study relates to personality, its measurement and its relationship to sport.

Application

At least one strategy for using knowledge of personality to improve sports performance: for example, use personality tests to

Now test yourself

46 Use Table 21.2 to identify two differences between wrestlers and gymnasts.
47 Use Table 21.2 to identify two differences between American footballers and gymnasts.
48 Outline two other findings from this study.

TESTED

Now test yourself

49 Suggest one conclusion that can be drawn from the findings of this study.

TESTED

identify potential athletes, use personality tests to match individuals to particular sports, use personality tests to identify personality traits that might hinder performance so these can be managed.

Now test yourself

50 Name one way in which knowledge of personality can be used to improve sports performance.

TESTED ☐

> **Exam tips**
>
> The question is likely to be worded generically so focus the specific strategy selected for using knowledge of personality to improve sports performance.
>
> Be able to apply at least one strategy for using knowledge of personality to improve sports performance to a novel situation.

Performing with others (Social)

REVISED ☐

Teams: for example, definitions of 'group' and 'team', team formation, team/group cohesion (social cohesion, task cohesion).

Coaching: for example, definition of 'coaching', coaching and performance.

Leadership: for example, definition of 'leadership', Lewin *et al.*'s leadership styles, Chelladurai's three types of leader behaviour, leadership and performance.

Now test yourself

51 Explain the difference between social cohesion and task cohesion.
52 Describe two of Lewin *et al.*'s leadership styles.

TESTED ☐

Key research: Smith *et al.* (1979): Coach effectiveness training: a cognitive-behavioural approach to enhancing relationship skills in youth sports coaches

Theory/theories on which the study is based

Good quality supervision is vital in youth sports – see the Official Rules (1977) of the Little League Baseball, page 18.

> **Exam tip**
>
> Be able to describe the concepts of 'teams', 'coaching' and 'leadership' in relation to sport.

The development of cognitive and behaviour change methods is highly applicable to intervention programmes designed to modify coaching attitudes, goals and behaviours in desirable ways. Cognitive-behavioural frameworks can be used to make coaches more aware of their behaviours, to create expectancies concerning the likely consequences of various coaching behaviours, to increase their desire to generate certain consequences rather than others, and to develop or enhance their ability to perform desirable behaviours effectively.

One way to improve the chances that engagement in youth sports is positive is to focus on the behaviour of the adults who have the most control over the child's experience, i.e. the sports coaches (Smith *et al.*).

Now test yourself

53 Outline why cognitive-behavioural frameworks may be useful for coaches.

TESTED ☐

Background to the study

The behavioural guidelines communicated to coaches in the training programme used in this study were empirically derived from a preliminary investigation involving 51 Little League coaches and 542 of their players (Smith, Smoll and Curtis, 1978). On the basis of empirical relationships between observed coaching behaviours, players' perceptions and recall of such behaviours, and players' attitudes, a series of behavioural guidelines was developed (Smoll, Smith and Curtis, 1977).

Smith, Smoll and Curtis (1978) found that children with low general self-esteem were responsive to differences in coaching behaviours in terms of their attitudes towards their coaches. Previous research by Smith *et al.* (1978) showed that children who played for highly reinforcing and encouraging coaches had significantly higher levels of post season self-esteem than those who were exposed to coaches who did not behave in this manner.

This study attempted to transmit and assess guidelines to coaches and to promote their utilisation with the aim of enhancing the ability of Little League Baseball coaches to relate more effectively with their players.

It was expected that cognitive changes would promote and mediate positive changes in overt coaching behaviours. Through the use of coach effectiveness training (CET) it was expected that there would be an increase in positive interactions between coaches and their players and positive interactions between team-mates.

The role of self-esteem as a moderator variable affecting children's reactions to trained and untrained coaches was also investigated with the following hypothesis: differences in attitudes towards trained and untrained coaches will be most pronounced for low self-esteem children.

Research method

This was a field experiment. The IV was whether the coach was assigned to the group who underwent the evening training session or to the no-treatment (control) group. The DVs were the observed behaviours of the coaches during games, players' perceptions of the coaches' behaviours and player attitudes towards themselves, the coaches, team-mates and the sport.

Data was gathered through observation (leading to the completion of the CBAS) and self-reports (via the self-monitoring forms, post-season interviews and the Self-Esteem Inventory).

Outline of the procedure/study

The initial sample consisted of 34 Seattle-area, male, Little League Baseball coaches. All of the coaches were involved at the major (10 to 12 year olds) and senior (13 to 15 year olds) levels of the programme. They coached in three leagues that had participated in the earlier investigation of relationships between coaching behaviours and players' reactions to the Little League experiences.

Eighteen coaches were randomly assigned to the experimental group and 16 were assigned to a no-treatment, control condition. The unequal group sizes allowed for a sufficiently large experimental group in case of no-shows for the training programme.

Three coaches in the control condition were lost during the course of the season due to team mergers or changes in residence. The final sample therefore consisted of 18 coaches in the experimental group and 13 coached in the no-treatment, control group. The mean age of these coaches was 36.10 years. They had an average of 8.37 years of coaching experience.

In addition, a total of 325 male players (82 per cent of those who played for the experimental and control coaches) were individually interviewed to gather data about their perceptions of the coaches' behaviours and their attitudes towards themselves, the coaches, team-mates and the sport.

The training package involved a number of techniques. As well as verbal and written presentation of the devised behavioural guidelines, modelling, behavioural feedback and self-monitoring were employed.

Now test yourself

54 Outline two anticipated effects of the coach effectiveness training programme.

TESTED ☐

Now test yourself

55 Describe the independent and dependent variables in this study.

TESTED ☐

Exam tips

Know the research method and sample.

Know how data was gathered.

Now test yourself

56 Describe the final sample in this study.

TESTED ☐

Answers at www.hoddereducation.co.uk/myrevisionnotes

Training procedures

Coaches in the experimental group were contacted by telephone and invited to participate in an evening training session. They were told that the results of the previous study conducted within their leagues would be described and guidelines would be presented and discussed. The training session lasted about two hours and was conducted by the researchers (Smith, Smoll and Curtis).

The explicit goals of the guidelines were to increase positive interactions between coaches and players, as well as team-mates, and to reduce fear of failure among players. The following is one excerpt from the written guidelines given to the coaches:

> Good plays:
>
> DO – REWARD! Do so immediately. Let the players know that you appreciate and value their efforts. Reward effort as much as you do results. Look for positive things, reward them, and you'll see them increase. Remember, whether the kids show it or not, the positive things you say and do stick with them.
>
> DON'T – Take their efforts for granted.

The verbal presentation was supplemented by the modelling by the experimenters of both desirable and undesirable methods of responding to specific situations (for example, player mistakes). In addition to the guidelines, coaches were given a written brochure which contained concrete suggestions for communicating effectively with players, gaining their respect and relating to parents.

Behavioural feedback was given through the use of the 12-category Coaching Behaviour Assessment System (CBAS) (Smith, Smoll and Hunt, 1977a). The coaches were observed during the first two weeks of the season by trained coders and were then mailed behavioural profiles reflecting their behavioural patterns during two complete games.

Self-monitoring was effected by the coaches completing a brief self-monitoring form immediately after each of their first ten games of the season. Self-monitoring was restricted to desired behaviours recommended in the guidelines. All of the coaches returned their completed forms.

Evaluation procedures

In order to assess the effects of the training programme on coaches and their players, the experimental and control coaches were compared in terms of observed behaviours during games, players' perceptions of the behaviours and player attitudes towards themselves, the coaches, team-mates and the sport.

Observed behaviours were recorded through the CBAS by 16 undergraduates who were trained over a four-week period. Player perceptions and attitudes were recorded and assessed through the use of a structured interview conducted at the end of the season.

The measure of the players' perception of the coaches' behaviour was presented as a recall test. The player was given a description and examples of each of the 12 CBAS behaviours and asked to indicate on a seven-point scale, ranging from 'never' to 'almost always', how frequently their coach had engaged in that behaviour in situations like those described.

Following the recall section of the interview, the boys indicated reactions to their participation and ability-related perceptions. This was

Now test yourself

57 Briefly outline the procedure followed in this study in relation to the experimental group.

TESTED ☐

done by giving the child a clipboard and asking them to record their own responses on a series of seven-point scales in such a way that the interviewer could not see them. Two examples of the questions asked are: 'How much do you like playing baseball?'; 'How good a baseball teacher is your coach?' The scales ranged, for example, from 'dislike a lot' to 'like a lot'/'very poor' to 'excellent'.

As part of the post-season interview, players were asked to complete an adaptation of Coopersmith's (1967) Self-Esteem Inventory as a measure of general (global) self-esteem. This consisted of 14 descriptive statements, each of which was rated on a five-point scale ranging from 'not at all' to 'very much like me'.

Key findings

Comparability of experimental and control coaches

No significant differences were found between the groups of coaches in terms of age, number of years of total coaching experience and number of years coaching baseball.

On other behavioural measures, the two groups were also deemed quite comparable.

Observed CBAS behaviour differences

A total of 26,412 behaviours were coded during four game observations of the experimental and control coaches. Each coach averaged 213.19 codable behaviours per game. The frequency data within the CBAS categories was converted to rate scores and it was found that the rate scores between the two groups did not differ significantly on either any of the 12 behaviour categories or the total of the combined categories.

Because the two groups did not differ in their level of activity, subsequent analysis focused on the distribution of behaviours within the categories. Table 21.3 shows the percentage of behaviours which fell into each CBAS category. Analysis showed that Reinforcement was the significant major discriminator between the two groups.

Table 21.3 Descriptive statistics showing differences between observed (CBAS) behaviours of experimental and control group coaches

Behavioural category	Experimental	Control
	Mean	Mean
Reinforcement	25.99	20.51
Non-reinforcement	3.28	2.77
Mistake-contingent encouragement	4.25	3.33
Mistake-contingent technical instruction	3.12	3.63
Punishment	1.48	1.67
Punitive technical instruction	0.62	1.04
Ignoring mistakes	1.70	1.73
Keeping control	1.18	1.46
General technical instruction	21.43	24.55
General encouragement	29.04	33.13
Organisation	4.80	4.67
General communication	3.11	2.30

Now test yourself

58 Outline how the observed behaviour of the coaches in both the experimental and control groups was recorded.
59 Outline how the players' self-esteem was measured.

TESTED

Now test yourself

60 Use Table 21.3 to identify the group that, on average, used general encouragement the most.
61 Use Table 21.3 to identify the group that, on average, used punishment the least.

TESTED

Differences in players' perceptions of coaching behaviours

After further ANOVA analysis, experimental group coaches were rated as more frequently engaging in Reinforcement, Mistake-contingent encouragement and General technical instruction, and less frequently engaging in Non-reinforcement, Punishment and Punitive Technical Instruction.

Player attitudes and self-esteem

Evaluative reactions to coach and team-mates: data indicated that children who played for the trained coaches did not differ in liking for baseball compared with those who played for the untrained coaches. However, they indicated greater enjoyment in having played for their coaches and a stronger desire to play for them in the future. They also rated the trained coaches as better teachers of baseball and evaluated the relationships which existed among team-mates more positively.

Post-season self-evaluations: on the measure of general self-esteem, no significant group difference was found. Likewise, the children's evaluations of their own baseball ability did not differ. However, significant differences were found in the children's perceptions of their coaches' and team-mates' evaluation of their skills. Children who played for the trained coaches felt that both their coach and their team-mates evaluated their skills more highly. No difference was found in the children's perception of their parents' evaluation of their skills.

Pre- and post-season self-esteem changes: total samples of children who played for the trained and untrained coaches did not differ in post-season self-esteem scores. However, self-esteem data obtained in similar interviews conducted the previous year was available for 75 of the children who played for the untrained coaches and for 112 children who played for the trained coaches which allowed for changes in self-esteem scores to be examined. Analysis showed a significantly higher level of self-esteem in the children who had played for the trained coaches. In addition, there was a significant increase in scores for the children who had played for trained coaches whereas the control group children exhibited no significant change in scores.

Self-esteem as a moderator variable: the total player sample was divided into high, moderate and low self-esteem groups. Analysis showed a significant groups effect only at the low self-esteem level, with the children with low self-esteem rating the coaches who had received the CET programme more highly than children in other self-esteem categories.

On the measure of how well team-mates got along with each other, significant main effects were found for both coach groups and self-esteem. Children who played for the trained coaches rated their teams as higher in intra-team attraction, as did children high in self-esteem.

Team records

Given the strong attitudinal differences found between children who played for the two groups of coaches, the researchers deemed it important to examine the potential influence of won–lost records.

> **Exam tip**
>
> Know the key findings and be able to draw conclusions from the findings.

> **Now test yourself**
>
> 62 Outline the difference found between the pre- and post-experimental scores in relation to self-esteem.
>
> TESTED ☐

The trained coaches had a mean winning percentage of 55 per cent, whereas for the untrained coaches this was 45 per cent. These findings were not statistically significant, however.

Conclusions

Training programmes exert a significant and positive influence on overt coaching behaviours and on player-perceived behaviours, as well as towards their coach/towards their team-mates/towards many aspects of their athletic experience.

Children who play for trained coaches develop positive self-esteem/develop more positive self-esteem than children who play for untrained coaches.

Children who play for trained coaches evaluate their coach/the interpersonal climate of their teams more positively than children who play for untrained coaches.

Self-esteem is an important moderator of attitudinal responses to coaching behaviours.

Application

At least one strategy for improving team performance: for example, team building/increasing team cohesion, coach development, use constructive feedback, use operant conditioning and positive reinforcement.

> **Exam tips**
>
> The question is likely to be worded generically so focus on the specific strategy selected for improving team performance.
>
> Be able to apply at least one strategy for improving team performance to a novel situation.

Audience effects (Social)

How an audience can facilitate or inhibit sports performance: for example, definition of '**social facilitation**', Zajonc's drive theory, Cottrell's evaluation apprehension theory, Baron's distraction–conflict theory, individual differences in audience effects, co-action and audience effects.

Home advantage: for example, explanations for home advantage and home disadvantage effects (for example, application of drive theory and evaluation apprehension theory, familiarity, crowd density and intimacy).

Key research: Zajonc *et al.* (1969): Social enhancement and impairment of performance in the cockroach

Theory/theories on which the study is based

Poor performance in group situations can be attributed to distraction (Gates and Allee, 1933). The presence of others can have a negative effect on performance (Gates and Allee, 1933). Conversely, the presence of others can lead to improvements in performance.

> **Now test yourself**
>
> 63 Outline the difference in won–lost records between the two groups of coaches.
>
> TESTED ☐

> **Exam tips**
>
> Know how the study relates to the component 'Sport and exercise psychology'.
>
> Know how the study relates to the topic 'Performing with others (Social)'.
>
> Know how the study relates to teams, coaching and leadership.

> **Now test yourself**
>
> 64 Suggest one conclusion that could be drawn from the findings of this study.
> 65 Outline one strategy that could be used to increase team performance.
>
> TESTED ☐

REVISED ☐

> **social facilitation** refers to the improvement in performance due to the presence of others. Social inhibition refers to an impairment in performance due to the presence of others.

> **Exam tips**
>
> Be able to describe how an audience can facilitate or inhibit sports performance.
>
> Be able to explain the term 'home advantage'.

Answers at **www.hoddereducation.co.uk/myrevisionnotes**

Zajonc (1965) suggested these two seemingly conflicting results could be reconciled if one assumed the presence of others to be a source of general drive (D). Therefore, as well as the presence of others being a source of specific cues, reinforcement and specific excitation (for example, as in aggression), it can direct behaviour by acting as a source of non-specific arousal which acts as a general energiser of all responses that are likely to be emitted in the given situation. It is assumed that the arousal effects would be those that are predicted by the Spence-Hull drive theory (Spence, 1956): if the animal's dominant responses are appropriate from the point of view of the experimental situation, the presence of others will enhance them and the resulting performance will appear as being improved. If these dominant responses are largely inappropriate, however, performance in the presence of others will appear as being impaired.

Socially facilitated increments in performance are usually found for behaviours that are either very well learned or instinctive (for example, Scott and McCray, 1967).

Background to the study

In 1933 Gates and Allee reported a study on the maze learning of isolated and grouped cockroaches (see Figure 21.4) in which they observed a clear inferiority of performance of the grouped subjects.

Other studies using animal or human subjects also found a deterioration of performance under social conditions (for example, Klopfer, 1958).

Research with humans, where information about the subject's response hierarchy was available prior to the tests of social effects, has provided substantial support for the drive theory of social facilitation (for example, Cottrell, Rittle and Wack, 1967). However, until this study, procedures of this sort had not been employed with animals as participants.

Zajonc *et al.* proposed that if a situation in which the cockroach's response tendencies would be largely 'correct' or 'appropriate' could be contrived, an increment rather than a decrement in performance should be obtained under social conditions. They proposed that in comparison with maze performance, this situation would provide a rather stringent test of the drive theory of social facilitation.

This paper therefore reports two experiments in which the performance of cockroaches in a maze and in a runway was compared under various social conditions with the aim of providing evidence for drive theory. In all the experiments socially mediated performance decrements in the maze and socially mediated increments in the straight runway were expected.

Research method

This study involved the use of two laboratory experiments, each of which used an independent measures design.

In Experiment 1:
- The independent variables were:
  - whether the cockroaches performed alone or in pairs (32 of the cockroaches)
  - whether the cockroaches performed alone or in pairs with an audience (40 of the cockroaches)
  - whether the cockroach/cockroaches had to traverse a maze or a straight runway (see Figure 21.5 on page 244).

Now test yourself

66 Define 'social facilitation'.
67 Outline one theory in relation to audience effects.
68 Outline Spence-Hull's drive theory.

TESTED

Figure 21.4 The participants were cockroaches!

Now test yourself

69 Outline the aim of this study.

TESTED

- The dependent variable was the starting latency and the time taken to reach the goal box so the guillotine gate could be lowered.

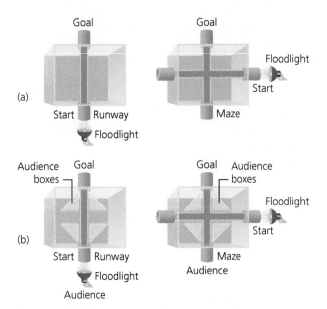

Figure 21.5 Runways and mazes used in the coaction and in the audience treatments of Experiment 1

In Experiment 2:
- The IVs were:
  ○ whether the cockroaches had to traverse a maze or a straight runway
  ○ whether the cockroaches had to traverse a maze/runway outfitted with mirrors alongside the vertical walls; whether the cockroaches had to traverse a maze/runway stimulated by the presence of olfactory cues associated with their conspecifics or whether the cockroaches had to traverse a maze/runway alone, in socially neutral conditions.
- The DV was the starting latency and the time taken to reach the goal box so the guillotine gate could be lowered.

Outline of the procedure/study

Sample

Experiment 1:
- 72 adult, female cockroaches.
- For at least one week prior to the first experimental trial they were housed in individual mason jars with screened lids and kept in the dark with a relatively constant temperature of 75 degrees Fahrenheit.
- They were fed an 'ad lib' diet of peeled and sliced apples – meaning this food was available at all times, with the quantity and frequency of consumption being the free choice of the cockroach.

Experiment 2:
- 180 female cockroaches.
- All cockroaches were kept in individual mason jars for four days prior to the experiment.
- One-third (60) of the cockroaches were assigned to the mirror condition (Mi), onethird to the odour condition (Od) and one-third to the solitary (Al) condition.

Now test yourself

70 Describe the independent variables in Experiment 1.
71 Describe the dependent variable in Experiment 2.

TESTED

Now test yourself

72 Identify the three testing conditions in Experiment 2.

TESTED

Procedure

Experiment 1

This experiment had two major purposes:
- To test the drive theory of social facilitation.
- To determine whether socially mediated effects obtained in cockroaches when the participants could not profit from cues provided by companions (i.e. an audience) would affect performance times.

Apparatus

The basic apparatus consisted of a 20 × 20 × 20 inch clear Plexiglass cube outfitted so as to house either a maze or a runway. A 150 watt floodlight served as a source of noxious stimulation.

The runway consisted of a straight track running between two opposite vertical walls and was 20 inches long. The maze was made of two runways, placed in the same plane and perpendicular to each other, thus forming a cross with the walls of the intersection removed. The paths in the runway and in the maze, namely those leading from the starting box to the goal box or to a cul-de-sac, were 20 inches long. To attract the cockroach to the goal box, an opaque cover, painted flat black on the inside, was placed over the box, making its interior dark. A flat black poster-board, covering the entire 20 × 20 inch area, was hung on the wall which held the goal box.

For the groups which had a passive audience, four 9 × 9 × 1 inch boxes with Plexiglass sides and tops and Bakelite floors were used. These boxes were placed inside the Plexiglass cube housing in such a manner that their floors were flush with the floors of the runway or the maze and their sides directly contiguous with the walls of the runway or the maze. When these boxes were in position, almost the entire extent of walls of the runway or maze was in direct contact with the sides of the audience boxes. Air holes in the sides of the boxes lined up with air holes in the walls of the runway and the maze to allow transmission of olfactory cues.

Procedure

Before each trial the runway (or the maze) was swabbed with alcohol and then allowed to dry thoroughly. The starting box and goal box were swabbed in the same manner before each set of ten trials.

The cockroach was placed in the starting box, which was covered with an opaque container similar to the one that covered the goal box.

Each trial began by removing the cover, turning on the floodlight and removing the guillotine door separating the opening in the starting box from the runway or the maze. No light other than that provided by the floodlight was present in the experimental room.

The trial was terminated when the cockroach (or the pair of cockroaches) entered the goal box and the guillotine gate was lowered behind it (or them), or in five minutes, whichever was earlier. The guillotine gate was always lowered immediately after the cockroach's last leg crossed the entrance of the goal box.

For the 32 animals involved in the co-action condition and the 40 that were involved in the audience condition:

- Half of the cockroaches worked in the runway and half in the maze.
- In addition, within each combination of condition and task, half of the animals were run in the alone condition and half in the social condition.
- In the co-action condition participants were placed into starting boxes in pairs.
- In the audience condition ten adult females were placed in each of the four audience boxes. A control group of 20 cockroaches, which was not to be exposed to a passive audience, worked with audience boxes in position, but empty and clean.
- All cockroaches run in the audience condition and in their proper control conditions were run individually.
- Starting latency consisted of the interval beginning with the opening of the guillotine gate of the starting box and ending at the time the last part of the roach's body left the starting box.

In all conditions the subjects were given ten consecutive trials, all separated by one-minute inter-trial intervals.

In short, cockroaches were observed alone and under two types of social treatments, co-action and audience, while they traversed either a straight runway or a maze.

Experiment 2

This experiment attempted to determine whether socially mediated effects such as those obtained in Experiment 1 would be produced if the immediate presence of conspecifics (members of the same species) were somehow curtailed or reduced.

Two conditions were employed. In the first condition the insects ran in mazes and runways which were outfitted with mirrors alongside their vertical walls. In the second condition regular runways and mazes were utilised, but the animals were stimulated by the presence of olfactory cues associated with their conspecifics.

These conditions were compared with one in which the insects were observed under solitary and socially neutral conditions.

Apparatus and procedure

An appropriately modified version of the apparatus from Experiment 1 was used.

In the Mi treatment a runway and a maze were used which were equipped with mirrors along the entire extent of the walls. Otherwise the apparatus was the same as in the alone condition of Experiment 1.

In the Od treatment the regular runway and maze from the audience condition of Experiment 1 were used which, it will be recalled, had holes drilled in their walls. An olfactory social stimulus was provided by placing an egg carton impregnated with the odour of conspecifics inside the housing of the apparatus directly beneath the maze or the runway.

The Al treatment was the same as the Od treatment except that a fresh clean egg carton, not impregnated with cockroach odour, was placed beneath the runway or the maze.

Now test yourself

73 Outline the purpose of Experiment 1.
74 Describe how each trial was started in Experiment 1.
75 Describe how latency was measured in Experiment 1.

TESTED

Now test yourself

76 Outline how an olfactory stimulus was provided in Experiment 2.

TESTED

The same procedure was used for scoring latencies and running times as in Experiment 1.

Key findings

Experiment 1

Table 21.4 shows the results for Experiment 1.

Table 21.4 Running time and starting latency in seconds for subjects tested alone, in co-action and in the presence of an audience

	Runway		Maze	
Treatment	Alone	Social	Alone	Social
Co-action				
Starting latency	8.25 (8)	6.88 (8)	10.56 (8)	11.19 (8)
Running time	40.58 (8)	32.96 (8)	110.45 (8)	129.46 (8)
Audience				
Starting latency	14.80 (10)	9.35 (10)	37.55 (10)	22.75 (10)
	62.65 (10)	39.30 (10)	221.35 (10)	296.64 (10)
Both treatments				
Starting latency	11.89 (18)	8.25 (18)	25.56 (18)	17.61 (18)
Running time	52.84 (18)	36.48 (10)	172.06 (18)	222.34 (18)

Note. Average of medians. Figures in parentheses indicate the number of cockroaches in each cell.

Cockroaches running in the maze co-action condition took longer to reach the goal box than cockroaches running alone (replicating the findings of Gates and Allee). However, cockroaches running in the runway co-action condition took less time to reach the goal box than the cockroaches that ran alone.

The same pattern of results was found for the audience condition. Running times and latencies were substantially shorter in the co-action cockroaches than in the audience groups.

To summarise, in both conditions (co-actions and audience) maze performance was impaired while runway performance was facilitated when compared with solitary performance.

Experiment 2

The interactions between conditions and tasks did not attain levels of statistical significance. However, with respect to total running times, both main effects and the interaction were significant.

Running times in the straight runway were not improved in the two social conditions (Mi and Od) – both Mi and Od participants took longer to traverse the runway than the Al participants. Maze-running in the Mi condition was facilitated, i.e. faster, whereas it was impaired for the Od condition, i.e. slower. See Table 21.5 on page 248.

Table 21.5 Running time and starting latency in seconds for subjects tested alone, with mirror and in the presence of conspecific odour

Treatment	Runway	Maze
Mirror		
Starting latency	27.38	28.88
Running time	77.21	160.71
Odour		
Starting latency	20.00	24.97
Running time	69.53	245.72
Alone		
Starting latency	22.67	18.33
Running time	55.67	219.63

Note. Average of medians. These means are based on 30 independent observations in each cell.

Conclusions

The presence of an audience of conspecifics is a sufficient condition for the enhancement of dominant responses, such that the performance of the subject in a one-alternative task is improved and the performance of the subject in a multi-alternative task is impaired. The mere presence of conspecifics is a source of general arousal that enhances the emission of dominant responses.

Enhancement as well as impairment of performance can be obtained with cockroaches, depending on whether a simple (straight run) or a complex task (a maze) was used, and therefore depending on whether the situation was more likely to recruit appropriate or inappropriate response tendencies.

The partial presence of conspecifics may have distracting effects. In order for drive effects to take place, the presence of conspecifics must be actual.

Partial presence, such as the presence of olfactory traces, is not sufficient to produce effects consistent with the drive theory of social facilitation. The presence of others can enhance performance in either well-learned or instinctive behaviours.

Application

At least one strategy for training for and playing spectator sports: for example, develop automatic processing through practice, develop psychological resilience, learn to manage arousal and anxiety levels, learn techniques to minimise the effects of distracters such as co-participants and/or an audience, train alongside others to reduce the negative effects of co-participants and/or an audience.

> **Exam tip**
>
> Know the key findings and be able to draw conclusions from the findings.

> **Now test yourself**
>
> 77 Outline one finding from Experiment 1.
> 78 Outline one finding from Experiment 2.
>
> TESTED ☐

> **Exam tips**
>
> Know how the study relates to the component 'Sport and exercise psychology'.
>
> Know how the study relates to the topic 'Audience effects (Social)'.
>
> Know how the study relates to how an audience can facilitate or inhibit sports performance.

> **Now test yourself**
>
> 79 Outline one strategy for training for and playing spectator sports.
>
> TESTED ☐

> **Exam tips**
>
> The question is likely to be worded generically so focus on the specific strategy selected for training for and playing spectator sports.
>
> Be able to apply at least one strategy for training for and playing spectator sports to a novel situation.

Answers at www.hoddereducation.co.uk/myrevisionnotes

Practice questions

Sport and exercise psychology

1 Describe Lewis *et al.*'s research into exercise and mental
   health.   [10]
2 Discuss the usefulness of studying exercise and mental health.   [15]
3 A group of students went to see a mental health practitioner at their university because their
   final exams were coming up in a month's time and they were feeling stressed, anxious and
   depressed. The mental health practitioner was not prepared to prescribe any medication and
   suggested the best thing for them to do was to relax and get more exercise. Use your
   knowledge of exercise and mental health to suggest at least one strategy the students could
   employ to improve their mental health.   [10]

ONLINE

Summary

By the end of this chapter you should:
● know how arousal can be optimised, anxiety
  controlled and measured in a sporting context,
  Fazey and Hardy's study, at least one technique
  for managing arousal and anxiety in sport
● be able to describe some benefits of exercise
  to mental health, Lewis *et al.*'s study, at least
  one exercise strategy to improve mental health
● be able to describe self-efficacy in relation to
  sport, sports confidence, imagery as used in
  sport, sports orientation, Munroe-Chandler
  et al.'s study, at least one strategy for
  motivating athletes
● be able to describe personality, its
  measurement and its relationship to sport,

Kroll and Crenshaw' study, at least one
strategy for using knowledge of personality to
improve sports performance
● be able to describe the concepts of 'teams',
  'coaching' and 'leadership' in relation to sport,
  Smith *et al.*'s study, at least one strategy for
  improving team performance
● be able to describe how an audience can
  facilitate or inhibit sports performance, the
  concept of 'home advantage', Zajonc's study, at
  least one strategy for training for and playing
  spectator sports.